Spanish Legacies

For Doug Massey,
distinguished colleague
and friend with
best collegial regards.

A. Portes

Princeton,
August 2016

# Spanish Legacies

*The Coming of Age
of the Second Generation*

Alejandro Portes,
Rosa Aparicio, and
William Haller

UNIVERSITY OF CALIFORNIA PRESS

University of California Press, one of the most
distinguished university presses in the United States,
enriches lives around the world by advancing scholarship
in the humanities, social sciences, and natural sciences. Its
activities are supported by the UC Press Foundation and
by philanthropic contributions from individuals and
institutions. For more information, visit www.ucpress.edu.

University of California Press
Oakland, California

Library of Congress Cataloging-in-Publication Data

Names: Portes, Alejandro, 1944– author. | Aparicio,
   Rosa, author. | Haller, William (William John), author.
Title: Spanish legacies : the coming of age of the second
   generation / Alejandro Portes, Rosa Aparicio, and
   William Haller.
Description: Oakland, California : University of
   California Press, [2016] | "2016 | Includes
   bibliographical references and index.
Identifiers: LCCN 2015047733| ISBN 9780520286290
   (hardcover : alk. paper) | ISBN 9780520286306 (pbk. :
   alk. paper) | eISBN 9780520961579
Subjects: LCSH: Children of immigrants—Cross-cultural
   studies. | Children of immigrants—Spain—Social
   conditions. | Spain—Emigration and immigration—
   Social aspects.
Classification: LCC JV6344 .P67 2016 | DDC
   305.230946—dc23
LC record available at  http://lccn.loc.gov/2015047733


25  24  23  22  21  20  19  18  17  16
10  9  8  7  6  5  4  3  2  1

In keeping with a commitment to support
environmentally responsible and sustainable printing
practices, UC Press has printed this book on Natures
Natural, a fiber that contains 30% post-consumer waste
and meets the minimum requirements of ANSI/NISO
Z39.48-1992 (R 1997) (*Permanence of Paper*).

*To the children of immigrants and their families in Spain, and especially to those who made this study possible*

# Contents

*Plate gallery located between pages 84 and 85*

# Preface

This book is the product of an eight-year-long collaborative effort between American and Spanish research institutions and scholars to produce the first reliable and representative study of the condition and future prospects of children of immigrants—the second generation—in Spain. The idea for the study was prompted by the convergence in time of two apparently unrelated events. The first was the completion in the United States of the Children of Immigrants Longitudinal Study (CILS), the first large-scale project of its kind yielding a novel theory of the process of second-generation growth and adaptation to American society. The study was completed in 2005. The second was a series of urban protests and unrest in a number of European cities, spearheaded precisely by immigrant youths—immigrants themselves, but mostly children of immigrants during the same year.[1] These events (*emeutes,* as they are called in France) indicated how little was known in European countries about young people of foreign origin growing up in their midst. Labor immigration and refugee migration to these countries had proceeded steadily since the onset of the guest-labor programs in the 1960s and 1970s, leading to a significant growth of the foreign population. By 2010, it had reached about 10 percent in France, 13 percent in Spain, and a remarkable 15 percent in Ireland.[2] As elsewhere, immigrants spawned a new generation that is growing up in a tense relationship between the culture and language of their parents and those of their new countries.

The outcomes of such a process are neither predictable nor necessarily benign. The larger the size of the foreign-born population, the more important these outcomes are. Unlike the first generation, born and raised in a foreign country and marked indelibly by its experiences there, the children are mostly here to stay, forming a potentially significant component of the young population of their adopted countries. Success or failure of their process of integration can have major social and political consequences for the cities and regions where they concentrate.[3]

Thus, this study was designed with two related goals in mind. First, to test the theoretical concepts and hypotheses stemming from the just-completed CILS project in the United States and, second, to create a body of factual information about the second generation in a West European nation. The first goal aimed at examining the extent to which the theory of segmented assimilation, the related notions of selective and dissonant acculturation, and competing hypotheses such as neo-assimilationism and "second-generation advantage" applied to a European context.[4] The second aimed at producing, for the first time, a statistically representative panel with which outcomes of the adaptation process from early to late adolescence could be traced and causal models of their determinants constructed.[5]

Spain was selected for two substantive reasons. First, among major European countries, it is the one where the foreign-born population has grown fastest, going from practically zero in the late 1980s to 13 percent in 2010, a figure comparable to that of the United States (12 percent), despite the much longer history of immigration to America.[6] Second, Spain was chosen because of its relative similarity to the United States in the national origins of both immigrant flows, having their primary source in Latin America.

Although several major U.S.-bound migrant flows, such as Asian Indians and Koreans, are scarcely represented among the foreign-born in Spain and, conversely, large immigrant nationalities on the Iberian Peninsula, such as Moroccans and Romanians, are relatively uncommon in America, there are a number of other remarkable overlaps. Filipinos, for example, are present in sizable numbers in both countries; so are the Chinese, who have managed to build a vigorous economic presence in major cities of both nations. Above all, Latin American nationalities—such as Bolivians, Colombians, Dominicans, Ecuadoreans, and Peruvians—are major components of the foreign-born population in both countries.[7] Without exaggeration, it can be said that the overseas Latin American population of the twenty-first century concentrates in the United States and Spain and that their children are growing up and adapting mainly to American and Spanish societies.

The methodology followed by this study, baptized by its Spanish initials, ILSEG (Investigación Longitudinal de la Segunda Generación), is described in detail in Chapter 4. The point to be emphasized here is that it replicated, in all major aspects, the research design followed by CILS in the United States—thus profiting, in multiple ways, from that earlier experience. The baseline survey was administered to a statistically representative sample of second-generation youths at average age 14, identified and interviewed in 180 secondary schools of metropolitan Madrid and Barcelona. The sample, stratified by geographic location in each city and by type of school (public versus private) came close to 7,000 cases, or approximately 1,700 more than the original CILS sample.[8]

The baseline survey for ILSEG was completed in 2008. Two years later, and replicating the CILS methodology, a random subsample of immigrant parents was interviewed face-to-face and by telephone, either in Spanish or in their native languages. This sample, numbering close to 2,000 cases, provides an independent check on children's reports about their families' background and socioeconomic status and allows us to construct causal models of key adaptation outcomes employing data from both parents' and children's surveys.

The original sample was then followed over time and re-interviewed four years later, when the respondents had reached average age 18. The tracking effort was successful, retrieving the majority of the original respondents. To this group was added a replacement sample composed of second-generation youths of comparable age not interviewed in the first survey. Finally, a Spanish native-parentage sample of the same average age was interviewed for comparative purposes. In total, these surveys, completed in late 2012, yielded upward of 7,000 cases, providing a wealth of information that is (1) statistically representative of second-generation youths growing up in the two principal Spanish cities, (2) comparable across time, and (3) comparable between native and foreign-origin populations.

This body of evidence presents a major opportunity and a challenge. Never before, to our knowledge, has a study of this scope been completed in Europe. The data afford the opportunity to meet the twin goals of the study, as described previously. Simultaneously, however, surveys of so many populations conducted at different points in time confront the analyst with a momentous task. Sifting through these various data files in order to arrive at reliable and valid conclusions of key integration outcomes is the challenge that this book attempts to meet.

We begin with three chapters that provide context for the quantitative, substantive analyses that follow. The first chapter is based on summaries of real-life histories based on a subsample of our respondents deemed emblematic of major trends in the data. The second presents a review of contemporary theories about the integration of children of immigrants, including those based on CILS, as well as other major studies in the United States and Europe. The third chapter is a review of existing evidence concerning recent immigration to Spain, including an examination of the pertinent literature produced by Spanish scholars and the main conclusions to be deduced from it.

These are followed by substantive chapters on the experiences, present situation, and attitudes of immigrant parents; the psychosocial and linguistic adaptation of their children; and their educational and occupational experiences, as they manifest themselves in late adolescence and young adulthood. These include both actual objective outcomes as well as ambitions and plans for the future. While not generalizable to other European nations, we expect that these results will provide a solid basis for comparative studies elsewhere. On their own, they provide a thus-far-unavailable reference point against which to contrast evidence from the American research literature and to test hypotheses and ideas derived from it.

The existing Spanish social science literature, reviewed in Chapter 3, emphasizes the unanticipated character of the massive human flows received by the country and the absence of societal or governmental blueprints to deal with them. Instead, challenges posed by the arrival and settlement needs of so many foreigners were handled in practical terms, confronting them on a day-to-day basis without an overarching model of integration. How this approach succeeded or failed in incorporating massive and diverse immigrant flows into Spanish society is a question not well answered so far. The availability of information from a large and representative sample of second-generation youths provides a reliable basis to begin doing so.

Results of the study are neither predictable nor conventional. A number of surprising convergences emerge in patterns of adaptation of adult immigrants and their children in the United States and Spain, as well as significant differences that cast the context of receiving immigrants in both societies in a new light. Similarly, outcomes of the adaptation process of the second generation in Spain are quite unexpected, given the absence of an overarching integration model or policy. For the readers' convenience, summaries of the main findings are provided at the end of each empirical chapter. Implications of the study for Spanish society (currently mired in a severe recession), for the future of immigration to Western Europe, and for theories of immigrant adaptation are examined in the final chapter.

An earlier, abbreviated version of results presented in this book was published in Spanish in 2014.[9] Its purpose was to make available to Spanish authorities and lay public the principal findings and policy implications of the study. Too often, researchers travel to other countries, collect data, and then publish results in English, neglecting the people and country left behind. We made it a priority to publish results in Spanish, making them accessible to a non-specialized audience. The present book presents the complete results of the study, including the full statistical analyses, and a systematic comparison between empirical patterns detected in Spain and those found by CILS for second-generation youths in the United States a decade earlier. We believe that such comparisons will be of prime interest for an American audience. Qualitative interviews, presented in the first chapter, provide context for these findings.

# Acknowledgments

A study of the size and complexity as the one presented in the following pages could not have been completed without the support and assistance of many institutions and people. Our first debt of gratitude is to the Spencer Foundation of Chicago and, in particular, its president, Michael McPherson, who had the vision of supporting a study in a foreign country to test theories and hypotheses developed originally in the United States and to fill a knowledge gap on the adaptation process of children of immigrants in non-American contexts.

The Spencer Foundation supported the entire initial survey of second-generation youths in Spain, conducted in 2007–8, as well as the subsequent parental survey. That survey was also supported by the Directorate of Immigration of the Community of Madrid. The initial survey, comprising a large, representative sample of children of immigrants in the schools of Barcelona and Madrid, could not have been conducted without the cooperation of the respective school superintendents (*Consejerías de Educación*) in the two metropolitan regions. We are indebted to the heads of the Superior Evaluation Council of the Catalonian Community, Joan Mateo, and of the General Directorate of Secondary Education, Jose Garcia-Patrón, for their enthusiastic support of this study.

Fieldwork for the original survey was conducted under the capable and diligent leadership of Yolanda Tomas, supported by a staff that included Maite Vidal, David Capretta, and, in Barcelona, Marc Sabadi. The enthusiasm and initiative displayed by this team were directly responsible for the success of what was at the time uncharted terrain, since a study of this kind had never been attempted before.

We also acknowledge with gratitude the cooperation of the dozens of school principals and teachers without whose assistance this survey of close to 7,000 school children could not have been completed. Two years after the initial survey, a study of parents of participating children was launched. It was conducted by the same team that carried out the original survey with the addition of new members Sileny Cabala, Giulio Tinessa, and Assia Fresegna. This parental survey was conducted via individual telephone interviews and completed in 2010.

To make the study longitudinal, as its name in Spanish (Investigación Longitudinal de la Segunda Generación) indicates, it became necessary to track the students over time and reinterview them. The Spencer Foundation, once again, came to the rescue by granting half of the necessary funds—provided that a Spanish or European source contribute the other half. A successful application to the *Plan Nacional* of the Spanish Ministry of Science and Innovation yielded the necessary funds to activate the Spencer grant and make the follow-up survey possible. By then the study, baptized as ILSEG for its Spanish initials, had moved its headquarters to the Ortega y Gasset University Institute of Madrid. Its director at the time, Jesus Sanches Lambás, was kind enough to advance the necessary funds to launch the survey while the American and Spanish grants were being processed.

Fieldwork for the follow-up survey began in the schools of metropolitan Madrid in the fall of 2011 and extended to those of metropolitan Barcelona in the spring of 2012. This effort was again led by Yolanda Tomas, supported by Maite Vidal and Samira Shaban. The efforts of this team yielded a sizable number of interviews with original respondents as well as a refresher sample of other second-generation students and a new sample of native-parentage youths for comparative purposes. All three surveys were completed in the same schools originally included in the 2007–8 sample. We are indebted to the ILSEG field team, led by Tomas, for its extraordinary achievements in organizing and completing this part of the study.

The retrieval rate of original respondents reached through fieldwork in the schools did not yield, however, a sufficient number of original respondents to permit authoritative analysis of trends over time. To supplement that effort, we turned to other means of sample retrieval, in particular contacts through social media via the Internet. This part of the survey was based at the Ortega y Gasset Institute and was led by Sileny Cabala with a team formed by Jaime Goez, Monica Mongui, and Assia Fresegna. This team labored through the summer and fall of 2012 using both the telephone and the Internet in a sustained effort to find ILSEG's original respondents. The team developed an ILSEG project blog and invited respondents to post messages in it and to help team members locate other cases. Such efforts, described in detail in Chapter 4, succeeded in bringing the retrieval rate to over 70 percent of the original sample. In total, over 7,000 cases were contacted and interviewed by the various 2011–12 surveys.

The size and complexity of this data set required a major effort of editing and statistical analysis. Research assistants working under the senior author at Princeton University and the University of Miami can be credited for a significant and indispensable contribution during this analytic stage. They included Jessica Yiu at Princeton and Adrienne Celaya, Aaron Puhrmann, and Bryan Lagae at Miami. The empirical chapters that represent the core of this book could not have been completed without their diligent and highly competent collaboration.

As the analysis of survey data was progressing, we became increasingly aware of the need to supplement quantitative results with in-depth, qualitative interviews of a subsample of our respondents deemed emblematic of key trends detected by the statistical analysis. This qualitative module of the project was supported by a final presidential grant from Spencer Foundation president Michael McPherson. The almost one hundred interviews completed as part of this module were conducted in person or via Skype in Madrid and Barcelona by Yolanda Tomas and Jaime Goez. A selection of these interviews forms the basis for Chapter 1. We are indebted to Yolanda and Jaime for their excellent contribution to this final stage of data collection.

At every stage of the project, we received support and wise advice from Professor Andres Tornos, s.j., of the University of Comillas in Madrid. His wide-ranging cultural and research experience yielded many valuable contributions to the successive phases of the study.

The many versions of the book's chapters were typed at Princeton by Christine Nanfra, who is also credited with assembling the bibliography and formatting the entire manuscript. We are deeply grateful to Christine for her intelligent and devoted collaboration throughout the entire publication process. Last but not least, our long-time editor at the University of California Press, Naomi Schneider, deserves credit for her enthusiastic and unwavering support of this book project since the its beginnings. As with many earlier projects over the years, her collaboration was indispensable in bringing the present one to successful completion.

# Figures

# Tables

# ONE

# Twelve Lives

## ANDREA

Born in Romania, Andrea came to live in Madrid ten years ago.[1] Her father arrived in 2003, she in 2004. Her father works as a truck driver and her mother as a nurse. The family is doing fairly well economically. Andrea, who is only 19, has already graduated from advanced secondary school and is enrolled at the university, pursuing a degree in psychology. By age 40, she wants to be a professional psychologist: "I am sure that I will. Studying you can get anywhere."

Andrea has been back to Romania five times but has no intention of living there. "I am sort of a fusion, part Romanian, part Spanish, but I will stay here." Her boyfriend is Spanish, also a university student, as are all of her friends. About Spain, she likes the people, the sociability, "everything in general." She has never felt discriminated against here.

In contrast, she is very critical of her own people: "Many Romanians come to Spain with bad intentions and others are influenced by this element; many children leave school early and neither work nor study." That is the reason why Andrea feels Romanians have not been successful in Spain. However, she is proud of herself and quite confident of her future. Living with both of her parents in a solid family situation, and succeeding so far in her studies, she has every reason to look forward to life in her new country.

## CHAIMAE

Chaimae was born in Morocco and came to Spain in the late 1990s. She is now 20 years old, lives with both of her parents, and is studying to be a dietitian with a scholarship from the Spanish Ministry of Education. Her father is a janitor and her mother works as a nurses' aid. Although she lives with both of her parents, she is already married. The husband, who is also Moroccan, lives with his own parents. Chaimae is Muslim; she goes to mosque occasionally but prays at home every day. In part because of her religion, she identifies as Moroccan. She has also suffered occasional discrimination: "In the street, somebody has yelled at me 'go back to your own country' or 'sh——moor.'"

Despite these incidents, Chaimae likes Spain, especially because of its climate. She plans to become a dietitian and work in the country. The worst thing for her is Spanish politics and politicians, whom she sees as responsible for the economic crisis. "If things do not improve in Spain, I may have to move to another country."

In her view, the biggest obstacle that Moroccans have faced in Spain is language, especially when they come very young: "Spanish children in school, they can be very cruel." Chaimae is, however, already fluent in Spanish. She does not feel particularly proud of herself but is confident that, by pursuing her studies, she will be successful professionally. Neither she nor her husband has plans for children at present. Her future depends on the work opportunities that appear after she completes her present training. Neither she nor her husband sees any incompatibility between their Muslim religion and pursuing successful lives in Spain.

## HERNAN

Born in Spain to Colombian parents, Hernan is now 20 years old and works as a waiter in a Mexican restaurant in Madrid, making 700 euros per month. His father returned to Colombia, and Hernan lives with his mother, who ekes out a living as a part-time seamstress and house-cleaner. He is no longer studying and instead aspires to become a soldier in the Spanish army. Hernan says that he identifies as Spanish but complains of having been discriminated against often "because of the color of my skin." Also, he did not do well in schools here, so he returned to Colombia: "I performed much better there," he says.

Aside from his stint as a student in Colombia, he has returned many times to that country. "I love Colombia; there are many things that I can do there that I cannot do here." Hernan gets carried away with these sentiments and finally affirms that "there is nothing that I like about Spain, but I am resigned to continue living here." Despite his Spanish birth, Hernan is in limbo between the two countries. He does not know what he wants. He says that most of his friends are Spanish, as is his girlfriend, and he has set his sights on joining the Spanish army. In the same breath, he recalls his positive experiences in his parents' country and says than he plans to return there. A broken family, a poor mother, and lack of support and success in his studies have put this young man at a loss about what to do with his life. At present, the only certainty is his waiter's job, the acceptance of his mother and his Spanish girlfriend, and the hope of a possible life as a soldier.

DIANA

Born in Spain of Filipino parents, Diana is 19 years old and is pursuing a technical degree in administration and finance while working fifteen hours per week. She works as a maid for three hours in the morning, a job for which she is paid 250 euros per month. She lives with her parents. Her mother also works as a maid in a hotel, and her father is a butler in a private home. Earlier in her life, Diana dropped out of school, joined a gang of girls, and engaged in public drinking and rowdy street parties, often broken up by police. What brought her back to her senses was religion. She is now a born-again Christian attending an evangelical church several times a week. "The Church really turned me around," she says; "once I joined, all the other bad stuff went away."

She has felt discriminated against "because of the color of my skin" but, in comparison with other problems, that has been a minor concern. The important things now are her religious conviction and her optimism for the future. By age 40, she wants to reach a high-level administrative position in a major Spanish firm. She is confident that she will get there because of her persistence and the good grades she is now getting in school.

Diana identifies herself as Spanish and plans to stay in the country. Most of her friends are Spanish, although her boyfriend is also Filipino. She plans to marry and leave her parents' home once she completes her studies and both she and her boyfriend find well-paying jobs. Despite the economic crisis, her religious faith makes her confident that this will happen. "It is just a matter of steady work and prayer," she says; "God will take care of the rest."

## LIOU

Born in Shanghai, Liou was brought to Spain at age 9. She was the second daughter of a couple that had to leave Shanghai because of the official one-child Chinese policy and, hence, the impossibility of enrolling Liou in school. She is now 20 years old, pursuing a career in business administration at the elite Carlos III University in Madrid. She still lives with her parents but works part-time in a luxury fashion clothing store. Much of her work involves translating for wealthy Chinese tourists. For this, she is paid about 750 euros per month.

Liou saves most of her salary because she lives with parents who support her. Like many other Chinese, the parents own a convenience store, and they have been quite successful in Madrid. They speak Chinese at home, and she uses it regularly at work. She calls herself Chinese but "once I get the Spanish nationality, I will call myself Spanish of Chinese ancestry," she says. This is, in part, because she plans for a highly successful career in Spain. By age 40, she sees herself as the manager of a large department store. "I'm certain I'll get there; I already have everything planned for the future."

She has never felt discrimination during her years in the country. "In early school, it was difficult because I could not speak the language," but now all of that is in the past: she interacts with wealthy customers, receives a good part-time salary, and her own elite university protects her. The Carlos III has just given her a scholarship to study business administration for one year at the University of Singapore. Her brother also received a scholarship from the Spanish government to study in Germany.

In her view, the Chinese have been quite successful in Spain because of their business skills, but they have failed to integrate into Spanish society. "The first generation, they just stay by themselves and don't go out; they seldom try to learn the language." By the second generation, it is all different. "We do mix and we're part of the youth of this country; we will stay." As an example, she cites herself: she still has some Chinese friends, but "seventy-five percent of my friends and relations are with Spaniards." For Liou, Spain is her home and the country where she expects a bright future."

## OTILIA ALEJANDRA

Otilia Alejandra was born in Romania and brought to Spain at age 12. Her father came in 2000 and was followed by Otilia and her mother.

Her parents moved to Spain "to give us a better life." Her father is a construction carpenter; her mother works cleaning houses. Otilia is 21 years old and already has an advanced degree in administration and finances (superior secondary level). She is already "in practices" after completing her studies. She now works and lives with her parents. For a while, she worked at the cafeteria set up by her father, but it went bankrupt.

Otilia is Russian Orthodox, and she goes to church occasionally. That religious identification is important to her, but she already identifies as Spanish. She plans to stay in Spain and to become a financial administrator. She is certain that she will succeed because of her good grades in school.

Nevertheless, she has had problems with discrimination. "The Spanish students pushed me around early in school"; "there are many people here that discriminate against us Romanians," she says. In Otilia's view, the problem is that some young Romanians commit violent robberies and "people develop terrible prejudice against them." Then "they classify all of us alike." This is not the case, however, with her Spanish professors, who have always treated her respectfully. Despite problems with discrimination "by some people," Otilia very much likes living in Spain. Most of her friends are Spanish, and she plans to obtain citizenship next year. She already has a steady boyfriend; he is Colombian.

JAVIER ANDRES

Born in Colombia, Javier Andres came to Madrid thirteen years ago. He is now 21 and studying in technical school to become a welder. He lives alone with his mother, since his parents divorced. The mother works as a nightclub waitress. From her earnings, she supports him so that he can study full time. Javier Andres had completed high school and sought to enter superior technical school to study computer logistics. Unfortunately, cuts in the education budget of the Community of Madrid reduced the number of available places in the technical school, and his application was rejected. Having nothing better to do, he enrolled in a private welding school. The course cost his mother 2,000 euros.

Javier Andres has been to Colombia twice but is not interested in preserving his parents' culture. He identifies as Spanish, plans to stay in the country, and aspires for the moment to work as a welder in a private firm. His plans to become a logistics engineer are on hold, but he hopes that he can go back to them in the future. Tall and handsome, Javier

Andres says he has never been discriminated against in Spain, though he admits that many young Colombians are. The stereotype among some Spaniards is that "all Colombians sell drugs."

Despite this, he likes living in Spain. He appreciates, in particular, the freedom and the public security—very different, in his view, from his native Colombia. Although he receives no support from his father and depends precariously on his mother's night-time job, he is confident that he will get ahead in life. "We are all in the same boat," he says; "in Spain, we are all trying to get out of the crisis." In this sense, he sees no difference between his own situation and that of young native Spaniards.

### EDWIN ANDRES

Ecuadorean by birth, Edwin Andres arrived in Spain when he was 6 years old. His parents came for economic reasons and to "give him a future." He is 22 years old and studies telecommunications in middle-technical school; he already worked in a radio station. His goal is to earn a degree in telecommunications and set himself up in business.

Although Edwin is not married, he already has a 2-year-old daughter and lives with the mother. They all live together in his parents' home. His father was a union organizer in Ecuador and has done rather well in Spain. He is in charge of maintenance and equipment in a Madrid sports club. He later got a job for his wife as cleaning supervisor in the same club, and more recently he employed Edwin's girlfriend in the same tasks. That sports club has been the family's economic salvation.

Edwin plans to live in Spain but will move to England if the economy continues to deteriorate. He wishes to keep "the little of my Ecuadorean roots that I was able to bring here." He likes Spain and identifies himself as "Spanish-Ecuadorean." He has never felt discriminated against—indeed, "people here have always treated me and my family well." At present, most of his close friends are Spanish; only a few are Ecuadorean.

In his view, the main problem of Ecuadorean youths in Spain is that they drop out of school: "they quit studying and join gangs; then they end up in prison or deported," he says. He knows several Ecuadoreans who have been deported. Luckily for Edwin, he did not abandon his studies and is solidly supported by his parents. While having a child at an early age represents a burden for the future, he is very confident that he will do well in Spain; in the worst case, he will move to another European country.

## ALI

Ali was born in Madrid of Moroccan parents who had come to Spain in the 1980s. He is now 21; he has quit his studies and works occasionally in informal jobs. His parents originally did very well in Spain. His father worked as a police officer in Melilla (a Spanish enclave city in North Africa), which facilitated getting an entry visa and housing in Madrid; he found a job in a Spanish enterprise, Dragados, that paid him a high salary. Unfortunately, however, he was then diagnosed with epilepsy and lost his job. The family currently depends on his invalid pension of 500 euros per month. Ali's mother is 52 and in ill health.

Ali was doing well in school through the first year of senior high school (*bachillerato*), which he successfully completed. During the second year, however, he ran into serious trouble with a professor, a racist in his view. "We were studying the Middle Ages and when the topic of Muslims came up, she called them 'moors' and looked at me directly, like provoking me." He let this and other incidents pass, but when she flunked him, he went to see her, arguing that other students who had performed at the same level had passed the course. The professor answered, according to Ali, that no matter how much he studied, she would not let him graduate.

Ali went to see the principal, collected signatures from fellow students, and filed a formal complaint. There was an investigation. In the end, according to him, professors at his school closed ranks in support of their colleague, and nothing was done. Indeed, another professor called the mother of his girlfriend (who was Spanish) to ask her "if she knew that your daughter is going out with a Muslim." Ali was expelled from his school and forced to enroll in another.

But it was not the same. For him, it was starting all over again, without his friends and in a strange environment. He had a serious bout of depression and decided to quit school. Since then, he has had occasional jobs working in bars, washing cars, and buying and selling things, but nothing steady. He still lives with his parents, but, given his situation, he cannot help them economically.

Ali plans to go back to school but not to senior high. Instead, he wishes to enroll in a mid-level technical career. Failing this, he plans to join his brother, who works as a hotel receptionist in Brussels. In addition to Arabic and Spanish, Ali speaks French and some English. Despite the incident with the professor and other episodes of discrimination, he still likes Spain and would like to live here. "I went to go visit my brother in Belgium and, in two weeks, the sun only came out once; I really missed Madrid."

Ali's friends are Spanish, Moroccan, and Latin American. Nationality makes no difference to him. Despite having been born in Spain, he does not consider himself Spanish, however: "The typical thing . . . here you're not Spanish, but Moroccan; when I go to Morocco, I am not Moroccan, but Spanish. In the end, it's all the same to me." In his opinion, Moroccans have not done well in Spain because of their backwardness. "Many of them are real Cro-Magnons [sic]. I have seen parents that do not allow their daughters to go out, that force them to wear a veil, to leave their studies early. Fortunately, my parents were more tolerant and did not object to my going out with a Christian girl."

Ali has no idea of what he wants to be by age 40. "To tell you the truth, since there is so much scarcity right now, I would only want a job, even one with many hours and low pay . . . enough to maintain myself, pay the rent, and eat. That would be enough." He does not stop to think where he really belongs. "To me, it's all the same, but when I feel attacked, I defend myself like anyone else would do. We all have our pride, and no one has the right to step on it."

Ambling from one petty job to another and without steady plans, it is clear that Ali has not recovered from that encounter with the racist professor and his dismissal from his high school. In his favor, he has a supportive family, friends from many origins, and a Spanish girlfriend who has not left him despite the problems he has to face.

## ASTRID

Astrid was born in Madrid of Peruvian parents. They arrived in 1991, and Astrid was born three years later. She is now 20 and studying to complete senior high school while working full time in a paintings and ceramics shop. Her parents have done fairly well in Spain. Her father is an upholsterer and has his own shop; her mother cleans houses. The family owns its own home and two cars. Astrid lives with them.

During her second year of senior high school, she confronted problems and flunked math, literature, and English. Her father was extremely upset and kept reproaching her for her failure. "You cannot stay in this house, doing nothing," he said. He talked to some of his friends and found her a job in a painting shop. The change turned out to be good for Astrid. She learned to paint, and, though she works full time, the job is not hard. "It's not like being a waitress or something," she says. She earns 1,100 euros per month and, living with her parents, saves most of it. Her paintings are sold for decoration to hotels and restaurants.

Astrid aspires to go to the university, and, for this reason, she decided to go back to school to complete an advanced secondary degree. She goes to night school after the work day. Her parents approve. She also plans to use her savings to go to an English- speaking country to perfect her knowledge of the language. "English has become an obsession with me," she says.

Later in life, she wants to be an executive or general manager of a large firm. To achieve this, she plans to enroll in the international commerce program in superior technical school after completing her last year of senior high. Astrid has traveled every five years with her family to Peru but does not plan to do so again in the future. "I get bored, I have nothing to do there; I would go only to see my grandparents before they pass," she says.

She is planning to stay in Spain and feels herself to be Spanish, but not "Spanish, Spanish"—"With the color of my skin, I can't, I have too much Peruvian blood." Though born in Spain, she is frequently asked where she comes from. "I look at myself in the mirror, and I know why," she says. Despite the difference, most of her friends are Spanish, and she feels very much at ease with them. Indeed, what she least likes about Spain is the presence of so many Latino (i.e., Latin American) youths. "I don't like Latinos," she says, "the way they dress, the noise they make, the bands they join. They are always breaking bottles, hitting cars, smelling of marijuana." Naturally, not all Latinos are like that; she also has several Latino friends, "but they do not do these things; they are like the Spanish, they know how to behave."

Most often typified as a Latina herself because of her skin color, Astrid rejects this to embrace a Spanish self-identity and a positive future in the country. Her parents, deep mestizos (people of "mixed blood") themselves, have paved the way by carving a good economic position in Madrid, finding her a good job, and strongly encouraging her to pursue her studies. It is for these reasons that Astrid sets herself apart from Latino migrants and, despite several incidents of discrimination, plans on a successful life in her country of birth.

## SARAH

Born in the Philippines, Sarah was brought to Spain at age 7. Her father is Spanish (Catalan), and her mother is Filipina. Sarah is now 18 and is completing her second year of senior high school. Interested since early high school in economics and marketing, she plans to enter the university to pursue a degree in business administration. She is certain that she will succeed.

Reasons for that certainty have to do with her privileged upbringing: her father is a senior executive of the Hilton Hotels chain in Spain and Portugal, in charge of expanding the firm into new cities; her mother is a high-fashion photographer. At home, the family speaks English, but Sarah is also fluent in Spanish and Philippine Tagalog. Living and studying in Barcelona, she also speaks Catalan, which she uses, at times, in conversations with her father.

However, Sarah sees herself not as Catalan or Filipina but as Spanish—"very Spanish," she says. Her distinctive physical features, inherited from her mother, do not represent, in her view, a disadvantage but quite the opposite: "It makes me unique, even exotic." Sarah has never felt discriminated against in Spain, and indeed all her friends are Spanish. From her childhood in the Philippines, she remembers only the cuisine and little else; she has never been back nor is interested in doing so.

Before settling in Barcelona, the family lived in Mallorca, where Sarah attended private Catholic school. She is currently pursuing her senior high studies in a Jesuit private school. Naturally, she identifies herself as Catholic, though she only goes to Mass from time to time. Religion is not really a big part of her life; she is focused mainly on her studies and her friendships. By age 40, she would like to be a financial broker—"I always loved the Wall Street thing," she says. However, she plans to stay in Spain and, if possible, in Barcelona.

As to the situation of other Filipino immigrants in Spain, she believes that they have been generally successful. "Every time that I pass in front of MACBA [the Contemporary Art Museum of Barcelona], I see lots of Filipinos and they all look happy and prosperous; I still have to see a homeless or poor Filipino here," she says. Fluent in English, successful in her studies, and with educated and supportive parents, Sarah faces an open future. For her, Barcelona—indeed, all of Spain—looks like her oyster.

## YASMINA

Yasmina was born in Spain to poor Moroccan parents. Her father worked for many years as a trucker in a Barcelona factory and is now retired; her mother stays at home. Yasmina is 19; she is completing her first year of senior high school after failing twice in the past. She aspires to reach the university, "to study tourism or English philology," she says.

The reason that she failed repeatedly in school is that she started going out with a group of kids, all Moroccan, who took her life in a different direction. "I had to be one hundred percent dedicated to them; every time that I started to study, they opened my 'WhatsApp' and demanded to know what I was doing." Her parents repeatedly told her to quit these friendships; they were all "marroquinists" [the colloquial term used in Barcelona to refer to Moroccans, or *marroquinos* in Catalan and Spanish] and very conflictive. They urged her to focus on her studies, which were key to her future.

Eventually, she complied: "Morally, I was destroyed; I did not know what to say or what to do. You had to be at their beck and call to keep them happy," she says of her former friends. Also, she went to Holland, where her cousin lived. There she saw her cousin and other Moroccan relatives who had completed their university degrees and lived normal, happy lives. "Right then and there, I decided that I wanted to be like them; I realized that I was wasting my life."

Yasmina finally left the Moroccan gang: "The boys were very bossy; they stole, drank, always partying; they had a lot of evil inside." She re-started her studies and is confident that she will complete senior high. Since this shift in her life happened relatively recently, she does not have a clear idea of what career she will pursue or what she wants to be later in life. "It's too soon for me to think about this, I'm only recovering now," she says.

Like her parents, Yasmina is a Muslim. They seldom go to mosque but pray at home often. Her mother wears a veil and insists on keeping her religious roots; her father is more tolerant: "He says that, if you're a good person, respect others, work, and take care of your children, it does not matter if you're religious or what religion you practice." Yasmina shares her father's views. She does not wear a veil and identifies herself as thoroughly Spanish. "After all, I was born here; this is all that I know."

Her brothers, older than her, are not religious and have fully integrated into life in Spain. One of them is in the Spanish army. Because of her past experiences, Yasmina is wary of new relationships and studiously avoids "other marroquinists." Her only close friend is an Indian girl with whom she studies every day. She would like to have more Spanish friends in the future. She also would like to live in a different neighborhood. "I have lived here all my life and need to leave behind the very bad memories of my past." Going back to Holland to spend some time with her cousin is also an option: "The important thing is to forget what happened and move on with my life," she says.

Although her parents are well established in their neighborhood, they fully support her new ambitions, with the father always reminding her that "she was born here." In Yasmina's opinion, the reason why many Moroccans have not succeeded in Spain is that they have a very narrow-minded view of culture and religion. "From the door outwards, the kids try to be like the Spaniards—they do try to improve their Spanish; but once they return home, it's all over; it is a different world . . . quite difficult to keep that balance." Failing to balance the demands of school and their families, many Moroccan youths end up on the streets. Having experienced that life, Yasmina is grateful to have pulled back thanks to the advice and tolerance of her parents and the example and support of her cousin in the Netherlands. Still, she is not particularly proud of herself: "I have not yet done much with my life, but that should come to pass," she concludes.

The stories of these twelve young people who were part of the ILSEG study illustrate the very different experiences of children of immigrants in Spain, whether born in the country or born abroad and brought to the country at an early age. Like in the United States, immigrants in Spain face multiple challenges as they confront the demands of life in a new country. Moving between two social and cultural worlds, these demands become even more complex for their children. How they deal with those challenges will determine both their future and the future of the immigrant communities to which they belong. This book is dedicated to examining their experiences and to identifying those factors that determine both individual outcomes and collective effects in the country that is now theirs.

# TWO

# Theories of Second-Generation Adaptation

The rapid growth of the immigrant population in the advanced world represents one of the most important demographic and social phenomena confronting these societies. By 2010, close to 13 percent of the population of the United States was foreign-born. In Spain, one of the European countries most heavily affected by the phenomenon, the foreign-born population was roughly the same (12 percent), despite the much more recent onset of migration flows and the negative effect on them of the economic recession starting in 2008.[1]

Unlike transfers of merchandise and capital, immigrant flows are composed of people and thus tend to have enduring social consequences. One of the most important is the re-constitution of families and the procreation of a new generation. Unlike adult immigrants, born and educated in a foreign society and whose outlook and plans are indelibly marked by that experience, their offspring commonly become full-fledged members of the host society and present it with new challenges. If their numbers are large, socializing these new citizens and preparing them to become productive and successful in adulthood becomes a major policy concern.

This is what has been happening in the United States as well as in Western Europe and, in particular, in Spain. The rapid growth and diversity of this young population have naturally sparked worries and questions about its future. In the absence of reliable information, all kinds of speculative notions have been advanced about the character and the effects on the host society of the new immigrants and their off-spring.[2] In this chapter, we review the various theoretical perspectives that have been advanced on this topic as a prelude for the presentation of our empirical results. However, it is necessary to begin with some important preliminary distinctions. Although public discourse and some academic essays treat this young population in blanket terms, the truth is that the term *migrant children* conceals more than it reveals because of the heterogeneity of its component groups.

First, there is a significant difference between children born abroad and those born in the host society. The first are immigrant children; the second are children of immigrants. The research literature points to major differences in the social and cultural adaptation process of these two categories. In between are children born abroad but brought to the host society at an early age, making them sociologically closer to the second generation. These are known as the "1.5 generation." A number of studies, notably those by Rubén Rumbaut, have analyzed the distinct patterns of linguistic and cultural development associated with birth-place and length of time since arrival.[3]

A second important distinction concerns countries of origin and soci-oeconomic background. Both in the United States and in Spain, it turns out that these dimensions overlap due to several historical contingencies. Immigration to the United States has become bifurcated into a high human capital flow—professional workers of various kinds coming to fill positions in high-tech industry, research centers, and health services—and a larger manual labor flow seeking employment in labor-intensive industries such as agriculture, construction, and personal serv-ices.[4] Professional migration comes primarily from Asia, being sourced mainly in India and China, with smaller flows from the Philippines, South Korea, and Taiwan. Manual labor migration comes overwhelm-ingly from adjacent Mexico and secondarily, from the countries of Cen-tral America and the Caribbean.[5] Although Spain has not deliberately promoted the migration of professional and scientific talent, significant differences in educational and occupational background are apparent between immigrants from other European countries and the Southern Cone of the Americas and those coming from other parts of the world. These differences will be examined in detail in Chapter 5.

To the extent that migrant workers, either professional or manual, return promptly to their countries of origin, no major consequences accrue to the host society. In reality, however, many of the migrants stay and either bring their families or create new families in their new places of settlement. In due time, the contingent geographical divide in the major sources of contemporary migration gives rise to different ethnic groups in the host society. In the United States, two such major groups have emerged: "Asians," by and large the offspring of highly educated migrants; and "Hispanics," the majority of whom are manual workers and their descendants. In Spain, as well, significant differences separate the children of white immigrants from Europe and certain countries of South America and those from sub-Saharan Africa, the Andean region, and the black Caribbean. Parental differences in phenotypes, education, and occupational skills can be expected to affect the process of adaptation in both national contexts.

The purpose of this book is to clarify how this process plays itself out in Spain. We tell the story of the Spanish second generation on the basis of a large-scale longitudinal study (ILSEG) that partially replicates the Children of Immigrants Longitudinal Study (CILS), which was completed in the United States between 1992 and 2005.[6] Because both studies used the same methodological blueprint, it is possible to move back and forth between them for comparison and clarification. Both studies are described in detail in Chapter 4. As a preview to the presentation of these comparative results, this chapter examines existing theories on the adaptation of the second generation, and the next chapter summarizes the history of immigration to Spain and the research literature bearing on it.

## THEORIZING THE FUTURE OF THE SECOND GENERATION

Little longitudinal research on the contemporary second generation has been conducted, so far, in Europe. The most prominent study on the topic is the Integration of the European Second Generation (TIES) project, based on a cross-national sample of young adults of Moroccan, Turkish, and Yugoslavian origins in several West European countries.[7] Although TIES contributed many significant findings, it was limited by the static nature of the data and the restriction of the sample to a few nationalities. A longitudinal design is necessary to establish causal order among determinants and outcomes of a dynamic process such as the adaptation of the second generation. Similarly, past studies in the United States indicate that this process can differ markedly among various nationalities.[8]

Investigation of the second generation in Europe has been given considerable impetus by a comparative project financed mainly by the

National Science Foundation of the United States to look at the situation of children of immigrants in American and West European schools.[9] That study did not collect original data, limiting itself to the use of existing cross-sectional information, including that produced by TIES. As a result, inter-country comparisons describe in detail differences in the educational systems between the United States and several European countries but do not advance any original theoretical notion. Furthermore, the use of existing survey data is commonly limited to one immigrant group per country, defined *a priori* as problematic. As in the case of TIES, this definition assumes what has to be investigated, thereby limiting the generalizability of results.[10]

Theorizing about second-generation adaptation has gone further in the United States, corresponding to the larger body of empirical research there. For that reason, we organize this review on the basis of theories formulated in the American context, with attention to West European variants when appropriate. Theoretical perspectives in this field can be grouped into two distinct schools that may be labeled "culturalist" and "structuralist." Culturalist views emphasize the relative assimilation of immigrants into the cultural, linguistic, and political mainstream; structuralist perspectives focus on the integration of newcomers into the socioeconomic hierarchies of the host society, concentrating on such topics as educational attainment, occupational achievement, wealth and poverty, and negative experiences compromising success in adult life. The cultural and structural experiences of assimilation can be decoupled. For instance, individuals who are fully assimilated into society's cultural/linguistic mainstream can still experience poor outcomes in education, occupation, and income. Conversely, they may not become fully integrated culturally and still do well economically.[11] Table 1 presents a summary of the views that will be reviewed next.

### Culturalist Perspectives

Views emphasizing the cultural, linguistic, and political assimilation of the second generation range from pessimistic to optimistic. At the pessimistic end of the spectrum is the belief, championed by Harvard political scientist Samuel Huntington, that children of immigrants are not assimilating.[12] In this view, certain groups, Hispanics in particular, have arrived in such large numbers in certain areas of the United States that they are not inclined to acculturate. Immigrants and their children resist learning English, place allegiance on the interests of their ethnic com-

TABLE I   AN OVERVIEW OF THEORETICAL PERSPECTIVES ON SECOND-GENERATION ASSIMILATION

| Perspective | Primary proponents | Views on assimilation | Empirical basis |
|---|---|---|---|
| Culturalist perspectives | | | |
| Hispanic challenge | Samuel Huntington | Pessimistic, not happening | Theoretical |
| Neo-assimilationism | Richard Alba and Victor Nee | Optimistic, occurring just as in past generations and transforming the mainstream of the host society | Secondary review of historical and contemporary data on immigrant cultural and linguistic assimilation |
| Structuralist perspectives | | | |
| Second-generation advantage | Philip Kasinitz, John Mollenkopf, Mary C. Waters, and Jennifer Holdaway | Optimistic, the second generation is situated in a social and cultural space that works to its advantage | Cross-sectional study of second-generation young adults in New York City |
| Generations of exclusion | Edward Telles and Vilma Ortiz | Pessimistic, Mexican Americans stagnating into the working class or assimilating into a racial underclass | Longitudinal study of three-plus genera-tions of Mexican Americans in Los Angeles and San Antonio |
| Segmented assimilation | Alejandro Portes and Rubén Rumbaut | Mixed, assimilation may help or hurt social and economic outcomes depending on parental human capital, family structure, and contexts of incorporation | Longitudinal study of second-generation youths in Southern California and South Florida from early adolescence into early adulthood |

SOURCE: Adapted from Portes and Rivas, "The Adaptation of Migrant Children," table I.

munities and home countries, and reject the ideals and norms of the host society. This view is rooted in the belief that American identity is intimately tied to the Anglo-Protestant culture of the founders of the country and that Catholic newcomers from Latin America, unwilling to adopt Anglo-Protestant ways, will form their own cultural and linguis-tic enclaves. Thus, children of immigrants who come from societies deemed to be culturally incompatible with Anglo-Protestant America will not advance much into the cultural and linguistic mainstream.[13]

Parallel views in Western Europe have been buttressed by the massive presence of non-Christian immigrants, primarily Muslims, and the widespread conviction that they do not wish to assimilate to the culture of the host societies. This pessimistic view is advanced not only by right-wing scholars but also by mass political movements that have succeeded in swaying the electorate in many countries. The formerly tolerant multicultural approach of the Netherlands, for example, has been abandoned under the influence of these views giving way to determined pro-assimilationist policies.[14] In Spain, Huntington-like arguments have focused on Moroccan and sub-Saharan Africans as their prime targets and have produced isolated attacks on them. Studies of immigrant youths have also targeted Moroccans *a priori* as most problematic. However, the policies of the Spanish national and regional governments have so far not been swayed by this perspective, encouraging instead ethnic tolerance and a gradual process of integration.[15]

Huntington's perspective is not rooted in any original empirical research; rather, it is a response to what he perceived to be the forces that prevent current immigrants from assimilating. Since Huntington's writings on the issue were speculative, critics had no difficulty refuting his assertions with evidence that immigrants are capable of assimilating culturally and linguistically. For instance, there is little evidence that children of immigrants avoid learning English or that non-English languages endure past the second generation in the United States. Sociologists have also found that levels of active participation in the American political system rise across generations and that descendants of Latin American immigrants follow the same course.[16] The rapid and decisive increase in the Hispanic vote in the 2012 presidential elections provides additional evidence of this trend.

In Western Europe, in general, and Spain, in particular, arguments that Moroccans and other Muslim and sub-Saharan immigrants do not wish to integrate to the host society are backed more by anecdotal evidence than by serious scientific research. As we will see, the available data on the second generation do not support these views.[17] Although not backed by hard evidence, the Huntington hypothesis is important because it resonates with segments of native public opinion and can, at times, decisively affect both electoral politics and public policy.

On the optimistic side of the culturalist camp are those authors who have returned to the traditional melting-pot theory and dusted it off for the twenty-first century. They argue that cultural and political assimilation continues to take place and that immigrants of today are no different in this respect from those of the past. They further argue that immigrants assimilate not into specific segments of society but rather into a broad "mainstream" that is simultaneously changed by them. The champions of this viewpoint, sociologists Richard Alba and Victor Nee, describe assimilation as "something that happens" to people while they are making other plans.[18] These plans, they argue, are to achieve economic success. In seeking success, immigrants come into contact with the cultural features of the mainstream and undergo linguistic and cultural assimilation. Therefore, though it may take time, the children of today's immigrants and subsequent generations will eventually join the body of society, even if they do not ultimately achieve upward mobility. Alba and Nee's thesis argues that exposure to the host culture and subsequent assimilation are inevitable.

Neo-assimilationism, as these views are known, draws support from historical evidence on the acculturation of descendants of European immigrants in the United States and other countries of immigration in the Americas who have, by now, become indistinguishable from natives. The experience of Italian, Portuguese, and Spanish migration to France and the Low Countries can also be cited in support of this view, as descendants of these earlier immigrants became thoroughly acculturated to these countries' sociocultural mainstream.[19] Spain is too recent a country of immigration to provide evidence for or against this hypothesis. Results from our study, to be presented in the following chapters, provide the first glimpse of the extent to which children of immigrants are joining the Spanish mainstream.

## Structuralist Perspectives

Like culturalist views, structuralist perspectives can be organized by their level of optimism about the future of immigrants and their children. As mentioned previously, they focus on the extent to which immigrants and their descendants succeed in the educational and occupational systems of the host society, regardless of their level of acculturation.

The "generations of exclusion" thesis paints a rather pessimistic picture of the future for some groups of immigrants and their children. This perspective describes immigrants as isolated from the opportunities for mobility offered by the host society, not because of their decisions to avoid assimilation but due to membership in ethnic and racial groups that are heavily discriminated against. According to this view, Mexican immigrants and their descendants in the United States move into communities and segments of society that have become racialized and marginalized. Past waves of immigrants from Europe were able to assimilate both culturally and economically by gradually elbowing their way into the more privileged "white" segments of the American racial hierarchy. In contrast, Mexican and other Hispanic immigrants, whose ancestry includes European roots, risk becoming a distinct "race" with consistently worse outcomes than whites—and comparable outcomes to those endured by black Americans.[20]

The research of sociologists Edward Telles and Vilma Ortiz into Mexican-American communities in Los Angeles and San Antonio over several generations form the basis of this immigrant racialization view. In 2000, Telles and Ortiz re-interviewed Mexican-Americans who had previously been part of a 1965 study on the social condition of the Mexican-American community. As a result, Telles and Ortiz were able to construct a thirty-five-year longitudinal data set covering the integration of the original respondents and their descendants into the third, fourth, and sometimes fifth generations. They found that most members of these latter generations still lived in predominantly Mexican neighborhoods, married within their ethnicity, and identified as Mexican. Although there were socioeconomic gains between the first and the second generations, that progress did not continue afterward: poverty rates in the third and fourth generations stayed consistently high, and educational attainment actually declined among their members. Telles and Ortiz attributed the disadvantage experienced by Mexican-Americans to lack of access to quality education, persistent discrimination, antagonistic immigration policies, and the reliance of the economy on cheap, ethnically defined labor.[21]

For groups other than Mexican-Americans, outcomes will vary according to the specific mix of resources and disadvantages linked with their racial/cultural features. Nathan Glazer and Daniel P. Moynihan, for example, noted that the various immigrant groups in New York City had lost their original language and culture but remained distinct from one another. In their view, "the whole point of the melting pot is that it did not happen."[22] Instead, ethnic groups, though transformed, maintained themselves as if separate organs of society. Jews, Italians, Puerto Ricans, and others organized themselves not only around ethnicity but also around common political and economic of resources. For some groups, such as Cubans in Miami, control over these political and economic resources has brought power and prosperity. Others, such as Mexican-Americans and Puerto Ricans, have been racialized and have been kept at the bottom of the income and occupational hierarchies.[23]

In Western Europe, the experience of marginalization and racialization of second- and even third-generation Turks in Germany and that of children of Turks and Moroccans in the Low Countries documented, among others, by the TIES project tends to support the "generations of exclusion" thesis. These youths have become fluent in the host country languages and adopted much of their culture without this acculturation translating into much educational or occupational mobility.[24] In this sense, they have come to resemble the experience of Mexican-Americans in the United States. The set of comparative studies in European countries and the United States assembled by Richard Alba and Jennifer Holdaway concludes on a similar note, even asserting that children of low-education immigrants are subjected to a system of "effectively maintained inequality" whereby any gains that they manage to make are neutralized by the greater power of the native upper and middle classes.[25]

According to the "generations of exclusion" hypothesis, we should expect children of immigrants in Spain to assimilate to the racial/ethnic categories assigned to them by the native majority. These identities would remain ensconced in their parents' ethnic origins, and their progress in the educational system would trail those of native Spaniards. Unlike Alba and Nee's earlier assimilationist views, children of immigrants would be integrating into Spanish society, but the process would not necessarily lead to joining an all-inclusive "mainstream." Instead, it could lead to their integration into specific subcategories of a racialized social structure.

Other scholars believe, however, that though immigrants may enter host societies as members of stratified racial groups, their children are able to use their location as participants in two societies and two cultures to their own advantage. This "second-generation advantage" thesis argues that, unlike native minorities, children of immigrants possess a wealth of cultural resources and can pick and choose from a wide set of alternatives when planning out the course their lives will take. They are, in Rumbaut's term, "translation artists."[26] Empirical support for the idea of second-generation advantage comes from a study of young adults in New York City conducted by Philip Kasinitz and his colleagues. Many of these youths were found living at home past high school or college age because their immigrant parents came from cultures where such living arrangements were not stigmatized. Members of the second generation also supplemented their searches for employment by tapping into their ethnic social networks. Rather than rely solely on newspaper ads, these youths learned of job opportunities through word of mouth in their communities. Along with resources embedded in their immigrant networks, many second-generation youths could also make use of resources and institutions established to aid native racial minorities achieve upward mobility.[27]

At the core of the "second-generation advantage" thesis is the belief that these youths are positioned at an intersection of several social and cultural currents and, as a result, the amount of information and support that they have at their disposal grants them a significant edge for mobility.[28] No evidence exists at present in Europe to back these ideas. As seen previously, historical records on South European immigrants in France and elsewhere tends to support the neo-assimilationism of Alba and Nee, whereas those of contemporary Turks, Moroccans, and sub-Saharians lean in the direction of Telles and Ortiz as well as Alba and Holdaway's racialization and exclusionism. If the "advantage" thesis were accurate, we would expect second-generation youths in Spain to race past their native-parentage peers, not by thoroughly acculturating to the mainstream but precisely by making use of resources embedded in two cultures. They should feature higher levels of ambition and perform better educationally and occupationally. In its emphasis on the advantages conferred by participation in two social systems and two cultures, this thesis comes to resemble a pivotal notion advanced by the next and last structuralist perspective.

Between the optimists and the pessimists lies a view that does not automatically predict positive or negative outcomes but instead takes a more nuanced approach toward the future of the second generation. The "segmented assimilation" thesis asserts that forces underlying second-generation advantage may indeed be at play, but different groups of immigrants face distinct barriers to upward mobility. The character of the co-ethnic community, governmental policies toward specific immigrant groups, and race and ethnicity can either increase or diminish the chances for successful integration by members of the second generation. These forces alone are not determinative of life outcomes, because the endowments and strategies employed by immigrant parents can also be vital in overcoming obstacles to upward mobility. This view does not focus so much on whether or not children of immigrants are assimilating but rather *into what segment* of the host society they assimilate. As a result, the process is seen not as automatically leading toward entry into the middle-class "mainstream" but as potentially leading in the opposite direction.[29]

The main barriers identified for successful integration by segmented assimilation are three-fold: racism; a bifurcated labor market; and the presence of deviant lifestyles as alternative adaptation paths. Racism against groups defined by natives as non-white negatively affects the self-esteem and aspirations of children of immigrants and can effectively bar them from educational and labor market opportunities. An increasingly bifurcated occupational structure requires advanced educational credentials to access the well-paying jobs that guarantee a middle-class lifestyle. This means that second-generation youths must seek and secure advanced degrees—often traversing, in the course of a single generation, a path that took descendants of earlier immigrants many decades to complete. The presence of street gangs, widespread sale of drugs, and crime in impoverished neighborhoods amounts to an alternative lifestyle, easily available to youths in these areas and attractive to those alienated from school discipline.[30]

Resources available to immigrant families to avoid these barriers are also three-fold: human capital; a favorable or neutral mode of incorporation; and community social capital. Immigrant parents with advanced levels of education are better situated to secure better paying jobs, move their families to secure neighborhoods with good schools, and otherwise steer their young toward higher ambition and educational achievement. Immigrants with legal documents and recipients of governmental assistance are beneficiaries of a positive mode of incorporation that places them in a much better position to confront barriers to successful integration than those with irregular status. Finally, second-generation youths growing up in cohesive co-ethnic communities profit from supportive social networks anchoring their self-images and strengthening their ambitions toward the future.[31]

Strong co-ethnic communities foster *selective acculturation,* a pattern in which children combine learning the language and culture of the host society with preservation of the parental language and key elements of the parents' culture. The theory asserts that selective acculturation is preferable for long-term adaptation than the full-barreled assimilation advocated by native mainstream institutions. Selective acculturation is a concept similar to "second-generation advantage," but it differs from the latter in that it is not a resource available to everyone and it depends for its existence on the cohesiveness of parental families and co-ethnic communities. It is, by and large, a collective rather than a purely individual resource.[32]

Depending on the variable geometry of barriers to successful adaptation and family and community resources to neutralize them, different personal trajectories can be anticipated. These are schematically presented in Figure 1. Segmented assimilation thus differs from the generalized optimism of neo-assimilationist and "second-generation advantage" views, agreeing that such outcomes are possible but only attainable when certain conditions are present. It also differs from the blanket pessimism of the generations-of-exclusion thesis or the recently coined "effectively maintained inequality" argument since, with the right combination of resources, barriers in the path to educational achievement and occupational integration can be surmounted. Many children of immigrants manage to accomplish this feat.

This model has been applied in several studies of immigrant children in Europe, including TIES. However, by being based on samples limited to a few nationalities and using a static cross-sectional design, these studies cannot provide an authoritative test of the model nor extend it in original directions. The same conclusion applies to the previously noted collection of comparative studies in the United States and West European countries.[33]

If segmented assimilation is applicable to the case of the second generation in Spain, we would expect patterned differences among immigrant groups contingent on their average parental human capital and modes of incorporation. We will also expect distinct paths of educational and occupational adaptation depending on the character of the co-ethnic community. Lastly, the key difference between culturalist and structuralist theories, noted at the start, should be kept in mind as we review empirical findings in the ensuing chapters. The different perspectives translate into contrasting predictions on children of immigrants' integration. They range from their educational and occupational aspirations to their performance in the educational system, self-identities and perceptions of discrimination, and labor market experiences. We examine next how each of these theories bears on different outcomes of the adaptation process.

## THE ROLE OF AMBITION

Much of the literature on immigrant adolescent adaptation focuses on the issue of aspirations and expectations. There is good reason for this, because sociological and psychological research has provided consistent evidence of the predictive power of these psychosocial factors on subse-

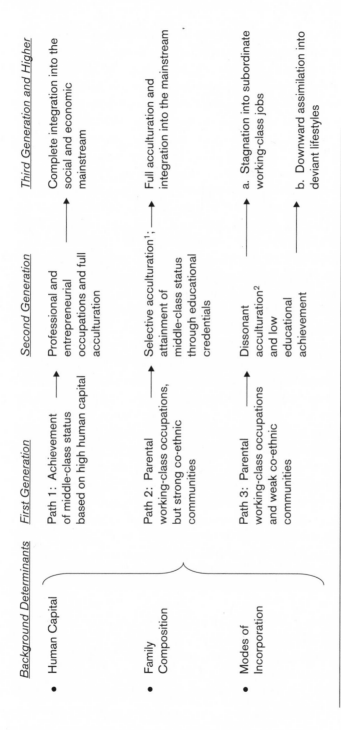

[1] Defined as preservation of parental language and elements of parental culture along with acquisition of English and American culture.
[2] Defined as rejection of parental culture and breakdown of communication across generations.

FIGURE 1. Paths of Mobility across Generations: A Model.
Source: Portes and Rumbaut, *Legacies*, fig. 3.1.

quent outcomes. The underlying rationale of this finding is straightforward: children and adolescents who aspire to a college-level education may or may not fulfill their goals, but those who do not aspire high will not get there. In that sense, adolescent aspirations function as a prerequisite—a necessary condition for subsequent achievement.

The main theoretical framework for the study of adolescent ambition has been the Wisconsin Model of Status Attainment, developed in the late 1960s and graphically reproduced in Figure 2. It posits that the influence of parental socioeconomic status is "filtered" through higher levels of ambition by the parents themselves, plus teachers and peers. These "significant others" directly affect the levels of aspirations of youths. Mental ability leads to higher grades that, in turn, reinforce aspirations both directly and indirectly through significant others. The model posits that educational aspirations are the prime determinant of educational attainment, whereas both educational and occupational aspirations play a similar role vis-à-vis occupational achievement.[34] In this sense, the model defines adolescent ambition as the key factor mediating between family and school influences and final outcomes of the status attainment process.

The literature on migrant children's aspirations in the United States, Western Europe, Australia, and Canada draw on a variety of sources—from nationally representative surveys to a number of convenience samples.[35] Some studies differentiate between *aspirations,* as symbolically ideal goals, and *expectations,* as realistic ones. Others lump the two categories as joint indicators of general ambition. Some studies focus on parental expectations, whereas others limit themselves to adolescents. Research in this field is beset by several problems, such as the reciprocal influence of aspirations and educational achievement and biases in children's reports of their parents' own goals and socioeconomic positions. Only longitudinal studies that include a parental survey are able to overcome these difficulties. CILS in the United States and ILSEG in Spain deliberately did so. Overall, the research literature tends to converge on five key predictions that extend or supplement the original Wisconsin model:

1. Immigrant parents tend to have high levels of ambition. On this point, the literature supports Grace Kao and Marta Tienda's concept of "immigrant optimism" and Alejandro Portes and Rubén Rumbaut's notion of "immigrant drive." Parental goals are commonly centered not so much on their own upward mobility but on that of their children.[36]

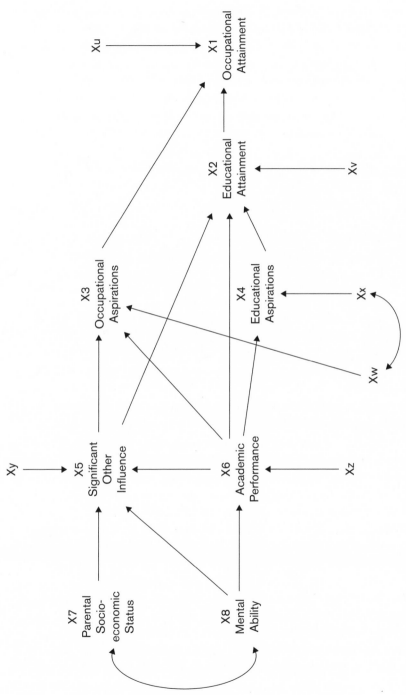

FIGURE 2. The Wisconsin Model of Status Attainment.
Source: Haller and Portes, "Status Attainment Processes," diagram 2.

Arrows from letter-subscripted variables are residual effects assumed to be uncorrelated with other determinants of each predicted (endogenous) variable.

2. There are major differences across nationalities. Immigrant groups with higher levels of human capital tend to produce higher and more stable aspirations; the opposite is the case with minorities of lower human capital. Differences across nationalities are reduced but do not disappear after introducing controls for parental characteristics. This is due to the contrasting modes of incorporation faced by different immigrant groups. This conclusion agrees with expectations from the segmented assimilation model.[37]

3. Parents and peers exercise strong effects on children's ambition. In agreement with the Wisconsin model, the effect of family socioeconomic status on children's ambition tends to be "filtered" through the parents' own goals and those of school peers. These effects vary cross-nationally: significant other influences are more powerful in relatively "open" educational systems, such as those of the United States, Australia, Canada, and Spain, and less so in the more structured and hierarchical systems of northern European countries, such as the Netherlands and especially Germany.[38]

4. Girls consistently exhibit higher ambition and performance than boys, and older youngsters, relative to their respective school peers, tend to have both lower aspirations and lower academic performances.[39]

5. Aspirations and academic performance are strongly interrelated, in line with the Wisconsin model. Children's ambition spurs greater school effort, but good academic results lead to pushing future goals upward. A causal loop thus exists between both variables. '

Specific studies have advanced findings that point toward additional significant trends. For example, Krista Perreira and her colleagues, as well as Patricia Fernández-Kelly, emphasize the idea of "cultural capital" brought from the country of origin. Although material capital may be higher among natives, cultural capital tends to be stronger among immigrants and their children, leading to a sustained achievement drive. In support of the "generations of exclusion" hypothesis, Perreira finds that this key resource dissipates by the third generation.[40]

The finding of a consistently high drive for achievement among immigrant parents, transmitted subsequently to their children, deserves additional comment. There is consensus in the literature that immigrants who come of their own free will are positively selected, relative to the sending country population, in terms of their determination and their motivation to succeed. They have to be in order to confront the many challenges and uncertainties of the journey. Immigrants of modest origins and those who confront a negative context of reception may center their ambitions not on what happens to them but rather on the future of their children. For this reason, the empirical literature registers high aspirations and expectations for children among parents of all nationalities and all socioeconomic origins, even the least educated.[41]

The sample of parents interviewed for CILS in the United States provides ample evidence of this trend. Seventy-four percent of the 2,442 immigrant parents interviewed during that survey expected their children to graduate from college, and, of these, close to 50 percent expected them to earn a postgraduate degree. Majorities of all immigrant nationalities expressed these goals—from those formed mostly by highly educated professionals, such as Filipinos and Chinese, to those composed mainly of manual workers, such as Mexicans, Salvadorians, and Haitians. Predictably, college and postgraduate expectations rose with parental education, but, even among parents with a high school education or less, two-thirds expected their children to achieve a college degree.[42] These ambitions are transmitted across generations, leading to high educational and occupational aspirations among the young.[43]

However, the early immigrant drive for upward mobility is not everlasting. The acculturating forces of the host society eventually prevail, leading to a progressive removal of children and grandchildren of immigrants from their cultural roots and, with it, a decline in the original drive. Other things being equal, the average socioeconomic status attained by an immigrant group depends on the moving equilibrium between its original level of ambition and the forces of acculturation. Once descendants have fully internalized the culture of the host society, the advantages conferred by the earlier immigrant drive cease and the group can be expected to remain at about the average educational and occupational levels reached up to that point.[44]

It is a common assumption in the popular migration literature that each successive generation achieves higher levels of status and wealth than the preceding one, but this is not always the case. A key finding in Charles Hirschman and Luis Falcon's now-classic study of educational differences among socioethnic groups in the United States is that immigrant groups that achieve high educational levels in the first or second generations preserve their advantage over time. In contrast, those that went no further than an average secondary education or less earlier on continue to experience educational and occupational disadvantages in subsequent generations.[45]

The "window of opportunity" created by earlier immigrant ambition tends to be fairly short-lived, as the assimilative influence of schools and native peers compel children to give up their original culture in order to become "like everyone else."[46] Naturally, better educated and more affluent immigrants can retard this process through various means, such as periodic trips back home, and tightly knit ethnic communities can employ their collective social capital for the same purpose. Immigrants of low human capital moving from place to place in search of employment are the least favorably situated. Lacking either the human or social capital to slow down acculturation, they are powerless as it inexorably transforms their children. Paradoxically, these youths are those most in need of preserving the original drive in order to overcome the many obstacles thrown in their path. This line of reasoning corresponds to the segmented assimilation model in predicting that selective rather than full acculturation tends to produce the better adaptation outcomes. It is also in line with "generations of exclusion" by pointing to some of the forces leading to stagnation across generations.

Although longer periods of residence in the host country may lead to a decline of the original achievement drive, they have a positive consequence—namely, greater fluency in the host country language. Other things being equal, host language fluency should lead to higher educational and occupational ambition because it facilitates ease of communication with the native majority.[47] Returning to the set of theoretical perspectives described earlier and summarizing this discussion, we find that culturalist theories have relatively little to say about the matter of immigrant children's aspirations, other than noting the significant effect of language acquisition. Overall, neo-assimilationism will predict a convergence of immigrant and native levels of ambition with the passage of time. Structuralist perspectives are more differentiated: the "generations of exclusion" and "second-generation advantage" views lead to opposite predictions—the first predicting lower aspirations, especially among more marginalized nationalities, and the second predicting an overall superiority of immigrant children's goals congruent with their alleged advantage.

Segmented assimilation theory advances a more qualified prediction: groups favored by higher levels of parental human capital and a positive mode of incorporation should register higher ambition levels. However, even lower-status parents will have high goals. The transmission of such goals across generations is governed by selective acculturation: good intergenerational relations should facilitate this conversion; the opposite situation would prevent it. Length of residence in Spain should have *no* net influence on youth's ambition. This is because greater knowledge of the language that would be a consequence of longer residence in the country and should lead to higher aspirations is counter-balanced by a declining achievement drive with the passage of time. Segmented assimilation converges at this point with neo-assimilationism in predicting growing convergence between immigrant and native youths, but predictions about effects on ambition of this increasing similarity are very different.

OUTCOMES

By average age 18, the effects of early ambition, parental socioeconomic status, parental modes of incorporation, and other variables should start to be translated into important social psychological dimensions such as self-identity, intergenerational relations, and perceptions of discrimination as well as tangible adaptation outcomes such as educational achievement and labor market entry. Negative outcomes highlighted by generations-of-exclusion and segmented assimilation theories as indicative of a downward path, such as early childbearing, unemployment, and incidents of arrest and incarceration, will also start making an appearance at this age. The ILSEG final surveys contain measures of all of these outcomes. We discuss them below, along with predictions stemming from the different theoretical perspectives outlined previously.

*Psychosocial Outcomes*

Important psychosocial adaptation outcomes include national/ethnic self-identities, perception of discrimination in the host society, and the evolution of intergenerational relations. Self-identities are a topic of a bourgeoning literature that have produced a vast array of findings across a number of nationalities and issues. The fascination of scholars with this topic is noteworthy because the same literature has shown that these identities are highly malleable, shifting significantly over time and across school contexts.[48] The question is how such a mutable and "soft" variable could have awakened so much interest. Part of the answer is that shifting self-identities lie at the core of the challenges faced by young people caught between two different cultural worlds and their conflicting pressures. For the most part, parents want them to preserve at least some elements of their own identity and culture, while the host society, particularly schools, pull in the opposite direction. As noted previously, migrant youths have been called "translation artists" as they struggle with and eventually learn to deal with these disparate expectations.

A second reason why self-identities are important is that, under certain circumstances, they can trigger collective mobilizations in opposition to the existing sociopolitical order. The massive and violent protests in the suburbs of French cities in 2005 and subsequent years were triggered largely by disaffected second-generation youths who mobilized against what they saw as their discriminated and permanently subordinate position in French society. Contrary to the "republican" ideology of the French state that distinguishes only between citizens and immigrants, failing to recognize specific ethnicities, these French-born youths often refused to call themselves French. Instead, many embraced the ethnic epithet with which many natives have disparaged them, *beurs*.[49]

Similarly, in the wake of Proposition 187 in California in 1994, American-born youths of Mexican origin mobilized in vast numbers against what they saw as a threat to their identity and that of their parents. This so-called "Save Our State" proposition did not explicitly target Mexican-Americans, just illegal immigrants in general. However, Mexican-American youths viewed it as anti-Mexican and anti-Latino, and they mobilized accordingly. In the wake of these events, many youngsters of this national origin chose to rescind the hyphenated label with which they had identified previously—Mexican-American—to call themselves just "Mexican."[50]

The identity options faced by second-generation youths in the United States include retention of the parental nationality, embracement of the host country nationality (i.e., "American"), in-between hyphenated identities (i.e., "Mexican-American"), and the pan-ethnic labels applied by natives, in blanket terms, to multiple nationalities (i.e., "Asian," "Black," or "Latino"). In Spain, national self-identity options divide naturally into retention of parental identities or adoption of a Spanish identification.[51] In the culturalist camp, pessimists such as Huntington would predict retention of parental nationalities, whereas optimists expect a gradual but sustained move toward host country identities. Among structuralists, the "generations of exclusion" thesis also leads to the expected retention of parental nationalities or adoption of a pan-ethnic label (i.e., "Latino") whereas the "second-generation advantage" thesis would be congruent with pan-ethnic labels, transitioning rapidly to full adoption of host country identities.

The segmented assimilation model predicts the adoption of different identities for youths following various adaptation paths. In this case, adoption of a Spanish self-identity would be appropriate for those advancing most rapidly into the mainstream on the strength of high parental human capital and a positive mode of incorporation, whereas a reactive identity based on a return to parental nationalities would be most common among those undergoing downward assimilation.

The research literature supports some of these predictions and questions others. As in the case of ambition, past findings converge on a limited set of theoretical predictions:

1. Place of birth and length of residence in the host society are powerful determinants of self-identity. The native-born second generation is significantly more likely to identify with Spain than youths born abroad. Other things being equal, the effect of length of residence on the 1.5 generation should run in the same direction.[52]

2. Parental effects on self-identity are complex. Higher parental status facilitates identification with the host society, insofar as it promotes a rapid entry into the Spanish mainstream. Having one Spanish-born parent should produce similar results, whereas both parents born in the same foreign country would lead in the opposite direction.[53]

3. Repeated incidents of discrimination by natives lower self-esteem and trigger reactive ethnicity among migrant youths. In the United States, this process often leads to adoption of a non-hyphenated national label (i.e., "Mexican") or migration from an American self-designation to a pan-ethnic one. In Western Europe, the deliberate adoption of disparaging epithets as self-identities, such as *beurs* in France, reflect the same reactive process.[54]

4. Phenotypically identified youths, such as blacks, mulattoes, mestizos, and Asians, would be more likely to experience discrimination and hence to develop a reactive ethnicity resistant to identification with the host society. Such ethnic labels are "thick" and are usually evaluated as important by those who adopt them. In contrast, children of white immigrants who adopt the non-hyphenated identity of the host society tend to regard this self-designation as less significant.[55]

Perceptions of discrimination is a second psychosocial outcome that can be expected to interact with self-identity and related variables but that represents, by itself, an indicator of problematic adaptation. Hence, the greater the number of second-generation youths who report having been discriminated against in the past, the worse the prognosis concerning the future course of their integration to Spain. Conversely, a low number of such perceptions would point toward a more optimistic assessment. Similarly, intergenerational relations (between parents and children) is both a predictor of other positive outcomes in late adolescence and an important result itself. Good intergenerational relations are an indicator of selective acculturation and, as such, should have positive effects on educational aspirations and attainment while helping protect youths from the negative effects of outside discrimination.

Among theoretical perspectives reviewed previously, the "generations of exclusion" approach would predict higher perceptions of discrimination and poorer intergenerational relations, especially among youths from lower-status and non-white nationalities, whereas the "second-generation advantage" thesis would be more optimistic about these outcomes. The segmented assimilation model predicts positive effects of intergenerational relations on other outcomes but also expects that close relations between parents and children will decline with time as assimilative pressures take over. In particular, intergenerational relations should deteriorate among the second generation "proper," where the cultural distance between parents and children is greater.

Self-esteem has also been the topic of a number of studies in sociology and social psychology. Morris Rosenberg's Self-esteem Scale has been the instrument of choice in this literature.[56] In the United States, repeated incidents of discrimination have been found to lower adolescent self-esteem among children of immigrants, as does a history of conflict with parents. These patterns have been reported among both Latin and Asian immigrants. Self-esteem is positively associated with both higher educational ambition and academic performance, although the causal direction of these associations has not been well established.[57] A longitudinal research design, seldom used in the past, would aid greatly in establishing causal order among these variables.

Interestingly, self-esteem does not appear to vary significantly among adolescents who adopt different self-identities. A possible reason is that the selection of one or another ethnic label is a form of protecting one's self-image, both among youths undergoing selective acculturation (associated with hyphenated identities) and among those adopting a more critical reactive stance. Lisa Edwards and Andrea Romero found, for example, that Mexican-descent youths engage in vigorous coping strategies as a way to protect self-esteem from external discrimination stress.

Engagement with co-ethnics and adoption of a pan-ethnic or non-hyphenated national identity figure prominently in these strategies.[58]

Taking advantage of the longitudinal character of CILS, Portes and Rumbaut developed a predictive model of self-esteem by selecting determinants at average age 14 and applying the Rosenberg scale to the same sample three years later.[59] The psychosocial profile of the second generation in Spain, including self-esteem, has not been examined exhaustively nor tracked over time in the past. The ILSEG surveys, described in detail in Chapter 4, afford the opportunity to do so, plus examine its determinants. They also will allow us to compare results systematically with those obtained in the United States. These comparisons will be presented in Chapter 6.

### Education and Labor Market Entry

Of all the early adaptation results, none is more important than educational attainment. This takes the form of academic grades and, crucially, no school abandonment. Dropping out of school to join the labor market at average age 18 represents, in most instances, a negative outcome. Although exceptions exist and will be noted, early employment commonly deprives youths of the chance to access the advanced credentials increasingly required for success in a bifurcated labor market. Our data also contain indicators of attitudes toward schools attended. A positive attitude toward their academic centers can be interpreted, in most instances, as indicative of an upward adaptation path. The role of earlier aspirations and expectations, highlighted by the existing literature and discussed previously, should be clearly reflected in educational and occupational outcomes by this age. This will be examined in Chapters 7 and 8.

Culturalistic perspectives have relatively little to say about educational outcomes. The negative views sponsored by Huntington and European critics of immigration lead to the overall expectation of lower academic performance and more negative attitudes toward school among immigrant students, especially among non-whites and non-Christians (e.g., Muslims). Conversely, neo-assimilationist views would predict the convergence of children of immigrants with native-parentage students, especially with the passage of time in both educational and occupational outcomes.

Structuralist views again line up on opposite sides, with the "generations of exclusion" approach predicting lower educational performance, early labor market entry, precarious employment, and more adverse school attitudes among poorer and marginalized groups, whereas "second-generation advantage" scholars would anticipate superior academic and occupational outcomes and more optimistic views of school. Segmented assimilation theory steers again mid-course, noting that a great deal depends on the socioeconomic background of families, the levels of parental expectations for their young, the character of the family, and intergenerational relations. The emphasis placed by the theory on parental modes of incorporation (i.e., the reception accorded to different groups by authorities and the native society at large) leads us to expect resilient differences among nationalities even after controlling for individual-level variables.

Segmented assimilation would predict a positive effect of Spanish language fluency on educational outcomes—a prediction shared with neo-assimilationism. It would also expect that parental human capital, the composition of the family, and selective acculturation as reflected in good intergenerational relations will affect decisively educational attainment, labor market entry, and school attitudes.

Educational and early occupational outcomes are central at this stage of the life course. If significant school abandonment and confinement of immigrants to the lower school tracks and precarious employment are detected by the analysis, success in Spanish society would be in serious question. The same would be the case if we were to find consistently inferior levels of ambition among second-generation youths or a uniformly negative stance toward their academic centers.

## Other Outcomes: Downward Assimilation, Language, and Future Goals

Psychological dimensions such as aspirations, self-identity, and self-esteem represent both a prelude and a determinant of tangible adaptation outcomes. As seen previously, they include educational achievement, labor market status, and early income. They also include events indicative of downward assimilations—such as early school abandonment, teenage childbearing, unemployment, and encounters with the police. Increasing knowledge and use of the host country language is another important dimension, as language fluency has been found to influence other adaptation outcomes, including educational goals and academic performance. Finally, the evolution of occupational goals over time is worth attention, as members of the second generation should have a clearer idea of how to orient their future occupational lives and how to achieve their goals. An analysis of the distribution and determinants of these goals will also be presented in Chapter 8.

Late adolescence is a suitable point in time to examine how the different theoretical perspectives described previously measure up to reality. Several of these theories predict uniform outcomes of the process of adaptation—whether entry into the "mainstream," "exclusion," or "second-generation advantage." The segmented assimilation model portrays a discrete plurality of trajectories and, as was seen in Figure 1, identifies three determinants of the process: parental human capital, family structure, and modes of incorporation.

The first ILSEG survey and its parental counterpart, to be presented and analyzed in Chapter 5, contain indicators of first-generation educational levels and occupational status. They also include indicators of family composition. As noted previously, modes of incorporation refer to the governmental, social, and community contexts receiving immigrant parents. In the Spanish case, modes of incorporation can be indexed by the legal status of parents in the country and by their phenotypical characteristics. As a number of studies, including those conducted previously in Spain, demonstrate, non-white immigrants can be expected to experience higher levels of discrimination and an overall more negative reception than others.[60] In combination with parental human capital and family composition, modes of incorporation can help us clarify the trajectories followed by first-generation migrants and the chances for upward mobility among their children.

The presence of a significant foreign element in the contemporary population of Spain has been a cause of celebration for some and of despair for others. Neither view is informed by reliable knowledge of the facts. The set of theories presented in this chapter provides us with a suitable frame of reference to understand what is actually taking place. More than the immigrant first generation, composed of persons socialized in foreign countries, it is the children who count as the embodiment of the long-term consequences of immigration. Born in Spain or brought there at an early age, these new Spaniards are slated to play major social, cultural, and political roles in the life of the country in the future. Their present situation, described in detail in the following chapters, will give us a clearer sense of what that future will bring.

# THREE

# The Recent History of Spain-Bound Immigration

The aim of this chapter is to highlight the main characteristics of immigration in Spain, seeking to place in context the findings of ILSEG on the integration of second-generation immigrants. We cover the background, figures, and causes of immigration to Spain; the diversity of immigrants and their places of settlement; the age, gender, education, and occupation of immigrants; the characteristics of children of immigrants in schools; previous studies on the subject in Spain; and the "Spanish model" of immigrant integration.

## BACKGROUND, FIGURES, AND CAUSES OF IMMIGRATION TO SPAIN

The first distinguishing characteristic of Spain-bound immigration is that, although flows of foreigners to the country started very late, they increased rapidly. It started late because, when its European neighbors began to receive immigrants in the mid-1950s, Spain was pushing millions of its rural population to emigrate.[1] However, forty years later, it began to receive immigrants at a rapid rate. Indeed, for a short period of time—called by some scholars the "Prodigious Decade" (1998–2008)[2]—Spain became the second largest recipient of immigrants from across the world, surpassed only by the United States. Through immigration, the proportion of foreigners settling in Spain has risen to 12 percent of the population, whereas in the United States, despite its much longer migratory history, this population group accounts for about 13 percent of the total.[3]

It is not easy to document the steps that brought about this drastic turnaround because the data collection mechanisms when the process started were not, by any measure, as detailed and complete as those that exist today. Thus, the earlier figures counted only foreigners with legal residence permits, omitting those who were unauthorized or in process of securing their papers. Even with this omission, the available data portray a massive rise in the foreign population. Hence, whereas between 1970 and 1980 the increment in legal foreign residents in Spain was only 2.3 percent, and between 1980 and 1990 was 5.2 percent, the rise from 1990 to 2000 reached 223.6 percent.

The question of the late onset of Spain-bound immigration is not difficult to answer. Since the end of the eighteenth century, in comparison with central and northern Europe, Spain had been declining economically and politically—giving rise to the malicious remark, born in France but internationally disseminated, that Europe, toward the South, ended in the Pyrenees. The dissemination of this slogan was bolstered by the fact that Spain did not participate in the 1914–18 "Great War," which was also called the "European War."

During the 1950s, when the European postwar migratory system was taking shape, Spain's position among nations declined even further. The Spanish Civil War (1936–39) left many open wounds; for decades the country endured the dictatorship of General Francisco Franco, who was widely repudiated in the international arena. In addition, it was attempting to transform its closed, stagnant, and predominantly agricultural economy into an industrial and service-based one, with the welter of hardships that unavoidably accompany such attempts. The process of industrialization and urbanization of the 1960s provoked a massive flow of agricultural workers to the cities. But Spain's labor market did not have the capacity to absorb all of this workforce. Consequently, large numbers had to emigrate, heading mainly toward other European countries, particularly Germany, France, and the United Kingdom.[4]

But if this holds true from the 1950s through the 1980s, why did more immigrants start flowing into Spain in the 1990s than to France, the Netherlands, or Germany? The country certainly changed dramatically during this time period: Franco and his dictatorship had disappeared; Spain was advancing toward modernization, and the economy rapidly internationalized; it had entered the European Economic

TABLE 2  THE FOREIGN POPULATION OF SPAIN

| | Population (absolute numbers) | | | | | | |
|---|---|---|---|---|---|---|---|
| | 1996 | 2000 | 2002 | 2005 | 2007 | 2009 | 2012 |
| Total | 542,314 | 923,879 | 1,977,946 | 3,730,610 | 4,519,554 | 5,648,671 | 5,736,258 |
| Men | 273,227 | 471,465 | 1,048,178 | 1,992,034 | 2,395,685 | 2,992,636 | 2,975,508 |
| Women | 269,087 | 452,413 | 929,767 | 1,738,576 | 2,123,869 | 2,656,035 | 2,760,750 |
| | Percentage of the Spanish population | | | | | | |
| | 1.3 | 2.2 | 4.7 | 8.4 | 10.0 | 12.1 | 12.1 |

SOURCE: National Institute of Statistics, Continuous Register of Inhabitants.

Community in 1986; the Welfare State greatly expanded; the structure of the labor market experienced important changes, among them the massive entry of women in its midst; and the country's image improved.[5] Before the 1990s, the small contingents of immigrants who arrived in Spain had been motivated mainly by adverse political situations in their countries of origin, as in the case of Argentineans and Peruvians, or were fleeing from destitution, exemplified by domestic workers from the Philippines and Dominican and Moroccan agricultural workers.

In the early 1990s, however, a number of scholars highlighted how the international media favorably portrayed Spain on the occasion of the Universal Exposition in Seville in 1992 and the Olympic Games in Barcelona that same year. These major events not only had positive economic effects but also produced favorable indirect impacts through media coverage. This created an important "pull" factor that had been absent previously.[6] Table 2 shows the evolution of the foreign population in Spain from the mid-1990s onward. By 2009, the 12.1 percent of the population that was foreign had made Spain the largest relative recipient of such flows in Europe, ahead of the United Kingdom or France (7 percent of the total population) or Germany (9 percent).

Yet the radical changes in immigration portrayed in this table could not be explained merely by changes in Spain's external image. Rather, the change in image was a consequence of the social, economic, and political changes that Spain had undergone. Lorenzo Cachón, who has studied the process in detail, notes that, in the 1990s when the foreign flows accelerated, the unemployment rate in Spain was quite high, so that it is impossible to attribute the origin of the process to an absolute scarcity of labor. For Cachón, one of the key factors was the enormous change experienced by the Spanish labor market because of the evolution of the educational levels of the native labor force and the diffusion of higher expectations among the popular classes. With the advent of democracy, workers acquired much greater negotiating powers.[7]

The number of young Spaniards who entered the labor market after completing an advanced education multiplied exponentially, increasing their expectations of better and better-paid employment than that which was the lot of their parents. The less prestigious and less well paid jobs were cast aside, thereby producing a segmentation of the labor market between the acceptable jobs of a primary sector and the increasing stigmatized occupations of a secondary one. Immigrant workers were increasingly channeled toward the latter.[8]

Hector Cebolla Boado and Amparo González Ferrer reinforce the point by noting that the secondary labor market is of extraordinary importance for the Spanish economy, whereas the number of native workers ready to work in it has become increasingly scarce. In their words:

> The economies of all the Southern European countries are characterized by a significant gap between the high demand for unskilled and semi-skilled labor and the low supply of native workers, better qualified and not inclined to work in these sectors. In Spain, like in its neighbors, successive regularizations (of the unauthorized foreign population) have permitted the satisfaction of unskilled labor demand.[9]

These would then be the main reasons for the dramatic turnaround of immigrant figures in Spain. But what type of immigrants arrived as a result?

## DIVERSITY OF IMMIGRANTS IN SPAIN

A salient characteristic of recent immigration to Spain is the great diversity of nationalities and regions of origin that often leads immigrants and their children to feel as different from each other as from the native population. The available data can be arranged by nationality and region, both of which are relevant as potential predictors of the adaptation path followed by the second generation. Table 3 presents results by national origin for the total number of immigrants and for Madrid and Barcelona, the two largest urban areas of immigration concentration.

TABLE 3    NATIONAL ORIGINS OF IMMIGRANTS TO SPAIN, 2012

| Country | Total | Madrid | Barcelona |
| --- | --- | --- | --- |
| Romania | 829,936 | 219,567 | 37,155 |
| Morocco | 651,207 | 84,799 | 141,636 |
| United Kingdom | 374,842 | 10,150 | 12,021 |
| Ecuador | 293,602 | 95,377 | 52,530 |
| Colombia | 246,451 | 58,868 | 29,197 |
| Germany | 179,069 | 9,361 | 14,218 |
| Bolivia | 178,463 | 42,357 | 42,692 |
| Bulgaria | 166,148 | 30,658 | 6,283 |
| Argentina | 163,545 | 15,125 | 19,031 |
| China | 149,070 | 46,425 | 40,514 |
| Peru | 123,748 | 5,188 | 27,821 |
| Portugal | 120,774 | 15,670 | 9,221 |
| Brazil | 104,098 | 18,201 | 14,836 |
| France | 101,625 | 15,476 | 21,645 |
| Dominican Rep. | 89,813 | 33,904 | 18,706 |
| Paraguay | 87,081 | 30,323 | 14,340 |
| Ukraine | 83,056 | 20,276 | 8,818 |
| Pakistan | 75,969 | 3,312 | 42,607 |

SOURCE: National Institute of Statistics, Continuous Register of Inhabitants.

It is worth noting that the flow of immigration to Spain occurred not as a steady movement but rather in "waves" of different nationalities. At the start of the 1990s, these waves were composed of Moroccans, Peruvians, Dominicans, and middle-class Argentineans expelled by the military dictatorship in their country. Afterward came Ecuadoreans, Colombians, and then Bolivians, taking advantage of the absence of visa requirements to enter Spain (a situation reversed subsequently). To the surprise of many scholars, the next wave was formed by East Europeans, primarily Romanians, who came in such numbers as to become the largest foreign nationality.

A key characteristic of immigration to Spain in comparison with the flows to its European neighbors has been the high proportion of migrants from Latin America and the Caribbean. By 2010, 37 percent of the foreign population of Spain came from that region, as opposed to less than 10 percent for the rest of Europe. The sources of these flows can be traced directly to the historical ties of Spain, as the former colonial power, with the Latin American republics and to the deliberate efforts of the Spanish government to preserve and strengthen such ties. As part of this effort, citizens of most Latin American countries could enter Spain without visas until relatively recently. Not surprisingly, the population of impoverished countries such as Bolivia, the Dominican Republic, Ecuador, and Peru took full advantage of the opportunity. This event led Cebolla Boado and González Ferrer to conclude that the "prodigious" decades of immigration to Spain (1990s and 2000s) would not have taken place without the mass influx of Latin Americans. Without it, the foreign flow would have been reduced to about half.[10]

Moreover, Spain's historical links with Latin America were complemented by similar ties between Spain and the Philippines and the Spanish colonization of Equatorial Guinea (1926–68) as well as those stemming from its protectorate of North Morocco (1912–56). Large migrant movements from Morocco were registered, and, though on a smaller scale than the two ex-colonies, all three added still more diversity to the incoming foreign population. Obviously, such vast differences in nationalities and regions of origin raise the question of the extent to which the course of adaptation followed by children of immigrants in Spain is determined by the countries and regions that their parents came from. In addition to differences stemming from the diversity of origins, new differences quickly emerged regarding areas of settlement. Most immigrants initially attempted to settle in the metropolitan areas of Madrid and Barcelona, but by the end of the twentieth century—and particularly during the first decade of the twenty-first century—their presence had extended to most Spanish regions, though Madrid and Barcelona still served as the main poles of attraction. Table 4 presents the relevant information.

## AGE, GENDER, EDUCATION, AND OCCUPATION

Figure 3 presents the pyramids by sex and age of the foreign-born population superimposed on the native Spanish population. As in the case of the United States and other countries of immigration, the migrant population is much younger among both males and females. The number of immigrants diminishes to almost nil after age 50, whereas, among natives, the number is still sizable between ages 50 to 80.

Concerning education, according to the figures provided by the National Immigration Survey of 2007,[11] the proportion of immigrants with an elementary education or less is actually lower than among Spaniards (22.63 percent of the immigrants versus 29 percent of the natives). Those completing basic secondary are similar in both

TABLE 4    FOREIGN POPULATION BY AUTONOMOUS COMMUNITIES
OF SPAIN, 2012

| Community | N | % |
| --- | --- | --- |
| Andalucía | 747,110 | 13.0 |
| Aragón | 173,111 | 3.0 |
| Asturias | 50,827 | 0.9 |
| Canarias | 310,841 | 5.4 |
| Cantabria | 39,313 | 0.7 |
| Castilla y León | 173,509 | 3.0 |
| Castilla-La Mancha | 236,049 | 4.1 |
| Cataluña | 1,186,779 | 20.7 |
| Ceuta | 5,812 | 0.1 |
| Comunidad Valenciana | 883,012 | 15.4 |
| Extremadura | 42,541 | 0.7 |
| Galicia | 112,183 | 2.0 |
| Islas Baleares | 242,570 | 4.2 |
| La Rioja | 46,373 | 0.8 |
| Madrid | 1,015,054 | 17.7 |
| Melilla | 11,264 | 0.2 |
| Murcia | 238,393 | 4.2 |
| Navarra | 69,623 | 1.2 |
| País Vasco | 151,894 | 2.6 |
| Total | 5,736,258 | 100 |

SOURCE: National Institute of Statistics, Continuous Register of Inhabitants.

populations (24.2 percent versus 26.2 percent), but many more immigrants than Spaniards have achieved an advanced secondary degree (32.1 percent versus 19 percent). Yet, among those with a college or postgraduate education, natives surpass the foreign population by a significant margin (26.4 percent versus 21.3 percent). It is not surprising that the foreign population comes primarily from a middling educational level because the poorly educated seldom possess the means to afford the considerable travel and other expenses of migration. At the other end, those achieving an advanced education are better situated to find good occupations at home, hence reducing the probability of having to find opportunities abroad. When the doors of the receiving country were opened by the absence of visa requirements and other facilities to immigration, it was the lower-middle classes in the sending countries that mostly took note. In general, the educational profile of the foreign population in Spain reflects this fact.

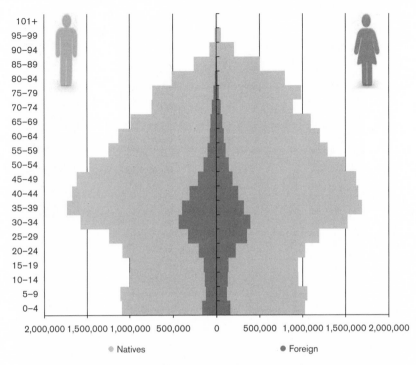

FIGURE 3. Population Pyramids of the Native and Foreign Populations in Spain, 2012.

However, a closer look at the figures shows that there are important differences between nationalities that cannot be ignored. The proportion of immigrants with an elementary education or less from European countries within and outside the European Union as well as from Latin America is below the average for all immigrants, but that of Asians is above average (27.9 percent) and that of Africans—mostly Moroccans—more than doubles that figure (49.2 percent). Similar differences appear regarding other educational levels. A look at the figures for tertiary education shows that Europeans largely surpass the average for all immigrants with a college or postgraduate education (32.1 percent), whereas the proportion of Latin Americans with this level of education is slightly below the average (18.6 percent) and that of Africans is far below that average (8.8 percent).

Figure 4 presents the sectoral distributions of the foreign and native economically active adult populations in Spain in two recent years. The two distributions are similar, both indicating the dominance of the

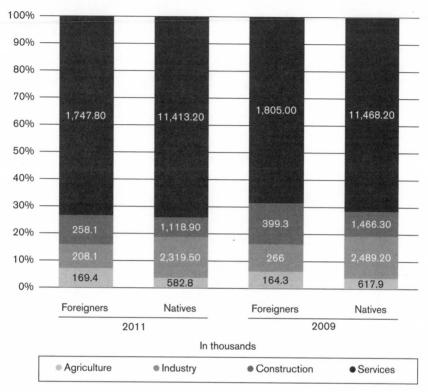

FIGURE 4. Occupational Sectors of the Native and Foreign Populations in Spain, 2012. Source: National Institute of Statistics, *Annual Surveys of the Economically Active Population*.

service sector. Migrants tend to be overrepresented in construction and natives in industry, but the differences are not large. These figures would seem to indicate a convergence among those who are employed, but they conceal the fact that immigrants are to be found mainly in the less skilled, poorly paid, and more precarious jobs.[12] This is true for all sectors and is well illustrated by domestic services in which working conditions are among the hardest and where immigrant women predominate.

It is therefore not surprising, especially considering the fact that construction was one of the sectors most affected by the economic crisis which started in 2008, that the unemployment rate for immigrants is considerably higher than that for natives. In 2011, 30.8 percent of the immigrant population was unemployed versus 20.5 percent of the native population. In spite of this, Josep Alonso, who has studied the matter carefully, points out that, in 2011, 83 percent of immigrant families had at least one working member. Thus, just about 17 percent or approximately 350,000 migrant-headed families lacked a regular source of income. In most cases, these families had no children, as their average size scarcely exceeded two members. Hence, the number of second-generation children suffering from long-term unemployment and serious poverty at home can be estimated to have reached no more than 10 percent of this population.[13]

## CHARACTERISTICS OF CHILDREN OF IMMIGRANTS IN SCHOOL

The presence of foreign children in Spanish schools registered an explosive increase in the 1990s in tandem with the rapid growth of the total immigrant population. The available figures are presented in Table 5. The data do not include children of immigrants who had secured Spanish nationality in each of the indicated years and who represent a considerable number, particularly in the later years. In 2012, for example, children of immigrants born in Spain who retained the nationality of their parents were only 415,773; others were already counted as Spaniards.[14]

Most of the children and adolescents counted in this table belong to the "1.5 generation" that is born abroad and brought to Spain at an early age. Most of what we know about this population is based on their school enrollment. The relevant data appear in Table 6. Once again, we note the rapid growth of the foreign population in Spanish schools. The speed of the process forced a rapid adaptation of school personnel to the new circumstances. Whereas only a few years before they were entrusted with the education of a homogenous native student body, now they had to contend with a rising number of foreign children, many of whom did not speak Spanish or came from poor academic backgrounds. To this challenge was added the rapid transfer of their children to other schools by native parents concerned about the deterioration of instruction and standards in schools affected by a rapidly rising number of foreign students.[15]

Naturally, the foreign-origin population is not homogenous. Children of Latin American parents come to school with full knowledge of Spanish and greater knowledge of Spanish culture, although many of

TABLE 5   THE FOREIGN-BORN POPULATION OF SPAIN, AGES 0–19

| Year | Total | Boys | Girls |
|------|-------|------|-------|
| 1996 | 96,975 | 49,724 | 47,251 |
| 2000 | 173,729 | 90,386 | 83,343 |
| 2002 | 358,532 | 185,574 | 172,959 |
| 2005 | 720,017 | 371,546 | 348,471 |
| 2007 | 875,091 | 451,971 | 423,120 |
| 2009 | 1,101,371 | 569,396 | 531,975 |
| 2012 | 1,118,274 | 578,644 | 539,630 |

SOURCE: National Statistical Institute, Continuous Register of Inhabitants.

TABLE 6   THE FOREIGN STUDENT BODY IN SPANISH SCHOOLS

| School level | 1997–8 | 2000–1 | 2005–6 | 2008–9 | 2011–12 |
|--------------|--------|--------|--------|--------|---------|
| Pre-elementary | 12,260 | 24,571 | 94,162 | 126,980 | 147,228 |
| Elementary | 34,923 | 59,386 | 228,842 | 308,896 | 272,316 |
| Basic secondary | 15,167 | 38,163 | 146,966 | 216,585 | 215,394 |
| Advanced secondary | 6,711 | 7,066 | 21,936 | 33,493 | 46,478 |
| Vocational/technical | 2,855 | 4,574 | 24,398 | 40,912 | 65,366 |
| Total | 72,335 | 141,916 | 530,954 | 755,587 | 781,446 |

SOURCE: Ministry of Education, *Datos y Cifras del Curso Escolar 2011/2012.*

these youths also come from poor schooling backgrounds in their respective countries. Others, like Romanians and Bulgarians, do not speak Spanish but come from countries with considerably more rigorous academic training, a legacy of their Communist-ruled past. The more common response of Spanish schools receiving a sizable number of foreigners has been to create "reception classrooms" *(aulas de acogida)* entrusted with accelerated teaching of Spanish and facilitating cultural transitions for this young population.

Overall, the response of Spanish schools, both public and private, to the challenge posed by the 1.5 and second generations has been proactive, seeking to rise up to it and integrate foreign students in the mainstream school population, without doing violence to their linguistic or cultural origins. Despite the mobilization of native parents against the growth of the foreign student population, educational authorities have consistently endeavored to respond to the needs of these students and integrate them into the mainstream. So far, however, the results of the *aulas* and, more generally, of the policies put in place by the authorities to cope with the needs of foreign groups have not been examined systematically on the basis of representative samples of the foreign-origin student population.

## PAST SPANISH RESEARCH ON CHILDREN OF IMMIGRANTS

Concerns and interest about the social integration paths of children of immigrants emerged from the very moment that immigration started to acquire visibility and importance in Spain. The first studies date back to 1991.[16] Very soon afterward, tensions emerged among teachers' and parents' associations concerned about the growing presence of foreign children in schools and the alleged degradation of the quality of education that this entailed. This was the first sign to school authorities that the situation could have long-term consequences for the educational system as well as for the overall integration of foreign youths to Spanish society.

Proof of this is that initial studies on the matter were financed by the Ministry of Education[17] and were focused on specific schools alleged to be the most affected by the foreign tide. Research at the time focused on the early school years, students aged 12 or younger. This was reasonable, since few immigrant children or children of immigrants were enrolled in secondary schools at the time. After the mid-1990s, researchers focused their attention on specific topics, including:

Demography: number and distribution of the foreign student population[18]

Approaches to their presence adopted by school authorities[19]

Successes and failures of the social integration process

Specific educational policies toward children of immigrants[20]

There were four major concerns guiding Spanish research at that time: the possible emergence of educational "ghettos" due to the concentration of a poor immigrant population in certain neighborhoods; the insufficient preparation of teachers and other school personnel to manage increasing cultural diversity; the levels of social integration achieved by foreign-origin students in schools following different policies; and the identification of the main factors determining success or failure of this process.

In retrospect, it is evident that, though many researchers had begun to focus their attention on migration issues, academic research in that earlier decade was based on small, local, and unrepresentative samples and without a common theoretical framework that would allow relating and comparing results from different studies. That situation was understandable, given the very recency of scholarly investigation on these topics. In addition, there was a great deal of dependency of research at the time on currents of public opinion and on the priorities of financing agencies, increasingly attuned to the orientations of the European Union. It would have been difficult for things to happen otherwise in the absence of the kind of scientific community that is capable of self-guidance and autonomous priorities.

The situation started to change by the end of the 1990s with the first academic migration conferences organized by the Ortega y Gasset University Institute of Madrid and the Institute for Migration Research of the University of Comillas. Gradually, research groups specializing on the topic emerged in various universities and started recognizing each other. They included, among others, the four research groups in Barcelona now brought together in the Centro de Estudios e Investigación sobre Migraciones, or CER, coordinated by Carlota Solé (GED-IME, EMIGRA, MIGRACOM, and GIPE-PTP); in Granada, under the leadership of Garcia Castaño; in the Autonomous University of Madrid, focused on Moroccan immigration and cultural relations; and the group in La Coruña, led by Antonio Izquierdo specializing in demographic issues. Other groups built around prestigious researchers soon followed, covering most parts of the Spanish territory.

Academic research on immigrants in Spain has accumulated by now a substantial portfolio of investigation and knowledge including, but not limited to, the following topics: social and cultural integration, levels of education, educational and social aspirations, experiences of discrimination in schools and, conversely, levels of tolerance in the same academic centers; and the evolution of national self-identities and interethnic relations among children of immigrants.[21] In particular, much attention has been dedicated in recent years to the publications of the Program for International Student Assessment (PISA), sponsored by the Organization for Economic Cooperation and Development (OECD) and focused on comparisons of educational achievement of secondary school students in Western Europe, Asia, and Oceania.[22]

## THE SPANISH MODEL: INTEGRATION
## WITHOUT A BLUEPRINT

Although the empirical research literature on immigration has registered rapid advances, most notably after publication in 2007 of the National Immigration Survey of Spain by the Instituto Nacional de Estadistica (INE), much of the published studies so far have focused on aggregate statistics or on the analysis of official policies toward immigration and immigrant integration. This literature includes notable contributions, including the works of Eliseo Aja, Joaquín Arango, Josep Alonso, Lorenzo Cachón, Miguel Pajares, Carlota Solé, Sonia Parella, and Ricard Zapata-Barrero.[23] For the most part, studies have had a historical orientation and a strong top-down focus on how governmental policy has shaped the course of events.

The overall conclusion of this literature is that Spain has approached the question of immigration and immigrant integration without a clear long-term perspective or an identifiable set of goals. Cebolla Boado and González Ferrer titled their book *Inmigración sin Modelo?* (*Immigration without a Model?*), and Zapata-Barrero refers to Spanish policy in this area as a "practical model," based on immediate responses to the issues of the day but without a pre-set vision of national identity or national community into which the foreign population should be integrated.[24]

In this respect, Spain differs sharply from its European partners, such as France, with its strong focus on full-fledged integration into its republican model, or Germany, with its long-term emphasis on blood ties defining who is and who is not entitled to membership in the national community.[25] The recent history of Spain, marked by the legacy of the long Franco dictatorship and major cultural and linguistic fractures among its regions, largely accounts for its differences from other countries.[26] A nation that, until recently, has been a net exporter of migrants and that is itself divided by multiple cultural differences could scarcely attempt to impose a monolithic assimilation model on its immigrants.

Instead, Spanish authorities opted for a pragmatic approach, seeking to integrate foreigners into the labor market and their communities of residence to the greatest extent possible. In general, Spain's policies toward its foreign population have been rather generous, as exemplified, among others, by the visa exemptions noted earlier, by repeated regularizations of immigrants in undocumented status, and by a proactive stance toward children of immigrants and immigrant children in schools.[27] Local governments have played a major role in this integration effort, devising specific policies tailored to the foreign communities in their midst. As Zapata-Barrero notes:

> In Spain, this dual role of immigrant associations, as an altruistic social movement providing welfare, is a reality. It is partly fostered by their relationship with government in general and local governments, in particular, in which the associations become "allies" of local politics in the design and, especially, in the implementation of policies.[28]

The stance taken by the Spanish government toward associations created by immigrants rounds the picture. In contrast to the United States, where the government has regularly adopted a *laissez-faire* attitude toward the organizational activities of immigrant communities,[29] in Spain, authorities have actively supported them to the point of financing many of these organizations and collaborating with them in "co-development" projects in their countries of origin.[30]

The pragmatic, day-by-day, and decentralized policies implemented by Spanish authorities toward the immigrant population could be criticized for their lack of long-term vision and clear goals. They have been disadvantageously compared with those of its European neighbors, such as France and Germany. Nevertheless, as Zapata-Barrero notes, "this lack of an identity debate has a positive effect: the lack of a regulatory framework for the appearance of anti-immigrant parties like those that have sprung up all over Europe since the 1980s."[31] Indeed, major xenophobic or anti-immigrant movements have had scant presence in Spain, and violent incidents against immigrants have been isolated and met with generalized public disapproval.

Furthermore, it is possible that the lack of pressure on immigrants to integrate as fast as possible into an idealized national community and the close attention to their needs and interests at the local level may have had superior integration consequences relative to the assimilationist policies implemented in other countries. In this regard, it is worth noting that the success of the United States in incorporating millions of immigrants from the most diverse origins has been due to a model that could also be labeled "integration without a blueprint." American authorities have seldom compelled immigrant groups to follow a particular course, allowing them instead to carve their own adaptation paths and create their own institutions.[32] This pragmatic approach bears close resemblance to that implemented by local and national authorities in Spain.

Yet there is little empirical evidence about the effects that this policy approach has had on the situation and attitudes of immigrants and their offspring. As noted previously, the literature on Spanish immigration has been mostly historical and theoretical, seldom coming down to the level of real immigrant outcomes. Most studies at close range have been ethnographic or based on small convenience samples. Specific exceptions exist, such as the longitudinal study of second-generation youths conducted by Estrella Gualda and her associates in Huelva.[33] This study anticipated, in several ways, the one to be described in the following chapters, employing the same basic methodological design.

For the most part, however, the existing empirical literature cannot answer the question of what generalized effects the non-identitary policies followed by governments in Spain have had on its immigrants and their children. Particularly problematic is the tendency in the journalistic and some of the qualitative social science literature to single out instances of failure or negative outcomes for attention. A single-minded focus on the so-called *bandas latinas* (Latin gangs) represents a common instance of this tendency, known in sociological methodology as the fallacy of "sampling on the dependent variable."[34] The consequences are biased conclusions that provide a distorted image of the population in question.[35]

Although qualitative interviews represent a valuable component of any in-depth inquiry into social reality, they must be subject to the discipline of generalizable results. The twelve life histories summarized in the opening chapter of this book are useful for providing real-life context for the findings to follow. By themselves, however, they do not add up to a comprehensive or reliable portrayal of second-generation integration in Spain.

CONCLUSION

It is in this context that the significance of the study described in the following chapters may be better understood. The historical and macropolitical studies of Spanish immigration have been useful in providing the necessary framework for ascertaining what is taking place on the ground. Such studies cannot provide answers, however, to the specific outcomes of the process of immigrant adaptation. Field studies conducted so far seek to answer these questions but, with the exception of the Huelva investigation by Gualda and her associates, they do not provide generalizable results.

ILSEG has sought to overcome these limitations through a design that includes large, statistically representative samples of second-generation youths in the two largest Spanish cities and that follows them over the course of adolescence. Results can provide authoritative answers to the question of what "integration without a blueprint" policies have led to in Spain and, by comparing them with findings obtained with a similar methodology in the United States, can place such findings into a cross-national comparative context. The following chapter presents details of the study's methodology, as implemented in both countries.

# The Longitudinal Study
# of the Second Generation

The study of the second generation, in Western Europe as in the United States, presents a series of challenges that differentiates it from research on the more stable adult population, including established first-generation immigrants. Acculturation, social adaptation, and self-identities among second-generation adolescents and young people are highly dynamic processes that can be expected to change significantly. For this reason, research designs that seek to follow this population over time are preferable to cross-sectional surveys. Static surveys of children of immigrants in early adolescence may well be representative of this universe at that time, but most of the outcomes captured—such as aspirations, self-esteem, and attitudes—are "soft" variables easily changeable over time.[1]

Conversely, surveys of second-generation adults are capable of capturing "hard" outcomes, such as education, employment and occupational status, income, marital status, and parenthood, but they censor the proportion of that population that fell by the wayside because of incarceration, other forms of institutionalization, destitution, or abandonment of the country. Such surveys thus sample the population of "survivors" from the traumas and challenges of adolescent adaptation and, for that reason, are prone to yield excessively optimistic accounts of this process.[2]

In addition, static surveys of young adults have difficulty constructing credible causal models of the factors that led to each "hard" outcome. This is because they depend on respondents' recall in order to construct indicators of key predictors, such as parental socioeconomic status in early adolescence, family composition at the time, characteristics of schools attended, and attitudes and aspirations. A long methodological tradition shows that the validity of such retroactive reports is dubious, as they tend to be colored by present realities.[3] The combination of biased samples and selective recall render causal accounts of the highly dynamic processes of acculturation and social adaptation in the transitional years of early and late adolescence problematic.[4]

Longitudinal designs for the study of the second generation can take two forms: panel studies, where the sample is followed over time and repeatedly interviewed at key life transitions, or cohort studies, where different samples of the same population are interviewed over successive time periods. The first method is capable of tracking *individual* change over time and identifying its determinants. The second method cannot do this but can identify *group* changes over time and highlight collective factors leading to them.[5] Such factors are traceable to the process of maturation of the target cohort and to historical events occurring in the interviewing periods.

An additional feature of longitudinal designs is their capacity to establish a clear temporal order between potential determinants and outcomes. This is particularly important in the study of highly dynamic processes such as immigrant acculturation and social adaptation. In the case of second-generation youths, for example, a correlation is observable between aspirations and academic achievement, but, with cross-sectional data, it is impossible to disentangle cause from effect. Similarly, self-esteem is positively correlated with good intergenerational relations, but again the causal order between these variables is ambiguous.

As already noted, another limitation of cross-sectional studies of young populations is that they rely on respondents' reports about family and parental characteristics. Such reports can be colored by the character of parent-child relations, the composition of the family, and its socioeconomic situation. Independent interviews with at least a random subsample of parents is necessary to establish the validity of such reports. Otherwise, causal analysis and models are at risk of endogeneity, where present outcomes color retroactive reports of alleged causes.[6]

Longitudinal studies designed to overcome the above limitations are difficult and expensive to carry out. They run the risk of excessive sample mortality in follow-up surveys, effectively denying the value of the entire exercise. The longer the time lag between the initial survey and successive ones, the greater their substantive value but also the greater the risk of substantial case loss. For example, a panel of students with a one-year lag between original and follow-up surveys is very likely to retrieve a large number or original respondents, but it is unlikely to yield significant results since little change can be expected over such a short time period. Conversely, a lag of three or more years is capable of revealing major time-linked changes in this young population, but it runs the risk of significant sample attrition.[7]

## STUDYING THE NEW SECOND GENERATION: THE CHILDREN OF IMMIGRANTS LONGITUDINAL STUDY IN THE UNITED STATES

This section describes in detail the Children of Immigrants Longitudinal Study (CILS) in the United States as background to the description of the ILSEG project in Spain and as prelude to the comparison of results from both studies in subsequent chapters. CILS focused on a baseline population of mean age 14, corresponding to the census estimate of the average for children of Asian and Latin American immigrants in the United States in 1990. In addition to this correspondence, there was another powerful reason to focus on this age group: at this early age, most children are still in middle school or junior high school, which makes it possible to generate representative samples by tapping the school population. At later ages, an unknown number drops out of school, biasing samples restricted to a student universe.[8]

The design of CILS called for taking large samples of students of foreign parentage in the eighth and ninth grades, ranging in age from 13 to 17, and following them for three to four years until their last year of high school. At that point, a second survey took place of all those students who had remained in school and were about to graduate as well as those who had abandoned their schooling. Through this strategy, it was possible to examine adaptation outcomes at the crucial school-to-work or school-to-college transition and, more importantly, to establish unambiguously the causal forces determining these outcomes. Hence, for example, a positive relationship between school grades and high parental aspirations may be due to the greater motivation for achievement spurred in the child by ambitious parents or, alternatively, to the adjustment of parental expectations to the child's actual performance. With surveys at two different points in time, one can establish the order of causation more confidently as well as examine how particular outcomes (in this case, grades) change over time.

In total, 5,262 students took part in the first survey. Their parents came from seventy-three different foreign countries. To be eligible for an interview, the student had to have at least one foreign-born parent and himself or herself be U.S.-born or have lived in the United States for at least five years. Thus, even the oldest foreign-born youths in these grades, age 17, would have had to arrive in the United States by age 12 to be included. This corresponds to a broad operational definition of second generation as native-born children of foreign parents or foreign-born children who were brought to the United States before adolescence.

The samples were drawn from forty-nine schools in the metropolitan areas of Miami/Ft. Lauderdale, Florida, and San Diego, California. These cities were selected because they represent two areas most heavily affected by the new immigration and because they serve as entry points to significantly different groups. Miami receives immigrants mainly from the Caribbean (especially Cubans, Haitians, Dominicans, Jamaicans, and other English-speaking West Indians), Central America (mostly Nicaraguans), and South America (primarily Colombians, Venezuelans, and Brazilians). San Diego is one of the main entry points and places of settlement for the large migrant inflow from Mexico; it also receives large numbers of Salvadorans and Guatemalans and is one of the cities preferred by immigrants from Asia, such as Filipinos, Vietnamese, Cambodians, Laotians, and, to a lesser extent, Chinese, Japanese, and Koreans.

In both cities, the sample design called for inclusion of schools in areas of heavy immigrant concentration as well as those where the native-born predominated. This strategy allowed for analysis of how various adaptation outcomes are affected by different school contexts. The San Diego school district is sufficiently diverse to contain both types of schools. Miami has been so heavily affected by immigration that most of its schools include large proportions of first- and second-generation students. For this reason, the sample encompassed the schools of Ft. Lauderdale (Broward County) where native-parentage students predominate. In addition, the CILS research team encountered a well-developed bilingual private school system in Miami, serving primarily the children of former Cuban exiles. Two such schools were included in the sample.

In terms of national origin, the sampling goal was to include roughly proportional numbers of students from the principal immigrant groups in each area while reserving approximately one-fourth of the interviews to represent smaller nationalities. This goal was met. As shown in Table 7, the major groups in both areas—Cubans, Nicaraguans, Colombians, and Haitians in South Florida; Filipinos, Mexicans, and

Vietnamese in Southern California—jointly constitute 75 percent of the sample. The remainder is represented by children of immigrants from sixty-six other countries.

Table 7 shows that the average age of the sample was 14 at the time of the survey and that it was evenly divided by sex and by grade in school. Similarly, about half of the respondents were native-born of foreign percentage (corresponding to a strict definition of the second generation), and the remainder are members of the 1.5 generation (born abroad but brought at an early age to the United States.) This first survey was conducted in 1992.

In 1995, three years after the original survey, the follow-up survey was launched. As seen previously, its purpose was to measure adaptation outcomes at a key juncture in the life of these youths when they left school for work or college. Whenever possible, interviews were conducted in school, first with the original ninth graders as they reached their senior year, and then with the original eighth graders as they, in turn, became seniors. For students who had dropped out or moved to other areas, questionnaires were completed in two other forms: either a member of the survey team visited the last known address and asked the student to fill out the schedule, or it was mailed to the student with an addressed, stamped envelope and instructions. In a few cases, students who had returned to their country of origin were located and interviewed by telephone.

The follow-up schedule repeated many questions from the original one in order to examine how the situation and outlooks of these children had changed over time. In addition, a number of items drawn from national surveys of comparable native-born students were included to allow analysis of similarities and differences between the two populations. A problem of potential bias exists because the follow-up survey did not retrieve all original respondents. The total follow-up sample was 4,288, or 81.5 percent of the original. The question is whether lost cases are random or whether they overrepresent a particular class of respondents. In the latter case, a sampling bias exists. To test this possibility, the researchers compared retrieved and lost respondents on their characteristics measured in the first survey and correlated presence in the follow-up with potential determinants, also ascertained in 1992–93.

Table 8 presents results of this exercise. By and large, results show that the follow-up sample faithfully reproduced the different categories of respondents in the original survey. For example, the second survey retrieved almost identical proportions of boys and girls, of native-born

TABLE 7    CHARACTERISTICS OF CHILDREN OF IMMIGRANTS INTERVIEWED
IN SOUTH FLORIDA AND SOUTHERN CALIFORNIA (CILS)

| Variable | N | % |
|---|---|---|
| Location: | | |
|   Miami/ Ft. Lauderdale | 2,842 | 54.0 |
|   San Diego | 2,420 | 46.0 |
| Grade in school: | | |
|   8th | 2,833 | 53.8 |
|   9th | 2,429 | 46.2 |
| Sex: | | |
|   Male | 2,575 | 40.9 |
|   Female | 2,687 | 51.0 |
| Length of U.S. residence: | | |
|   U.S.-born | 2,507 | 47.6 |
|   10 years or more | 1,426 | 27.1 |
|   9 years or less | 1,329 | 25.3 |
| U.S. citizen: | | |
|   Yes | 3,335 | 63.4 |
|   No or does not know | 1,329 | 25.3 |
| Father's education: | | |
|   Less than high school | 2,172 | 41.3 |
|   High school graduate | 1,889 | 35.9 |
|   College grad or more | 1,201 | 22.8 |
| Mother's education: | | |
|   Less than high school | 2,163 | 41.1 |
|   High school graduate | 2,034 | 38.7 |
|   College grad or more | 1,065 | 20.2 |
| National origin: | | |
|   Cuban | 1,226 | 23.3 |
|   Filipino | 819 | 15.6 |
|   Mexican | 755 | 14.4 |
|   Vietnamese | 370 | 7.0 |
|   Nicaraguan | 344 | 6.5 |
|   Colombian | 227 | 4.3 |
|   Haitian | 178 | 3.4 |
|   Jamaican | 156 | 3.0 |
|   Laotian | 155 | 2.9 |
|   Other West Indian | 116 | 2.2 |
|   Dominican Republic | 104 | 2.0 |
|   Cambodian | 95 | 1.8 |
|   Chinese | 72 | 1.4 |
|   Hmong | 53 | 1.0 |

| | | |
|---|---|---|
| Other Latin American | 365 | 6.4 |
| Other Asian | 91 | 1.7 |
| Other (Middle East, Europe, Canada, etc.) | 136 | 2.6 |
| Language spoken at home: | | |
| English | 371 | 7.0 |
| Spanish | 2,931 | 55.7 |
| Tagalog/other Philippine | 756 | 14.4 |
| Vietnamese | 326 | 6.2 |
| Lao | 158 | 3.0 |
| Hatian Creole | 150 | 2.8 |
| Chinese | 98 | 1.8 |
| Cambodian | 82 | 1.6 |
| Hmong | 51 | 1.0 |
| Other languages | 100 | 1.9 |
| No information | 41 | 0.8 |
| Household type: | | |
| Father and mother present | 3,338 | 63.4 |
| Parent and step-parent | 692 | 13.2 |
| Single parent | 1,061 | 20.2 |
| Other | 171 | 3.2 |

SOURCE: Portes and Rumbaut, *Legacies*, table 2.2.

and foreign-born youth, and of U.S. citizens versus noncitizens. Similarly, the proportions represented by different nationalities in both surveys are very similar. There is a slight tendency for children from intact families (both parents present) to be overrepresented in the follow-up survey. With this exception, all other differences are statistically insignificant.

An important limitation of the original survey was that information on the families was obtained indirectly from relatively young teenagers. For this reason, the data on families and parents were quite limited. It is obvious that the social context provided by immigrant parents plays a decisive role in the adaptation outcomes of their children. For this reason, it was deemed vital to extend the interviews conducted with a small group of parents following the first survey to a sizable subsample. This larger parental survey took place simultaneously with the follow-up of students in their senior year.

Many immigrant parents did not speak English fluently and, for this reason, the questionnaire had to be translated and the interview conducted face-to-face. In total, this instrument was translated into eight languages: Spanish, Haitian Creole, Philippine Tagalog, Cambodian,

TABLE 8   ORIGINAL AND FOLLOW-UP SURVEYS IN SOUTH FLORIDA AND SOUTHERN CALIFORNIA (CILS)

| | | Miami/Ft. Lauderdale | | | | San Diego | | | |
| | | First survey | | Follow-up survey | | First survey | | Follow-up survey | |
| Variables | Values | N | % | N | % | N | % | N | % |
|---|---|---|---|---|---|---|---|---|---|
| Sex | | | | | | | | | |
| | Male | 1,366 | 48.1 | 1,046 | 47.0 | 1,209 | 50.0 | 1,023 | 49.6 |
| | Female | 1,467 | 51.9 | 1,179 | 53.0 | 1,211 | 50.0 | 1,040 | 50.4 |
| Age (1992) | | | | | | | | | |
| | 13 or less | 549 | 19.3 | 468 | 21.0 | 479 | 19.8 | 419 | 20.3 |
| | 14 | 1,284 | 45.2 | 1,024 | 46.0 | 1,046 | 43.2 | 908 | 44.0 |
| | 15 | 804 | 28.3 | 594 | 26.7 | 736 | 30.5 | 617 | 29.9 |
| | 16 or more | 205 | 7.2 | 139 | 6.3 | 158 | 6.5 | 119 | 5.8 |
| Length of U.S. residence | | | | | | | | | |
| | Nine years or less | 596 | 21.0 | 467 | 21.0 | 733 | 30.3 | 605 | 29.3 |
| | Ten years or more | 739 | 26.0 | 582 | 26.2 | 687 | 28.4 | 583 | 28.3 |
| | U.S.-born | 1,507 | 53.0 | 1,176 | 52.9 | 100 | 41.3 | 875 | 42.4 |
| U.S. citizen | | | | | | | | | |
| | Yes | 1,886 | 66.4 | 1,461 | 65.7 | 1,449 | 59.9 | 1,260 | 61.1 |
| | No/don't know | 956 | 33.6 | 764 | 34.3 | 971 | 40.1 | 803 | 38.9 |
| Household composition | | | | | | | | | |
| | Father and mother present | 1,649 | 58.0 | 1,385 | 62.2 | 1,689 | 69.8 | 1,517 | 73.5 |
| | Parent and step-parent | 450 | 15.8 | 306 | 13.9 | 242 | 10.0 | 182 | 8.8 |
| | Single parent | 658 | 23.2 | 478 | 21.5 | 403 | 16.7 | 310 | 15.0 |
| | Other | 85 | 3.0 | 56 | 2.5 | 86 | 3.5 | 54 | 2.7 |

| | | N | % | N | % | N | % | N | % |
|---|---|---|---|---|---|---|---|---|---|
| Father's education | Less than high school | 1,066 | 37.5 | 809 | 36.4 | 1,106 | 45.7 | 924 | 44.8 |
| | High school graduate | 1,010 | 35.5 | 793 | 35.6 | 879 | 36.3 | 754 | 36.5 |
| | College graduate or more | 766 | 27.0 | 623 | 28.0 | 435 | 18.0 | 385 | 18.7 |
| Mother's education | Less than high school | 891 | 31.4 | 676 | 30.4 | 1,272 | 52.6 | 1,050 | 50.9 |
| | High school graduate | 1,319 | 46.4 | 1,037 | 46.6 | 715 | 29.5 | 616 | 29.9 |
| | College graduate or more | 632 | 22.2 | 512 | 23.0 | 433 | 17.9 | 397 | 19.2 |
| National origin | Cuban (public school) | 1,042 | 36.8 | 820 | 36.9 | 2 | 0.1 | 2 | 0.1 |
| | Cuban (private school) | 183 | 6.5 | 146 | 6.6 | 0 | 0.0 | 0 | 0.0 |
| | Nicaraguan | 340 | 12.0 | 277 | 12.4 | 4 | 0.2 | 4 | 0.2 |
| | Colombian | 223 | 8.0 | 181 | 8.1 | 4 | 0.2 | 4 | 0.2 |
| | Haitian | 177 | 6.2 | 134 | 6.0 | 1 | 0.0 | 1 | 0.0 |
| | West Indian | 253 | 9.0 | 189 | 8.5 | 19 | 0.8 | 12 | 0.6 |
| | Mexican | 28 | 1.0 | 21 | 0.9 | 727 | 30.0 | 578 | 28.0 |
| | Filipino | 11 | 0.5 | 8 | 0.4 | 808 | 33.4 | 716 | 34.7 |
| | Vietnamese | 8 | 0.3 | 7 | 0.3 | 362 | 15.0 | 303 | 14.7 |
| | Laotian | 1 | 0.0 | 1 | 0.0 | 154 | 6.4 | 143 | 6.9 |
| | Cambodian | 1 | 0.0 | 1 | 0.0 | 94 | 3.8 | 88 | 43 |
| | Hmong | 0 | 0.0 | 0 | 0.0 | 53 | 2.2 | 50 | 2.4 |
| | Other Latin American | 411 | 14.6 | 317 | 14.3 | 58 | 2.4 | 41 | 1.9 |
| | Other Asian | 22 | 0.8 | 40 | 1.8 | 118 | 4.9 | 107 | 5.3 |
| | Other | 120 | 4.3 | 83 | 3.8 | 16 | 0.5 | 14 | 0.7 |
| Totals | | 2,842 | 100.0 | 2,225 | 100.0 | 2,420 | 100.0 | 2,063 | 100.0 |

SOURCE: Portes and Rumbaut, *Legacies*, table 2.3.

Lao, Hmong, Vietnamese, and Chinese. Because of the complexity of locating and interviewing so many non-English-speaking parents, the survey was conducted with a probability sample representing 50 percent of the student follow-up. The parental sample was drawn randomly, but with differential probabilities by national groups in order to ensure sufficient representation of smaller nationalities, especially those composed of immigrants of more modest socioeconomic background.

The goal of this strategy was to produce sufficient parental interviews with immigrants of all nationalities. As shown in Table 9, this goal was met, as the survey yielded sizable numbers of Haitian, West Indian, Nicaraguan, and other Latin American parents in Miami/Ft. Lauderdale and of Vietnamese, Laotian, Cambodian, and Hmong parents in San Diego. The larger nationalities—Cubans, Mexicans, and Filipinos—are proportionally underrepresented, although they still constitute the greater absolute numbers in the parental as well as in the student surveys. Table 9 also shows that the majority of interviewed parents had been in the country for a considerable length of time, averaging 21.6 years, and that most had become U.S. citizens.

Results of the CILS study have been published in a number of academic articles and in two books: *Legacies: The Story of the Immigrant Second Generation* and *Ethnicities: Children of Immigrants in America*. Both appeared in 2001.[9] The data from the study were subsequently placed in the public domain and have been intensively used since then by other scholars and students.[10]

## THE LONGITUDINAL STUDY OF THE SECOND GENERATION IN SPAIN (ILSEG)

ILSEG was deliberately patterned after CILS as a means to develop reliable data about the present situation and future prospects of the second generation in Spain and to facilitate comparison with American results. Like CILS, the new study adopted a panel design in order to measure individual change, as well as collective change, over time. Repeated cross-sectional surveys of student populations, most prominently the OECD-sponsored Program for International Student Assessment (PISA), can provide representative figures for successive student cohorts and assess collective changes over time. They cannot, however, trace, individual change or create the basis for causal models at this level. In addition, general surveys of student populations tend to contain limited information on foreign-born and foreign-parentage youths.

TABLE 9   BASIC DEMOGRAPHIC CHARACTERISTICS OF IMMIGRANT PARENTS (CILS)

| Variable | Miami/Ft. Lauderdale | | San Diego | | Totals | |
|---|---|---|---|---|---|---|
| | N | % | N | % | N | % |
| Parent's country of birth: | | | | | | |
| Cambodia | — | — | 85 | 6.4 | 85 | 3.5 |
| Colombia | 83 | 7.4 | 3 | 0.2 | 86 | 3.5 |
| Cuba | 384 | 34.2 | 2 | 0.2 | 386 | 15.8 |
| Haiti | 75 | 6.7 | — | — | 75 | 3.1 |
| Jamaica/West Indies | 99 | 8.8 | 4 | 0.3 | 103 | 4.2 |
| Laos (Hmong) | — | — | 46 | 3.5 | 46 | 1.9 |
| Laos (Lao) | — | — | 140 | 10.6 | 140 | 5.7 |
| Mexico | 8 | 0.7 | 321 | 24.4 | 329 | 13.5 |
| Nicaragua | 203 | 18.8 | 3 | 0.2 | 206 | 8.4 |
| Philippines | 1 | 0.1 | 359 | 27.2 | 360 | 14.7 |
| Vietnam | 1 | 0.1 | 248 | 18.8 | 249 | 10.2 |
| Other Latin America | 207 | 18.5 | 17 | 1.3 | 224 | 9.2 |
| Other Asia | 11 | 1.0 | 64 | 4.9 | 75 | 3.1 |
| Other country | 51 | 4.5 | 26 | 2.0 | 77 | 3.2 |
| Relationship to child: | | | | | | |
| Parent | 1,081 | 96.3 | 1,289 | 97.8 | 2,370 | 97.1 |
| Step-parent | 17 | 1.5 | 3 | 0.2 | 20 | 0.8 |
| Guardian | 25 | 2.2 | 26 | 2.0 | 51 | 2.1 |
| Gender: | | | | | | |
| Male | 338 | 30.1 | 583 | 44.2 | 920 | 37.7 |
| Female | 785 | 69.9 | 735 | 55.8 | 1,520 | 62.3 |
| Marital status: | | | | | | |
| Married | 847 | 75.5 | 1,106 | 83.9 | 1,953 | 80.0 |
| Divorced/separated | 209 | 18.6 | 126 | 9.6 | 335 | 13.7 |
| Widowed | 39 | 3.5 | 64 | 4.9 | 103 | 4.2 |
| Other | 28 | 2.4 | 23 | 1.6 | 51 | 2.1 |
| If married, partner's relationship to child: | | | | | | |
| Biological father/mother | 713 | 84.2 | 1,001 | 90.5 | 1,714 | 87.8 |
| Step-parent | 119 | 14.1 | 88 | 8.0 | 207 | 10.5 |
| Other | 15 | 1.7 | 17 | 1.5 | 32 | 1.7 |
| Present citizenship: | | | | | | |
| Foreign | 514 | 45.8 | 675 | 51.3 | 1,189 | 48.7 |
| U.S. | 609 | 54.2 | 643 | 48.7 | 1,252 | 51.3 |
| Year of arrival in U.S.: | | | | | | |
| Before 1960 | 43 | 3.8 | 37 | 2.8 | 78 | 3.2 |
| 1960–69 | 292 | 26.0 | 121 | 9.2 | 412 | 16.9 |
| 1970–79 | 330 | 29.4 | 551 | 41.8 | 882 | 36.1 |
| 1980–84 | 303 | 27.0 | 368 | 27.9 | 671 | 27.5 |
| 1985 and after | 155 | 13.8 | 241 | 18.3 | 398 | 16.3 |
| Totals: | 1,123 | 100.0 | 1,319 | 100.0 | 2,442 | 100.0 |

SOURCE: Portes and Rumbaut, *Legacies*, table 2.5.

ILSEG is the product of a collaborative effort between the Center of Migration and Development at Princeton University and the Ortega y Gasset University Institute of Madrid with the explicit aims of filling the gap in the existing research literature and producing comparative data with earlier CILS results. Prior studies of the second generation in Europe have been cross-sectional and focused on a few foreign nationalities.[11] To accomplish the goals of the study, we sought the cooperation of education authorities in the Spanish communities of Madrid and Barcelona—the two principal areas of concentration of immigrants in Spain. Once obtained, we proceeded to draw random samples of secondary schools in each of the two metropolitan area, stratified by type of school (public versus private) and by geographical area. Complete lists of schools were made available for that purpose by the respective education authorities (*consejerías*). This stratified random sample maintained a constant sampling fraction by school type and by region within each metropolitan area, making the sample statistically representative of the target universes.[12]

Within each school, all eligible students were included. As in CILS, "second generation" was defined as children born in Spain, or brought to the country at an early age with at least one foreign-born parent. By convention, those born in the host country are defined as the second-generation "proper," whereas those brought at an early age from abroad are defined as the "1.5 generation."[13] Most immigrant youths in Spain attend public schools, but a significant minority has found its way into state-supported private schools, mostly Catholic-affiliated.[14] One of the important questions for analysis is whether the self-identities, future plans, and self-esteem of these youngsters vary by type of school. Geographically, the sample was also stratified by region to ensure that all schools in each metropolitan area were included. Because of the concentration of schools in the respective central cities, a simple random sample would have excluded those in many suburban areas. In total, 180 schools took part in the study: 101 in Madrid, and 79 in Barcelona. Of these, 111 were public schools, and the rest were private.

Basic secondary education in Spain is compulsory, and its students are, overwhelmingly, in their early adolescent years. These two features are methodologically convenient because they guarantee that a school-drawn sample will be representative of the respective age cohort, since almost all of its members are still in school. The study targeted the first three years of basic secondary school (*enseñanza secundaria obligatoria*, or ESO) because they include the population of average age 13–14 that represented the universe of interest. At this age, almost all children are

TABLE 10   BASIC DEMOGRAPHIC CHARACTERISTICS OF THE SECOND GENERATION
IN SPAIN, 2008

| Variable | Values | Barcelona | Madrid | Totals |
|---|---|---|---|---|
| Sex | Male (%) | 54.13 | 48.54 | 51.38 |
| | Female (%) | 45.87 | 51.46 | 48.62 |
| Age | Mean | 13.48 | 14.36 | 13.91 |
| | Median | 13 | 14 | 14 |
| Country of birth | Spain (%) | 15.94 | 13.56 | 14.77 |
| | Abroad (%) | 84.06 | 86.44 | 85.23 |
| Years of Spanish residence (for respondents born abroad) | Mean | 6.14 | 6.78 | 6.45 |
| | Median | 5 | 6 | 5 |
| Family composition | Lives with both natural parents (%) | 65.80 | 66.87 | 66.32 |
| Year in secondary school | 1st | 33.59 | 8.77 | 21.67 |
| | 2nd | 34.73 | 54.40 | 44.18 |
| | 3rd | 31.68 | 36.83 | 34.15 |
| Knowledge of Spanish: | | | | |
| Speaks: | Little (%) | 3.69 | 1.05 | 2.39 |
| | Some (%) | 5.68 | 3.45 | 4.58 |
| | Well (%) | 23.86 | 22.95 | 23.42 |
| | Perfectly (%) | 66.77 | 72.55 | 69.61 |
| Understands: | Little (%) | 3.03 | 0.78 | 1.93 |
| | Some (%) | 3.50 | 2.37 | 2.95 |
| | Well (%) | 18.09 | 19.46 | 18.76 |
| | Perfectly (%) | 75.38 | 77.39 | 76.36 |

SOURCE: ILSEG.

enrolled in school, and they are sufficiently mature to be able to fill out a simple questionnaire.

The total student sample size was 6,905: 3,375 in Madrid and 3,530 in Barcelona. With a constant sampling fraction, the sample is self-weighting with respect to the total universe and each sampling strata. This sample is thus considerably larger than that provided by CILS's baseline survey. Table 10 presents ILSEG's basic demographic characteristics, broken down by each metropolitan area. For the questionnaire employed in this survey, go to www.ucpress.edu/978052028629-0.

In 2010, approximately two years after completion of these surveys, the project undertook a new study of parents to complement the data obtained from the children. To this end, letters were sent to the home addresses supplied by students with an attached questionnaire to be completed by their parents. The letter explained the goals of the project and promised an incentive in the form of a monetary prize to be awarded by public lottery among those returning completed questionnaires. Reminders were sent to parents not responding to the original letter. In total, approximately 700 usable questionnaires were obtained, a figure that represented less than half of the target sample for the parental survey—1,750 cases, or one-fourth of the children's sample. The project team then turned to telephone data supplied by students and spent the entire summer and part of the fall of 2010 calling home numbers in Madrid and Barcelona. The team kept a moving tally of completed questionnaires to ensure that they would be roughly balanced between both cities and that all major nationalities in the original survey were represented.

In total, interviews were completed with 1,843 parents, representing 28 percent of the original student survey. The major nationalities in both surveys are identical. In the parental sample, they include Ecuador (28.0 percent), Morocco (10.5 percent), Colombia (7.8 percent), Peru (6.7 percent), the Dominican Republic (5.5 percent), and Romania (5.1 percent). Among second-generation children born abroad, the corresponding figures were Ecuador (28.6 percent), Morocco (7.1 percent), Colombia (8.4 percent), Peru (6.1 percent), the Dominican Republic (5.2 percent), and Romania (5 percent). No other nationality in either sample exceeded 5 percent. This survey provides the necessary data to assess parental effects and, hence, avoid the endogeneity problem referred to above. Table 11 presents descriptive characteristics of the ILSEG parental survey. The parental questionnaire can be found online at www.ucpress.edu /9780520286290.

## TRACKING THE ILSEG SAMPLE OVER TIME

Three years after the original 2008–9 student survey, the follow-up was launched. Its purpose was to obtain information on a set of adaptation outcomes in the strategic school-to-work transition. As noted earlier, surveys in early adolescence can only capture background and psychological variables, such as aspirations and self-esteem that point toward alternative adaptation paths but do not guarantee actual outcomes. By ages 17–18, such outcomes have started to crystallize. This is especially the case in a country like Spain, where many youths quit study after basic secondary in order to enter the labor market.[15]

TABLE II    SOCIODEMOGRAPHIC CHARACTERISTICS OF THE ILSEG PARENTAL
SAMPLE, 2010 *(N = 1,843)*

| Characteristic | Barcelona | Madrid | Total |
|---|---|---|---|
| Age, mean years | 42.0 | 43.2 | 42.6 |
| Gender (female) (%) | 66.0 | 69.2 | 67.7 |
| Has Spanish citizenship (%) | 34.3 | 41.0 | 37.9 |
| Years in Spain (mean) | 10.7 | 11.9 | 11.4 |
| Language spoken at home (%): | | | |
|    Spanish | 71.7 | 77.5 | 74.8 |
|    Catalan | 2.1 | 0.0 | 1.0 |
|    Other | 26.2 | 22.5 | 24.2 |
| Knowledge of Spanish (average)[1] | 3.4 | 3.6 | 3.5 |
| Family structure: | | | |
|    Both biological parents present (%) | 73.8 | 67.9 | 70.8 |
| Education (%): | | | |
|    Less than secondary | 48.9 | 42.2 | 45.6 |
|    Secondary | 34.7 | 40.1 | 37.5 |
|    Some university | 9.6 | 8.8 | 9.2 |
|    University graduate | 6.8 | 8.9 | 7.7 |
| Employment situation (%): | | | |
|    Employed | 57.2 | 60.7 | 59.0 |
|    Unemployed | 22.5 | 23.7 | 23.1 |
|    Disabled, other | 20.3 | 15.6 | 17.9 |
| Occupational status (average)[2] | 86.4 | 85.1 | 85.8 |

SOURCE: ILSEG parental survey.

1. Knowledge of Spanish Index (KSI). Range: 1 (lowest) to 4 (highest).

2. PRESCA Scale of Occupational Status for Spain. Range: 60–235.

The follow-up survey aimed at covering a range of possible outcomes, from objective events to subjective outlooks and opinions.
(The full questionnaire can be found online at www.ucpress.edu
/9780520286290.) These are the most important.

Educational Attainment:
   Completed school years
   Still attending school
   Type of school attended (public versus private)
   Top and average grade in last year of school

Reasons for dropping out of school
Plans to return to school
Occupational Attainment:
Present occupational situation
If working, occupational status
If working, hours per week
If working, type of occupation (formal versus informal)
If working, place of employment
Income:
Personal
Family
Family Situation:
Number of persons in household
Type of persons with whom respondent lives
Legal status of home (owned, rented, etc.)
Legal Status in Spain (citizen, legal resident, processing legal residence, without papers):
Of self
Of parents
Marital Status:
Of self
Of parents
Indicators of Downward Assimilation:
Dropped out of school
Unemployed and looking for work
Family income below poverty level
Joined a gang during last 3 years
Has been incarcerated during last 3 years
Has had one child or more during last 3 years
Self-identity:
National self-identification (Spanish/foreign nationality)
Importance of national self-identification
Social Relations:
Character of relationship with parents
Number of friends
Ethnicity/nationality of friends
Goals for the Future:
Educational and occupational aspirations (ideal)
Educational and occupational expectations (realistic)

*Tracking the Sample*

The follow-up survey began by soliciting the cooperation of school systems in the two target metropolitan areas, Madrid and Barcelona. The two secondary school superintendencies agreed to collaborate with the study and sent letters to that effect to all selected schools. These letters and subsequent communications by both superintendencies were vital for obtaining the agreement of school principals to participate. Once letters were sent to the target schools, the next step was to send teams of two interviewers to each of them. Teams were formed by experienced field-workers who had taken part in the first phase of the project. Their goals were:

To identify and re-interview all original respondents still in school

To obtain information on the whereabouts of those no longer in school

To identify other second-generation students in that school and interview them

To select and interview a sample of native-parentage students

Questionnaires were self-administered in group sessions, supervised by a member of the field team. Each team carried a list of respondents originally contacted in the respective school. Inquiries were made with the school principal and other officials on the whereabouts of absent respondents. The information thus gathered was incorporated into the tracking file for each case. The field teams hence completed the following tasks:

Contacting and re-interviewing all respondents still attending the original school

Gathering information on respondents who had changed schools or dropped out

Creating a new second-generation replacement sample

Creating a new native-parentage sample

This phase of the project took place sequentially: in metropolitan Madrid from October 2011 to January 2012, and in Barcelona from February to May 2012. In effect, the school survey sought to accomplish simultaneously three goals: to create a panel of individuals tracked over time; to create a cross-sectional sample of the same population over time, and to create a comparative sample of native-parentage youths. Although the school-based effort satisfactorily accomplished the last two goals, it fell short of the first. This happened because, as just noted, many students abandoned school early to enter the labor market. Hence, we had to turn to alternative retrieval paths.

From the initial student survey, we had personal identifiers for 5,240 respondents. Their names and telephone numbers provided the basis for the next phase of the tracking and retrieval effort. The second phase commenced before the termination of the first in Madrid and concurrently with it in Barcelona. It consisted of telephone calls to track and interview other respondents on a one-by-one basis. For this purpose, the team in charge of this phase of the study made use of the following information:

Telephone data from the original survey (2008)

Re-actualized data from the parental survey (2010)

New data gathered during school visits (2012)

Phone calls were made from the project's office located at the Ortega y Gasset University Institute in Madrid. To avoid overlap with the school fieldwork, calls were organized sequentially: first to respondents not found in the Madrid schools, then to those not located in the schools in Barcelona. Interviewers read to each respondent an introductory statement emphasizing the voluntary character of their participation and the incentive to do so (the chance to win one of three prizes of 1,500 euros each, to be chosen by lottery among all participating respondents).

## Facebook and Tuenti

Although the second-generation replacement sample and the native-parentage sample were completed without difficulty through school visits, that phase of the study plus the second one, based on telephone interviews, had only limited success in locating our original respondents. In Madrid, for example, only 793 cases or just 26 percent of the original traceable sample ($N = 3,002$) had been located by both means by the end of March 2012. This situation prompted a search for alternative retrieval paths. Members of the research team noted that ready access to Internet social networks has become nearly universal and that most youths use them regularly. In Spain, the most popular are Facebook and Tuenti.

Using the names of original respondents as basic data, Internet searches were organized in each of these networks. After a match was made, a message was sent inviting the person to become a "friend." If the invitation was accepted, a second message was sent explaining the purpose of the study and the incentives to participate. At that point, several contingencies could occur:

a. The person identified was the original respondent and agreed to fill out the questionnaire online or by telephone;

b. The person identified was not the original respondent; or

c. The person identified was the original respondent but objected to or raised questions about the study.

If "c," then an interactive process followed, including online "chats" with a member of the project team and referral of the person to the project's webpage in each of the networks. In most cases, the process successfully led to an acceptance. Interaction with located respondents did not end with completion of the questionnaire; they were invited to join the field team and thus become part of the study. This network-building process took several forms: regular messages informing respondents of the project's progress and welcoming new participants; the creation of a blog where respondents were invited to post photos as well as messages about themselves; and requests for leads or referrals to other school peers who took part in the original survey. The ILSEG blog is accessible online at https://proyectoilseg.wordpress.com/.

To stimulate referrals, a process of emulation was set up among graduates of schools included in the study's first wave. A list of such schools was included in the blog. Respondents were invited to support the project's team by providing leads so that his or her school would become one of the "winners." In the same message, they were encouraged to post photos, videos, or other materials about themselves in the ILSEG blog.

This Internet tracking effort had several important consequences. First, it increased dramatically the number of located respondents. Second, it became itself a source of information about the activities, opinions, and plans of a sizable number of these youths. Third, it created an emergent social phenomenon in the form of a rapidly growing network of contacts between members of the project's team and respondents, as well as among the latter themselves.

A final step of the retrieval process involved revisiting the original schools and requesting the cooperation of its personnel to locate respondents not yet found. This was not an easy task because many principals objected that supplying such information ran contrary to legal protection of personal data in Spain. To overcome this objection, the field team countered with the letters of authorization issued by school superintendencies; a statement about the use of the information obtained for exclusively scientific purposes; and the guarantee of such use by the human subjects protection agencies (institutional review boards) of Princeton University and the Ortega y Gasset University Institute.

The complexity of the sample retrieval effort is illustrated in Figure 5. It presents a flowchart, developed by the project's field team, representing the successive steps taken in the quest for original respondents. Through these various means, the ILSEG field team succeeded in retrieving 3,811 cases or 73 percent of the original traceable sample by the end of fieldwork in November 2012. For comparison, the first CILS follow-up survey in the United States retrieved 81.5 percent of the original sample (see Table 8), and the second, conducted in 2002–3, yielded 68.7 percent. Table 12 presents the final ILSEG follow-up sample broken down by city, type of survey, and mode of retrieval. In addition, the second survey yielded a replacement sample of 1,534 additional second-generation respondents and 1,965 native-parentage students. Both have the same average age and gender profiles as the retrieved sample. In total, the data set for the following analysis comprises 7,310 young adults of both sexes.

SAMPLE MORTALITY

Following the CILS methodology, we investigated next the extent to which the ILSEG follow-up sample is biased with respect to the original one or represents it fairly. For this purpose, we compared first the two samples over a series of objective variables measured in the first survey. Table 13 presents the results. Over a lengthy array of variables, differences between the two samples are quite small. Although several reach statistical significance, this is due to the large sample size. More telling is the Cramer's V coefficient of strength of association that is indifferent to sample size. With few exceptions, this coefficient does not exceed .10, indicating very little bias in the follow-up survey relative to the original one.

Another test for sample attrition can be performed by constructing a new variable, "Missing," in the follow-up survey and correlating it with a series of objective and psychosocial variables measured in the original one. Results are presented in Table 14. As shown there, the correlations

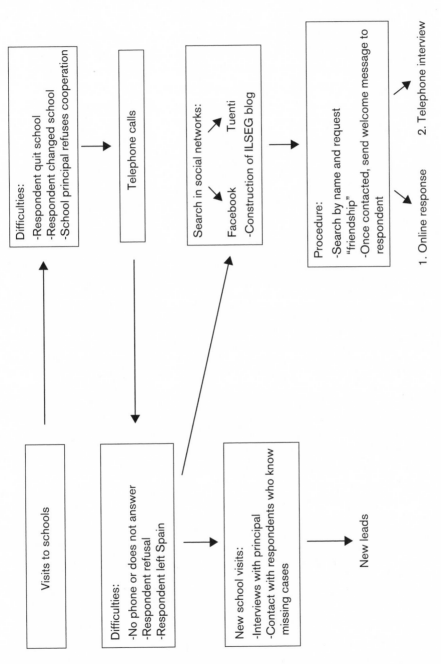

FIGURE 5. Flowchart of Sample Retrieval Steps, ILSEG Follow-up Survey, 2012.
Source: ILSEG field team, 2012.

TABLE 12   FOLLOW-UP SURVEY OF THE SECOND GENERATION IN SPAIN AND SUPPLEMENTARY SAMPLES, 2012

| City | Interviewed in school (%) | Telephone interview (%) | Leads by school personnel (%) | Internet social networks[1] (%) | Leads by other respondents through social networks (%) | Total | Replacement sample[2] (%) | Native parentage sample[2] | Grand total |
|---|---|---|---|---|---|---|---|---|---|
| Madrid | 28.9 | 69.7 | 63.5 | 55.1 | 54.3 | 50.2 | 60.2 | 46.4 | 54.4 |
| Barcelona | 71.1 | 30.3 | 36.5 | 44.9 | 45.7 | 49.8 | 39.8 | 50.6 | 45.6 |
| Total | 100.0 | 100.0 | 100.0 | 100.0 | 100.0 | 100.0 | 100.0 | 100.0 | 100.0 |
| N | 1,182 | 669 | 342 | 904 | 714 | 3,811 | 1,534 | 1,965 | 7,310 |

SOURCE: ILSEG follow-up survey, 2012.

1. Facebook and Tuenti.

2. Interviewed in schools.

TABLE 13   FREQUENCY DISTRIBUTIONS OF ORIGINAL AND FOLLOW-UP ILSEG SURVEYS ON OBJECTIVE VARIABLES

| Variables | Original sample (2008) | Follow-up sample (2012) | Cramer's V |
|---|---|---|---|
| Gender (male) | 51.3 | 48.8 | .054 |
| Age: | | | .088 |
| 12 or less | 14.1 | 15.6 | |
| 13 | 25.6 | 24.7 | |
| 14 | 31.4 | 30.7 | |
| 15 | 20.2 | 21.5 | |
| 16 or more | 7.2 | 8.9 | |
| Country of birth (Spain) | 14.8 | 17.2 | .076 |
| Knowledge of Spanish: | | | .017 |
| Poor | 9.3 | 8.7 | |
| Fair | 33.5 | 34.9 | |
| Good | 25.6 | 25.1 | |
| Excellent (fully fluent) | 31.6 | 31.3 | |
| Family composition: | | | .080 |
| Lives with both biological parents | 66.4 | 67.6 | |
| Other family arrangements | 33.6 | 32.4 | |
| Father's employment situation, 2008: | | | .018 |
| Employed | 90.1 | 90.6 | |
| Unemployed/other | 9.9 | 9.4 | |
| Father's educational attainment: | | | .028 |
| Less than university | 81.2 | 80.2 | |
| Some university or more | 18.8 | 19.8 | |

(continued)

TABLE 13 (*continued*)

| Variables | Original sample (2008) | Follow-up sample (2012) | Cramer's V |
|---|---|---|---|
| Mother's employment situation, 2008: | | | |
| Employed outside home | 78.2 | 79.1 | .022 |
| Housework, other | 21.8 | 20.9 | |
| Mother's educational attainment: | | | |
| Less than university | 78.0 | 76.8 | .030 |
| Some university or more | 22.0 | 23.2 | |
| Biological father's country of residence, 2008: | | | |
| Spain | 87.9 | 88.3 | .013 |
| Other | 12.1 | 11.7 | |
| Father has Spanish nationality (yes) | 48.3 | 49.0 | .016 |
| Biological mother's country of residence, 2008: | | | |
| Spain | 91.0 | 92.1 | .033 |
| Other | 9.0 | 7.9 | |
| Mother has Spanish nationality (yes) | 49.1 | 49.5 | .009 |
| City of residence, 2008: | | | |
| Madrid | 48.5 | 50.1 | .037 |
| Barcelona | 51.5 | 49.9 | |
| Type of school attended, 2008: | | | |
| Public | 82.3 | 82.9 | .017 |
| Private | 17.7 | 17.1 | |

TABLE 14 CORRELATIONS OF "MISSING" IN THE
FOLLOW-UP SURVEY WITH ORIGINAL SURVEY VARIABLES,
2008–12

| Variable | Correlation[1] |
|---|---|
| Gender (female) | −.054 |
| Age | −.082 |
| Birthplace (Spain) | −.076 |
| Knowledge of Spanish[2] | −.004 |
| Years of Spanish residence | .096 |
| Lives with father and mother | .080 |
| Family socioeconomic status[3] | .037 |
| Number of older siblings | −.028 |
| Number of younger siblings | −.027 |
| Father's employment status (employed) | .018 |
| Father's occupational status[4] | .031 |
| Father's educational attainment | .028 |
| Mother's employment situation (employed outside home) | .022 |
| Mother's occupational status[4] | .016 |
| Mother's educational attainment | .030 |
| Father's country of residence (Spain) | −.013 |
| Father's years of Spanish residence | .059 |
| Father has Spanish nationality | −.016 |
| Mother's country of residence (Spain) | −.033 |
| Mother's years of Spanish residence | .067 |
| Mother has Spanish nationality | .052 |
| Self-esteem[5] | −.036 |
| Familism[6] | −.029 |

1. Present in follow-up survey = 1; Else = 0.

2. Composite index (KSI) of self-reported ability to understand, speak, read, and write the language. See Table 17.

3. Composite index (FSES). See Table 17.

4. Scores in the PRESCA-2 scale of occupational prestige in Spain. See Table 17. Sample limited to employed parents.

5. Scores in Rosenberg's Self-esteem Scale. See Table 17.

6. Scores in Familistic Attitudes Index. See Table 17.

are uniformly low, failing to indicate a significant bias from one sample to the next.

The close similarity between both samples can be appreciated more fully by a detailed breakdown of country of birth. These results are presented in Table 15. As can be seen, the two series closely parallel each other, with the only difference exceeding 1 percent being registered among those born in Spain, the second generation "proper." The Cramer's V

TABLE 15 COUNTRY OF BIRTH OF ORIGINAL AND FOLLOW-UP
ILSEG SAMPLES

| Country of birth | Original sample | Follow-up sample |
|---|---|---|
| Spain | 14.8 | 17.2 |
| Argentina | 2.7 | 2.4 |
| Bolivia | 4.6 | 4.4 |
| Bulgaria | 1.3 | 1.4 |
| Chile | 1.2 | 1.4 |
| China | 3.5 | 2.1 |
| Colombia | 7.9 | 7.5 |
| Cuba | 0.5 | 0.3 |
| Dominican Republic | 4.9 | 4.5 |
| Ecuador | 26.3 | 27.3 |
| Equatorial Guinea | 0.8 | 1.0 |
| Morocco | 6.7 | 6.4 |
| Peru | 5.8 | 5.8 |
| Philippines | 1.6 | 1.8 |
| Poland | 0.6 | 0.6 |
| Romania | 4.7 | 4.7 |
| Ukraine | 0.9 | 0.9 |
| Venezuela | 1.2 | 1.2 |
| Other, Eastern Europe | 0.5 | 0.6 |
| Other, Western Europe | 2.1 | 2.1 |
| Other, Asia | 3.1 | 2.8 |
| Other, Central America | 3.9 | 3.5 |
| Other | 0.4 | 1.0 |
| Total | 100.0 (N = 6,872) | 100.0 (N = 3,767) |

coefficient of strength of association exceeds .10 in this case (V = .13), but this is primarily due to the large number of national categories rather than to significant discrepancies among them.

A final fortunate twist to these results is that the replacement sample, designed to compensate for sample attrition in the follow-up survey, closely resembles the latter in most objective variables. There was no reason to anticipate this pattern, since the replacement sample was collected exclusively in schools, and many members of the original sample had left school by 2012. Yet, as results in Table 16 demonstrate, the two samples are similar over an array of important variables. This evidence is presented in two forms—as means and percentages, and as correlations of selected variables with a new variable, "Survey Type," which was coded "1" if part of the follow-up and "2" if part of the replacement sample.

| Variable | Follow-up sample | Replacement sample | Correlation with "survey type" |
|---|---|---|---|
| Gender (male) (%) | 49.37 | 51.89 | −.002 |
| Age (mean) | 17.45 | 17.18 | .084 |
| Born in Spain (%) | 18.92 | 24.51 | −.062 |
| Years of Spanish residence (mean) | 9.58 | 9.02 | |
| Family situation (%): | | | |
| Both biological parents present | 64.30 | 64.68 | −.004 |
| Mother only | 26.83 | 26.21 | |
| Other | 8.87 | 9.09 | |
| Legal situation (%): | | | |
| Spanish nationality | 52.79 | 53.91 | −.007 |
| Residential parents | 38.44 | 39.58 | |
| Other | 8.77 | 6.51 | |
| Enrolled in school (%) | 84.57 | 99.54 | .215 |
| Country of birth (%): | | | |
| Spain | 17.2 | 24.5 | .114[1] |
| Argentina | 2.4 | 1.7 | |
| Bolivia | 4.4 | 4.2 | |
| Chile | 1.4 | 0.7 | |
| China | 2.1 | 2.3 | |
| Colombia | 7.5 | 5.9 | |
| Cuba | 0.3 | 0.5 | |
| Dominican Republic | 4.5 | 3.8 | |
| Ecuador | 27.3 | 24.9 | |
| Equatorial Guinea | 1.0 | 0.0 | |
| Morocco | 6.4 | 5.8 | |
| Peru | 5.8 | 7.1 | |
| Philippines | 1.8 | 0.6 | |
| Poland | 0.6 | 0.5 | |
| Romania | 4.7 | 4.8 | |
| Ukraine | 0.9 | 0.3 | |
| Venezuela | 1.2 | 1.1 | |
| Other, Eastern Europe | 2.0 | 1.8 | |
| Other, Western Europe | 2.1 | 1.6 | |
| Other, Asia | 2.8 | 2.7 | |
| Other, Central America | 3.5 | 2.8 | |
| Other | 3.07 | 2.4 | |
| Father's education (%): | | | |
| Secondary or less | 81.1 | 76.4 | −.053 |
| At least some college | 18.9 | 23.6 | |

(continued)

TABLE 16    *(continued)*

| Variable | Follow-up sample | Replacement sample | Correlation with "survey type" |
|---|---|---|---|
| Father's employment situation (%): | | | |
|   Not working | 37.6 | 33.5 | –.039 |
|   Employed | 62.4 | 66.5 | |
| Mother's education (%): | | | |
|   Secondary or less | 79.3 | 76.4 | –.031 |
|   At least some college | 20.7 | 23.6 | |
| Mother's employment situation (%): | | | |
|   Not working outside home | 29.7 | 31.0 | .013 |
|   Employed outside home | 70.3 | 69.0 | |
| Totals | 100.0 | 100.0 | |
| N | 3,805 | 1,528 | |

1. Cramer's V coefficient.

As seen in Table 16, these correlations are uniformly insignificant, with the predictable exception of current school enrollment—which is universal among new respondents but only partial among original ones. The similarity between both samples means that their members can be considered as part of the same universe of second-generation youths at average ages 17–18. The sample can, therefore, be merged in subsequent analyses, significantly increasing its statistical power and representativeness. As noted at the start of this chapter, tracing *individual* adaptation outcomes over time can only be done with longitudinal data, provided by the follow-up survey. However, for measuring average *group* differences over time, the merged longitudinal and replacement samples are appropriate, increasing the validity of these comparisons.

In synthesis, the 2012 surveys were successful in producing an unbiased subsample of the original 2008 sample and in adding to it a similar new sample that faithfully reproduces most objective characteristics of original respondents. Based on these findings, it will be unnecessary to introduce corrections for sample attrition in the ensuing analysis of substantive outcomes or analyze the replacement survey separately. In addition, as was indicated in Table 12, the research team was successful in completing a sizable survey of native-parentage students with whom results for second-generation youths can be systematically compared.

TABLE 17 COMPOSITE INDICES, ILSEG SURVEYS, 2008–13

| Variable | Description | Surveys | Range |
|---|---|---|---|
| Knowledge of Spanish | Sum of reported ability to understand, speak, read, and write Spanish. From "poor" to "fluent." Internal consistency reliability (alpha) is .89. | Baseline; parental; follow-up; replacement; native-parentage | 1–4 |
| Knowledge of a foreign language | Sum of reported ability to understand speak, read, and write a foreign language. From "poor" to "fluent." Internal consistency (alpha) is .78. | Baseline; parental | 1–4 |
| Family socio-economic status | Sum of standardized occupational status scores for father and mother plus education in years for both. Index standardized to mean, zero; standard deviation, 1. | Baseline; parental | −1.58 to 4.46 |
| Self-esteem | Ten-item Rosenberg Scale adapted to Spain. Sums of scores divided by 10. Internal consistency (alpha) is .732 (Madrid) and .694 (Barcelona). | Baseline | 1–4 |
| Familism | Three-item index adapted from CILS questionnaire. Internal consistency (alpha) is .49. | Baseline; follow-up; replacement; native-parentage | 1–3 |
| Occupational status | Scores in the PRESCA-2 scale of occupational prestige in Spain.[1] Parental occupations, parents', and children's occupational aspirations and expectations re-coded in PRESCA scores. | Baseline; parental; follow-up; replacement; native-parentage | 45–270 |
| Intergenerational relations | Four-item scale adapted from original CILS questionnaire to measure relations between respondents and their parents. Internal consistency (alpha) is .63. | Baseline; follow-up; replacement; native parentage | 1–3.75 |
| Attitudes toward school | Ad-hoc scale developed to measure opinions toward academic centers among respondents at average age 18. Internal consistency (alpha) is .60. | Follow-up; replacement; native parentage | 1–4 |
| Downward assimilation index | Count variable of number of events indicative of negative adaptation events (dropping out of school; teenage parenthood; unemployment, etc.). | Follow-up; replacement; native-parentage | 1–6 |

1. Carabaña and Gomez-Bueno, *Escalas de Prestigio Ocupacional.*

## INDICES

The data from the various surveys allow the construction of a number of indices of significant predictors and outcomes. Whenever possible, the questionnaires endeavored to measure such variables by a plurality of items in order to increase the reliability of the resulting measures. In some cases, such as self-esteem, variables were measured by a standardized index, adapted to the Spanish setting. In others, such as the Index of Intergenerational Relations, we developed our own indicators.

In most instances, complex indicators purport to measure the same underlying latent dimensions and, hence, measures of internal consistency (such as Cronbach's alpha) are appropriate. In a few cases, however, we constructed count variables indicating the number of events or instances indicative of a broader process. Such events need not be related to one another, therefore, measures of internal consistency are inappropriate. Item components of specific indices and scales are described in subsequent chapters, when appropriate. Table 17 presents a summary of these indices, their source, and their range and average scores.

# Daily Life of Immigrants and Their Children in Spain: Scenes and Images

*Photos by Javier Schejtman*

The following images illustrate aspects of daily life among immigrant children and their families in Spain. They provide a sense of the great diversity of this population and their visible presence in numerous institutional settings in Spanish society.

PLATE 1. Ecuadorian pupils at a secondary school in Madrid.

PLATE 2. Best friends: Spanish and Dominican teenagers during recreation at a secondary school in Madrid.

PLATE 3. Dominican mother and children in a Madrid park.

PLATE 4. Groups of students during recreation in the school playground of a multiethnic secondary school in a working-class area of Madrid.

PLATE 5. University students in Moncloa, the university district of Madrid.

PLATE 6. Students
entering the underground
station at the Complutense
University campus in
Madrid.

PLATE 7. "NiNIs": Latino youths who neither work nor study, in a deprived area of Madrid.

PLATE 8. Equal and different: the joy of being together.

PLATE 9. A lesson in a special program for youths of immigrant origin who have left school.

PLATE 10. Mother and daughter of Dominican origin in the office of an immigrant organization in Madrid.

PLATE 11. Young Muslim, Latino, and Asian girls listening to a lecture in Madrid.

PLATE 12. Students of Asian origin at a secondary school in a working-class area of Madrid.

PLATE 13. Adolescent pupils during recreation at a multiethnic secondary school in a working-class area of Madrid.

PLATE 14. Second-generation youth in Madrid asserting their status as first-class citizens in Spain.

PLATE 15. Youths of sub-Saharan origin in a vocational training course.

PLATE 16. Classmates of different ethnic backgrounds in a vocational training course.

PLATE 17. Moroccan woman after picking up her child from school in a working-class area of Madrid.

PLATE 18. Latina tutor and pupils during after-school remedial classes held by an NGO in Madrid.

# FIVE

# Immigrant Parents

*Spain and the United States*

Accounts about immigrants commonly focus on their struggles in the labor market and their efforts to gain social acceptance. An equally important task is coping with growing children, whose problems and crises can derail the best laid-out family plans. General trends exist, of course, and we will examine them shortly, but equally important are variations around these averages. Not everyone is chosen for success, and, together with many immigrants on the way to fulfill their ambitions, there are others who encounter nearly insurmountable obstacles to do so. As seen in Chapter 2, determinants of alternative adaptation paths in the first generation depend largely on what parents bring with them—their levels of human capital and ambition—and the social context that receives them. Together with family structure, these factors are expected to go on and affect the alternative paths of adaptation followed by their children.

In this chapter, we focus on trends and variations uncovered by the ILSEG parental survey and combine them, when appropriate, with existing data for the immigrant adult population of Spain. The analysis includes both objective data on the socioeconomic situation of immigrants and subjective evaluations and attitudes, as reported by our respondents in 2010. In addition, we make use of the available data from the CILS parental survey to present meaningful cross-national comparisons.

## WHAT THEY BRING ALONG

Overall, the level of human capital brought by immigrants to Spain is rather modest. As shown in Table 18, less than 25 percent of the parental sample had at least some university education, and only about 10 percent had achieved a university degree. Accordingly, 90 percent were employed in subordinate manual and non-manual occupations. These figures compare with those of the Spanish National Immigration Survey, a representative sample of the country's immigrant population conducted in 2006–7, according to which only 20 percent of the foreign-born population had achieved some university education, with about 40 percent having reached only basic secondary schooling. Only about 10 percent of that sample was found in upper non-manual occupations, figures very similar to our ILSEG sample.[1]

Figures from the CILS parental survey in the United States are surprisingly similar. Just 20 percent of those parents had reached the university, and two-thirds had a high school diploma or less. As a result, only 19 percent held a professional or managerial occupation at the time of the interview (1995–96).[2] Hence, in Spain in 2010, as well as in America a decade and a half earlier, immigrant parents possessed a modest level of human capital, equivalent to a secondary education, and their occupations were overwhelmingly in the unskilled, semi-skilled, or subordinate white-collar categories.

To the extent that intact families represent an asset for the adaptation of second-generation youths, immigrant parents are in a relatively solid position according to our data. Over 70 percent of them are married. The rest cohabit with their partners (7 percent), are divorced (13 percent), widowed (2 percent), or live by themselves. These figures are quite similar to those reported for immigrant parents in the United States by the CILS survey, wherein 63.2 percent of children were living with both biological parents and another 13.2 percent with a parent and a step-parent.[3]

Concerning modes of incorporation, the available data from the ILSEG parental sample provides two indicators: nationality of origin, and legal status in the country. Country of origin is important because specific nationalities are associated with certain phenotypical and cultural characteristics that promote greater or lesser receptivity among the native population. Since Lloyd Warner and Leo Srole's classic study of Yankee City, the general expectation is that the closer an immigrant group is to the phenotypical, religious, and linguistic characteristics of the native population, the greater its acceptance and the faster the assimilation process.[4] In the case of Spain, non-white (black, mestizo,

TABLE 18   EDUCATION AND OCCUPATION OF IMMIGRANT PARENTS IN SPAIN, 2010[1]

|  | Barcelona | Madrid | Total |
|---|---|---|---|
| Education (%): |  |  |  |
| Basic secondary or less | 40.90 | 37.96 | 38.90 |
| Secondary or technical | 35.40 | 39.06 | 37.71 |
| Some university | 13.26 | 11.49 | 12.34 |
| University degree or more | 9.22 | 11.49 | 10.40 |
| Other | 1.22 | 0.00 | 0.65 |
| Total | 100.00 | 100.00 | 100.00 |
| Occupation (%): |  |  |  |
| Manual Workers[2] | 49.76 | 58.07 | 54.12 |
| Lower white-collar workers[3] | 41.92 | 31.95 | 36.69 |
| Foremen, managers, professionals | 8.32 | 9.98 | 9.19 |
| Total | 100.00 | 100.00 | 100.00 |
| N[4] | 865 | 949 | 1,814 |

SOURCE: ILSEG parental survey, 2010.

1. Based on responding parent's characteristics; spouses reported characteristics closely reproduce those presented herein.

2. Includes domestic servants, bricklayers, waiters, and self-employed informal workers.

3. Includes clerks, other office workers, mechanics, and technicians.

4. Missing data excluded.

and Asian immigrants from sub-Saharan Africa, Asia, the Caribbean, and the Andean region of South America) can be expected to encounter less receptiveness among the Spanish population, in racial terms, than immigrants from other European countries or the mostly white southernmost countries of South America (Argentina, Chile, and Uruguay). Similarly, by reason of religion, immigrants from predominantly Muslim countries, such as Morocco and Pakistan, can be expected to meet a less welcoming reception in Catholic Spain than those from Christian and, especially, Catholic countries.[5]

Table 19 presents the distributions of the ILSEG parental sample by country of origin. Two traits are immediately apparent. First, a large number of nationalities contribute to the Spain-bound migrant flow, despite its recency. An economic development process that lasted scarcely two decades attracted migrants from over sixty different nations.[6] This number attests both to the fluidity of migrant flows in the contemporary world and to the attractiveness acquired by Spain during the post-1990 period of sustained economic growth. Second, there is a high diversity of the migrant inflow in terms of the very characteristics identified by Warner

TABLE 19    NATIONAL ORIGINS OF THE ILSEG PARENTAL
SAMPLE, 2010

| Country of birth[1] | Number | % |
|---|---|---|
| Ecuador | 575 | 31.0 |
| Morocco | 195 | 10.5 |
| Colombia | 145 | 7.8 |
| Peru | 125 | 6.7 |
| Dominican Republic | 102 | 5.5 |
| Romania | 95 | 5.1 |
| Bolivia | 92 | 5.0 |
| China | 84 | 4.5 |
| Pakistan | 45 | 2.4 |
| Philippines | 43 | 2.3 |
| Argentina | 38 | 2.1 |
| Bulgaria | 27 | 1.5 |
| Chile | 27 | 1.5 |
| Ukraine | 25 | 1.4 |
| Venezuela | 25 | 1.4 |
| Other[2] | 215 | 11.3 |
| Total | 1,858 | 100.0 |

1. Nationalities with at least twenty-five cases in the sample.
2. Immigrants from forty-seven other countries.

and Srole as decisive in the process of social integration—race, religion, and language. Thus, in this sample, we find sizable contingents of predominantly non-white immigrants from Africa, Asia, the Caribbean, and the Andean region of South America; Muslims and other non-Christians from Morocco, Pakistan, China, and other Asian countries; and non-Spanish-speaking migrants from Romania, Bulgaria, and other European, African, and Asian countries. The process of incorporation of immigrants from such varied nationalities can be expected to differ significantly.

National origins of the immigrant population of Spain are, unlike its educational and occupational levels, quite different from that of the United States. In the latter, the dominant nationalities include Mexicans, Filipinos, Chinese, Cubans, Nicaraguans, and Vietnamese. The only major overlapping nationalities in the CILS and ILSEG samples are Colombians and Filipinos.

The other indicator of mode of incorporation is the legal status of immigrants in the country. Naturally, migrants who have achieved some form of legal status, especially citizenship, are in a much stronger position to defend their rights and invest in businesses with confidence.

TABLE 20    PARENTAL YEAR OF ARRIVAL AND LEGAL STATUS IN SPAIN

|  | Barcelona | Madrid | Total |
|---|---|---|---|
| Year of arrival (mean) | 1999 | 1998 | 1998 |
| Standard deviation | 6.0 | 6.9 | 6.5 |
| Current legal status of self: | | | |
| Has Spanish nationality (%) | 34.3 | 41.1 | 37.9 |
| Current legal status of spouse: | | | |
| Has Spanish nationality (%) | 32.6 | 42.2 | 37.4 |
| N | 865 | 949 | 1,814 |

SOURCE: ILSEG parental survey, 2010.

Clearly, immigrants do not gain the host country nationality on arrival, but the ability to do so in a timely fashion can be regarded as an indicator of a more positive context of reception, as well as offering better prospects for the future. As seen in Table 20, although immigrant parents in the sample had spent about ten years in Spain on average at the time of the interview, only about one-third had gained access to the Spanish nationality; the rest were in various temporary statuses—from those awaiting residency papers to those still in an irregular situation.

These figures compare with those reported by the Spanish National Immigrant Survey of 2006–7, where average length of residence in the country was again ten years, but where the proportion holding Spanish nationality dropped to 21 percent. This lower proportion is attributable to the inclusion in the national survey of younger, unattached individuals, whereas the ILSEG sample is limited to older parents who tend to be more interested in regularizing their status in order to ensure family stability and well-being.[7] Remarkably, immigrant parents in the CILS survey also averaged ten years of residence in 1995–96, but, unlike immigrant parents in Spain, half had acquired U.S. citizenship. The difference may be attributable to differences in the legal naturalization regime in both countries. In the United States, legal immigrants are eligible for citizenship after five years; in Spain, except for Latin Americans and Filipinos, the required minimum period is ten years.[8]

## VARIATIONS BY NATIONALITY

Significant differences exist among nationalities in Spain, not only in the phenotypical and cultural characteristics discussed previously but also in indicators of human capital and legal status in the country. These are portrayed in the following tables. Table 21 breaks down the ILSEG parental sample by nationality, education, type of employment, and parental occupational status; Table 22 presents the distribution by length of residence in Spain and possession of Spanish nationality. All differences are highly significant statistically. In the case of education, parents who attended a university or achieved a university degree range from less than 5 percent among the Chinese to 50 percent among Argentineans and Venezuelans. The diversity in occupational status scores is equally large—from 73 points among Ukrainian immigrants to 130.4 for Venezuelans.[9]

Length of residence in the country and citizenship are equally varied. These data are presented in Table 22. Whereas immigrant Filipinos have lived in Spain for an average of seventeen years, Bulgarians have only done so for eight. These differences in length of residence are reflected in the acquisition of the country's nationality: 63 percent of Filipinos have done so, but only 4 percent of Bulgarians. No Ukrainian parent in the sample had naturalized, whereas Dominicans, another long-resident group, topped the list at 73 percent Spanish nationals. These differences in parental human capital and modes of incorporation are important because, like in the United States, they can be reflected in different adaptation outcomes among children. In particular, segmented assimilation theory predicts divergent adaptation paths, depending on parental endowments and contexts of reception. Left to examine are determinants of immigrant parents' performance in the Spanish labor market and their attitudes and goals toward their own and their children's futures. These results can also be compared with those obtained by CILS a decade earlier.

## DETERMINANTS OF PARENTAL OCCUPATION AND INCOME

Tables 23 and 24 present regressions of parental occupational status and income on relevant predictors. Parental status is given in PRESCA-2 occupational prestige scores, a continuous measure developed specifically for the Spanish labor market.[10] Accordingly, we use ordinary least squares to estimate effects. Income is given in five ordinal categories— from "less than 500 euros" to "4,000 or more." We employ an ordered logistic regression routine to estimate this model. All models use listwise deletion of missing data and robust standard error to adjust for the (school) clustered character of the original sample.

TABLE 21   NATIONAL DIFFERENCES IN EDUCATION, EMPLOYMENT TYPE, AND OCCUPATIONAL STATUS OF IMMIGRANT PARENTS, 2010

| | Education[1] | | Occupation[1] | Occupational status | |
| Nationality | Secondary or technical (%) | Some university or more (%) | Non-manual, supervising, and professional occupations (%) | Mean score[2] | N |
|---|---|---|---|---|---|
| Ecuador | 36.2 | 23.2 | 6.3 | 81.5 | 574 |
| Morocco | 22.0 | 11.8 | 6.1 | 78.5 | 195 |
| Colombia | 42.1 | 24.8 | 6.3 | 84.3 | 145 |
| Peru | 42.4 | 32.0 | 5.2 | 81.4 | 125 |
| Dominican Rep. | 42.6 | 14.8 | 2.6 | 80.6 | 101 |
| Romania | 67.4 | 9.5 | 7.6 | 78.1 | 95 |
| Bolivia | 31.9 | 18.7 | 0.0 | 73.9 | 91 |
| China | 53.8 | 4.8 | 23.2 | 109.1 | 84 |
| Pakistan | 11.1 | 15.6 | 3.9 | 93.3 | 45 |
| Philippines | 25.6 | 53.5 | 0.0 | 77.1 | 43 |
| Argentina | 31.6 | 55.3 | 36.4 | 110.7 | 38 |
| Bulgaria | 55.6 | 29.6 | 5.6 | 75.5 | 27 |
| Chile | 48.2 | 32.0 | 27.8 | 101.4 | 27 |
| Ukraine | 58.3 | 37.5 | 0.0 | 73.2 | 25 |
| Venezuela | 20.0 | 56.0 | 47.6 | 130.4 | 25 |
| Other | 34.7 | 29.5 | 17.1 | 97.7 | 173 |
| | Pearson's Chi square = 254.55 p < .000 Cramer's V = .262 | | Chi-square = 130.83 p < .000 Cramer's V = .353 | F-test = 14.52 p < .000 $R^2$ = .149 | |

SOURCE: ILSEG parental survey, 2010.

1. Figures are for responding parent only; reported figures for spouses are available and follow the same pattern reported here. "Less than secondary" in the reference category.

2. Mean scores in the PRESCA-2 occupational prestige scale for Spain (see Carabaña and Gomez-Bueno, *Escalas de Prestigio Ocupacional*).

TABLE 22 DIFFERENCES IN LENGTH OF RESIDENCE AND SPANISH NATIONALITY
OF IMMIGRANT PARENTS, 2010

| Nationality | Length of Spanish residence (years) | Has Spanish nationality (%) | N |
|---|---|---|---|
| Ecuador | 10.5 | 44.3 | 574 |
| Morocco | 16.5 | 29.1 | 195 |
| Colombia | 9.8 | 43.9 | 145 |
| Peru | 10.5 | 55.2 | 125 |
| Dominican Rep. | 12.8 | 72.6 | 101 |
| Romania | 7.8 | 5.4 | 95 |
| Bolivia | 7.7 | 18.0 | 91 |
| China | 10.6 | 6.2 | 84 |
| Pakistan | 10.2 | 17.8 | 45 |
| Philippines | 17.0 | 63.0 | 43 |
| Argentina | 9.9 | 43.2 | 38 |
| Bulgaria | 8.2 | 3.7 | 27 |
| Chile | 12.2 | 37.0 | 27 |
| Ukraine | 8.9 | 0.0 | 25 |
| Venezuela | 13.6 | 48.0 | 25 |
| Other | 12.6 | 26.6 | 173 |
| | F-test = 14.52 | Chi-square = 130.83 | |
| | p < .000 | p < .000 | |
| | $R^2$ = .149 | Cramer's V = .353 | |

SOURCE: ILSEG parental survey, 2010.

Predictors in both models include age (linear and quadratic effects), gender, length of Spanish residence in years, a binary indicator of holding Spanish nationality, a binary indicator of marital status (married), knowledge of Spanish, and education. As described in Chapter 4, knowledge of Spanish is an index composed of the sum of reported abilities to understand, speak, write, and read the language. The alpha coefficient of internal consistency for the parental Knowledge of Spanish Index (PKSI) is a high .85. Educational attainment is an ordinal-level variable coded into the five categories reported in Table 18. The models are presented in two sections. The first includes the predictors just listed. The second adds the effects of country of origin for all national groups in the sample with at least twenty-five cases. "Other countries" are the reference category.

Looking at results in the first section of Table 23, we see that significant and positive effects on occupational status are associated with gender (male), length of Spanish residence, and education: males exhibit a

| Predictors | Occupational status | | | |
| | I | | II | |
| | Coeff.[1] | t-ratio | Coeff.[1] | t-ratio |
|---|---|---|---|---|
| Age | .863 | .66 | 1.147 | .91 |
| Age squared | −.011 | −.74 | −.014 | −.97 |
| Gender (male) | 15.894*** | 8.13 | 14.726*** | 8.04 |
| Civil status (married) | 1.786*** | 1.16 | .439 | .29 |
| Length of Span. residence | .520** | 3.40 | .466** | 2.67 |
| Knowledge of Spanish | −.257 | −.18 | 1.134 | .73 |
| Has Spanish nationality | −.090 | −.05 | 1.572 | .93 |
| Education:[2] | | | | |
| Upper secondary or vocational | 5.437*** | 3.70 | 4.320* | 2.91 |
| Some university | 11.954*** | 2.59 | 12.166*** | 4.97 |
| University graduate or more | 26.511*** | 6.74 | 22.581*** | 6.51 |
| Country of origin:[3] | | | | |
| Morocco | | | −20.441*** | −4.96 |
| Colombia | | | −9.547* | −2.21 |
| Peru | | | −16.215*** | −4.11 |
| Dominican Rep. | | | −12.621** | −3.15 |
| Romania | | | −11.875** | −3.00 |
| Bolivia | | | −15.534*** | −4.34 |
| China | | | 15.095* | 2.59 |
| Philippines | | | −23.960*** | −4.96 |
| Bulgaria | | | −19.583*** | −4.22 |
| Ukraine | | | −21.375*** | −3.87 |
| Venezuela | | | 26.631* | 2.43 |
| Ecuador | | | −13.435*** | −3.99 |
| Constant | 51.712 | | 51.787 | |
| F-test | 15.59*** | | 10.69*** | |
| R[2] | .162 | | .282 | |
| N | 1,247 | | 1,247 | |

SOURCE: ILSEG parental survey, 2010.

1. Ordinary least squares regression coefficients with robust standard errors.

2. Secondary education or less is the reference category.

3. All nationalities numbering at least twenty-five cases were included in this model. Only those with statistically significant effects are included. "Other nationalities" ($N = 47$) is the reference category.

* $p < .05$

** $p < .01$

*** $p < .001$

TABLE 24 DETERMINANTS OF FAMILY INCOME AMONG IMMIGRANT PARENTS IN SPAIN, 2010

| Predictors | High income | | | |
| --- | --- | --- | --- | --- |
| | I | | II | |
| | AMEs[1] | z-ratio | AMEs[1] | z-ratio |
| Age | .011 | 1.38 | .008 | 0.97 |
| Age squared | .000 | −1.79 | .000 | −1.36 |
| Gender (male) | .024* | 2.00 | .023* | 2.02 |
| Civil Status (married) | .133*** | 10.77 | .119*** | 10.00 |
| Length of Span. residence | .002# | 1.93 | .002* | 2.39 |
| Has Spanish nationality | .010 | 0.94 | .028** | 2.67 |
| Knowledge of Spanish | .022** | 2.56 | .021* | 1.96 |
| Education:[2] | | | | |
|     Upper secondary or vocational | .073*** | 6.37 | .054*** | 4.88 |
|     Some university | .104*** | 6.21 | .084*** | 5.38 |
|     University graduate or more | .207*** | 9.80 | .161*** | 8.50 |
| Country of Origin:[3] | | | | |
|     Morocco | | | −.186*** | −7.51 |
|     Colombia | | | −.078*** | −3.48 |
|     Peru | | | −.083*** | −3.38 |
|     Dominican Rep. | | | −.181*** | −6.12 |
|     Romania | | | −.082*** | −3.27 |
|     Bolivia | | | −.140*** | −5.06 |
|     Philippines | | | −.111** | −3.04 |
|     Argentina | | | .085* | 2.20 |
|     Ecuador | | | −.010*** | −5.23 |
| Wald chi square | 263.25*** | | 368.48*** | |
| Pseudo-R[2] | .092 | | .143 | |
| N | 1,629 | | 1,629 | |

SOURCE: ILSEG parental survey, 2010.

1. Average marginal effects.

2. Less than secondary is the reference category.

3. "Other countries" is the reference category. Only significant nationality effects are included.

# p < .10

* p < .05

** p < .01

*** p < .001

net 15-point advantage in occupational prestige; each additional year in the country increases this status by half a point. Parents who reached a university education hold a net 12-point prestige advantage, increasing to 26 points among those who attained a college degree. No other predictor in the original model is statistically significant. When we add country of origin, two things happen. First, the coefficient of determination ($R^2$) almost doubles in size, indicating a significant improvement in explained variance. Second, a number of nationalities display significant effects. The table omits all non-significant nationality effects. Relative to the "Other" category, composed largely of West European and North American nationalities, many Latin American, North African, Asian, and East European groups are at a disadvantage. Notable, in particular, is the 20-point occupational status gap for Moroccan parents that rises to 24 points among Filipinos. Their case is significant because, as just seen, Filipino immigrants are among the longest-living nationalities in Spain, and they tend to have above-average educational credentials.

The only nationalities displaying a significant occupational advantage relative to the reference category are the Chinese and the Venezuelans. Despite very low levels of educational attainment, Chinese parents score high in the occupational status measure because of being classified as "owners" or "managers" of their own businesses. As was seen in Table 21, Venezuelan parents are the most educated in terms of university completion, and this is reflected in their occupational profile, even after controlling for educational attainment. With these exceptions, the pattern of results in Table 23 is attributable to differences in modes of incorporation and, in particular, the commonly subordinate position of phenotypical and culturally distinct minorities coming from less developed countries.

Multivariate models for income also include a quadratic term for age to capture the frequently non-linear effect of this predictor. Since the dependent variable is ordinal, we use ordered multinomial logistic regression and transform the coefficients into average marginal effects (AMEs), corresponding to higher incomes. Thus transformed, results are interpretable as the percentage change in the dependent variable associated with a unit change in the predictor, controlling for other variables.

The first section of Table 24 shows that high incomes among immigrant parents in Spain are the preserve of educated, married males. A college degree increases the probability of achieving a high income by 21 percent relative to parents with a secondary education or less. This is the strongest effect in the model. Even those with an incomplete university education have a net 10 percent advantage. Males also have a significant income advantage that increases to a net 13 percent for those married, relative to single or divorced parents. This result is in agreement with the importance assigned to family structure by segmented assimilation theory, as noted before.

As seen in the second section of the table, country of origin makes a very large difference in family incomes. Since human capital (such as age or education) is statistically controlled, these differences are attributable to the wide differences in modes of incorporation experienced by immigrant groups in Spain. Relative to the "Other" category, constituted primarily by parents from West European and North American countries, North African and many Latin American and Asian immigrants are at a significant economic disadvantage. The net probability of Moroccans reaching a high-income level is minus 19 percent relative to the reference category, a highly significant effect. The same is approximately true for immigrants from the Dominican Republic. Incomes are somewhat higher for Bolivians, Colombians, Ecuadorians, and Peruvians, though all these nationalities register significant negative effects. Only Argentineans exhibit an economic advantage, exceeding by 8 percent the average income for others. Modes of incorporation, associated with phenotypical and cultural differences among immigrant nationalities, thus appear to make a strong contribution to explained variance in economic status.

Despite differences in measurement and a fifteen-year gap, results from the CILS parental survey are similar. As in Spain, males displayed a significant economic advantage that translated into a net $7,795 of additional annual individual income relative to comparable females. A post–high school education increased annual incomes by $5,120 in comparison with less educated parents, an advantage that reached $7,265 among those with a college degree. As in Spain, length of residence also translated into higher incomes, adding an estimated net $165 for each additional year of residence.[11] In the United States, immigrant minorities that experienced a negative mode of incorporation for racial or legal reasons also suffered severe penalties in the labor market. In this case, Mexicans experienced a net $1,910 net gap in annual income relative to statistically equivalent immigrants from other nationalities. The disadvantage rose to a notable $5,930 for Haitians.[12]

These results, as well as those presented for Spain, are congruent with predictions advanced by human capital theory on the economic effects of education and additional labor market experience.[13] They also reproduce familiar gender and marital status differences on economic outcomes. Aside from these, the most important results are the large and numerous differences across immigrant nationalities when standard human capital predictors are controlled; these differences say something important about the context of reception experienced by various immigrant groups and their divergent experiences of success and failure in the host labor market. It remains to be seen to what extent such outcomes impinge on the adaptation of the second generation, a question to be examined in subsequent chapters.

## PARENTAL AMBITION AND ITS DETERMINANTS

As noted in Chapter 2, the research literature on educational and occupational achievement has singled out the role of adolescent aspirations as a key determinant. Beginning with the classic Wisconsin Model of Status Attainment, the same literature has also identified parental socioeconomic status and parental expectations as being major causes of adolescent ambition.[14] Results demonstrating the causal link between aspirations and subsequent achievement have been based on longitudinal studies in the United States that singled out ambition as a necessary condition for adult attainment.[15] In this chapter, we examine determinants of parental ambition; in Chapter 7, we will examine how they affect children's aspirations and attainment.

Parental ambition is broken down for this analysis into two dimensions: educational aspirations or idealistic goals, and educational expectations or realistic ones. Table 25 presents a breakdown of both dimensions in the parental survey. As a point of comparison, we also present a similar breakdown from the children's original survey in 2008. As can be seen in the table, parental aspirations and expectations were much higher than among their offspring. Seventy-seven percent of parents aspired to a university degree for their youths, but only 40 percent of the latter set their sights that high. Expectations were much lower for both generations, but, whereas 46 percent of parents realistically expected their children to attain a university or a post-graduate degree, only 23 percent of their young agreed. These results hold, without major differences, in both Madrid and Barcelona and among all immigrant groups, regardless of their socioeconomic status or language ability. Results are in line with the hypothesized decline in the immigrant achievement drive brought about by acculturation, as discussed in

TABLE 25 EDUCATIONAL ASPIRATIONS AND EXPECTATIONS PLUS LIFE PLANS
FOR PARENTS AND CHILDREN IN SPAIN, 2008 AND 2010

| Characteristic | Parents[1] (%) | | | Children[2] (%) | | |
|---|---|---|---|---|---|---|
| | Madrid | Barcelona | Total | Madrid | Barcelona | Total |
| Aspirations for child: | | | | | | |
| Secondary or less | 4.98 | 5.57 | 5.26 | 25.64 | 28.05 | 26.86 |
| Technical degree | 17.20 | 12.72 | 15.07 | 21.64 | 15.14 | 18.35 |
| Some university | 1.97 | 3.64 | 2.76 | 14.21 | 15.67 | 14.96 |
| University graduate | 59.68 | 62.84 | 61.19 | 29.13 | 31.14 | 30.13 |
| Postgraduate | 16.17 | 15.23 | 15.72 | 9.38 | 10.03 | 9.70 |
| Expectations for child: | | | | | | |
| Secondary or less | 12.98 | 17.06 | 14.93 | 45.07 | 43.57 | 44.32 |
| Technical degree | 32.60 | 25.49 | 29.21 | 22.33 | 18.12 | 20.20 |
| Some university | 5.83 | 13.20 | 9.39 | 11.89 | 13.51 | 12.70 |
| University degree | 39.25 | 33.45 | 36.48 | 15.61 | 18.69 | 17.17 |
| Postgraduate | 9.25 | 10.80 | 9.99 | 5.10 | 6.11 | 5.61 |
| Future life plans for child: | | | | | | |
| Live in Spain | 84.69 | 85.35 | 85.00 | 27.24 | 24.54 | 25.90 |
| Move elsewhere | 15.31 | 14.65 | 15.00 | 72.76 | 75.45 | 74.10 |

1. ILSEG parental survey, 2010.

2. ILSEG baseline student survey, 2008.

Chapter 2. Immigrant parents aim very high, but their children, confronted with difficult realities on the ground, set their sights lower.

For comparison, results obtained by CILS in the United States differ significantly. Immigrant parents in America voiced similarly high levels of ambition as their peers in Spain: 74 percent expected their children to graduate from college and, of these, 50 percent expected them to attain a postgraduate degree—figures rather similar to those yielded by the ILSEG parental survey. However, the sharp drop in children's aspirations and expectations relative to those of parents in Spain did not occur in the United States. Sixty-seven percent of second-generation youths there aspired to a university degree, and 44 percent expected to attain it, a figure that doubled the proportion of their peers in Spain who held similar beliefs.[16]

Despite the time lag and other differences between surveys, this gap in levels of ambition is noteworthy. It indicates that, while immigrant parents hold very similar levels of ambition for their young, the latter adjust their aspirations and expectations according to the possibilities and opportunities that they perceive in their immediate social context. The "immigrant drive" thus held much better among second-generation youths in America in the 1990s than among their Spanish counterparts a decade later.

A final notable discrepancy between parents and their children in Spain is in future life plans: the overwhelming majority of immigrant parents (85 percent) wished and expected their young to stay in the country, but only one-fourth of the latter agreed. The rest wished to move elsewhere, primarily to North America (23 percent) or other West European countries (15.8 percent). This discrepancy suggests that, though most immigrants envision Spain as their final country of destination, most of their children see the country, at least in adolescence, as a platform for moving elsewhere. This stance could be interpreted as disaffection from the host society, but, paradoxically, it also reflects acculturation since it is in line with plans by many native-parentage young people to also move abroad, at least temporarily.[17]

We focus next on determinants of parental ambition. For this analysis, we consider both parental aspirations and expectations, broken down into the categories shown in Table 25, plus a measure of parental participation in school activities. The Parental School Involvement Index (PSII) is a summated measure of standardized scores in four items indicating actual parental participation in school-related activities.[18] As predictors for each of these variables, we use the parent's age, gender, years of residence in Spain, marital status, acquisition of Spanish nationality, family socioeconomic status, and knowledge of Spanish. As shown in Chapter 4, family socioeconomic status (FSES) is a summated index of educational achievement and occupational status plus those of the spouse, if any, plus family income. The index is standardized to mean 0 and standard deviation 1. Coding of other variables has been described previously.

Table 26 presents ordered multinomial logistic regressions for parental aspirations and expectations and ordinary least squares results for the PSII scale. All regressions employ list-wise deletion of missing data and robust standard errors. Results are quite similar across the three dependent variables: family socioeconomic status and knowledge of Spanish are the principal determinants of parental school involvement, exceeding five times their respective standard errors. Lesser but still significant positive effects on PSII are associated with marital status (married) and length of residence in the country. With this array of variables controlled, most individual nationalities have no significant effect, with

TABLE 26   DETERMINANTS OF IMMIGRANT PARENTS' SCHOOL INVOLVEMENT
AND AMBITION IN SPAIN, 2010

| Predictor[1] | School Involvement Index | | Educational Aspirations | | Educational Expectations | |
|---|---|---|---|---|---|---|
| | Coeff.[2] | t | Coeff.[3] | z-ratio | Coeff[3] | z-ratio |
| Age | −.005 | −2.2* | −.009 | −0.9 | −.009 | −1.2 |
| Sex (female) | −.024 | −0.8 | .161 | 1.2 | −.038 | −0.3 |
| Years of Spanish residence | .008 | 3.0** | .005 | 0.4 | .020 | 2.1* |
| Has Spanish nationality | −.018 | −0.6 | −.079 | −0.6 | .062 | 0.6 |
| Marital status (married) | | 2.4* | .044 | 0.3 | .017 | 0.2 |
| Socioeconomic status (FSES) | | 5.7*** | 580 | 5.4*** | .750 | 9.2** |
| Knowledge of Spanish (PKSI) | | 7.7*** | .417 | 3.6*** | .239 | 2.6*** |
| National Origins:[4] | | | | | | |
| Argentina | | 1.1 | −1.031 | −2.1* | −.213 | −0.5 |
| Bolivia | | 0.90 | .038 | 0.1 | .219 | 0.8 |
| Bulgaria | | 0.06 | −.438 | −0.9 | .182 | 0.4 |
| Chile | | 0.7 | .357 | 0.5 | −.612 | −1.5 |
| China | | −10.1*** | −1.682 | −5.3** | −1.726 | −5.7*** |
| Colombia | | 2.2* | −.202 | −0.6 | −.146 | −0.6 |
| Ecuador | | 1.1 | .257 | 1.1 | −.489 | −2.8** |
| Philippines | | −1.1 | −.484 | −1.2 | −.445 | −1.4 |
| Morocco | | 0.7 | −.460 | −1.7# | −.075 | −0.3 |
| Peru | | 0.6 | −.459 | −1.5 | −.077 | −0.3 |
| Dominican Rep. | | −0.5 | −.106 | −0.3 | −.604 | −2.4* |
| Romania | | 0.6 | −.787 | −2.5* | −.463 | −1.8# |
| Pakistan | | 1.1 | .303 | 0.7 | .214 | 0.7 |
| Ukraine | | 0.1 | −.246 | −0.4 | −.493 | −1.3 |
| Venezuela | | 0.0 | .161 | 0.2 | −.516 | −1.1 |
| Constant | 2.538 | | −1.42 | | −.505 | |
| R² | .221 | | — | | — | |
| Pseudo R² | | | .067 | | .060 | |
| Chi square | | | 157.59*** | | 214.65*** | |
| N | 1,699 | | 1,705 | | 1,700 | |

SOURCE: ILSEG parental survey, 2010.

1. See text for explanation.

2. Ordinary least squares unstandardized coefficients.

3. Ordered logistic coefficients.

4. Rest of the sample is the reference category.

# p < .10

* p < .05

** p < .01

*** p < .001

the notable exception of the Chinese. Chinese parents are far less likely to involve themselves in school programs or activities, and the corresponding negative coefficient is very strong, exceeding ten times its standard error.

Determinants of parental educational aspirations and expectations are largely the same as for school involvement. In both cases, parental socioeconomic status and knowledge of Spanish are the principal determinants, each associated with higher levels of ambition. Several significant effects are also associated, however, with specific nationalities, all of them reducing aspirations or expectations relative to the "Other" category. The strongest and most consistent effect is associated with the Chinese—their levels of educational ambition are far lower than for all other nationalities in the sample.

The disparity between these findings and the high levels of educational ambition reported among Chinese immigrant parents in the United States is noteworthy.[19] Since family socioeconomic status and knowledge of Spanish are controlled, this result cannot be attributed to higher poverty or lack of linguistic fluency. A unique characteristic of Chinese immigrants in Spain is their extraordinary orientation toward entrepreneurship, as seen previously. In our sample, one-fourth of Chinese parents are self-employed, a proportion that exceeds five times that of the next highest entrepreneurial group. This orientation accounts for the positive effect of Chinese origin on occupational status (see Table 23), because Chinese parents are coded as "managers" or "owners" of their firms. Separate analysis of the ILSEG data indicates that Chinese parents transmit this entrepreneurial orientation to children, in effect substituting it for high aspirations in the conventional educational system.[20]

As further evidence of this trend, one-third of Chinese children in our 2008 sample preferred to "leave school early in order to learn a business trade," a far higher proportion than in any other nationality in the sample. The number of Chinese youths thinking that "it is very important to get good grades in school" is just 39 percent, far below all other nationalities. Chinese migrants in Spain are thus a group of rather modest socioeconomic background who, nevertheless, have managed to carve a viable and profitable business niche for themselves. Perceiving upward mobility via the educational system to be blocked for various reasons, including racial discrimination, these immigrants "bet" on the expansion of their firms as the most viable mobility path for themselves and their children.[21]

With this notable exception, results of this analysis indicate overall high levels of educational ambition among immigrant parents in Spain, congruent with the hypothesis of a strong achievement drive and very similar to patterns detected by CILS in the United States. Parents' ambition, as well as their involvement in their children's school, is conditioned primarily by their own education and knowledge of the language. This result is in line with the expected influences of human capital brought from the home country. Married couples also exhibit higher levels of ambition, in agreement with the importance of family structure emphasized by segmented assimilation theory. Most parents also display a positive attitude toward Spain, reflected in their strong preference for their children to remain in the country. Children's lower levels of ambition are interpretable as a result of the advance of the process of acculturation, as discussed in Chapter 2. In contrast with second-generation youths in America, those in Spain appear to assess their educational chances and possibilities in the host society more negatively, thereby reducing the original immigrant drive.

## PERCEPTIONS OF DISCRIMINATION AND OTHER ATTITUDES

Three-fourths of immigrant parents report that they have been "rarely or never" discriminated against. However, and as in other variables examined previously, there are significant nationality differences in these perceptions. As seen in Table 27, just 12 percent of Ukrainians and 16 percent of Venezuelans report being discriminated against, but the figure rises to 35 percent among Filipinos and a remarkable 75 percent among the Chinese. The Cramer's V coefficient indicates a strong association between national origins and these perceptions. The obverse of the picture is given in the second column of Table 27, which reports the extent to which co-nationals support each other in Spain. Sixty-one percent of the sample perceives strong support from their co-ethnics, but the figure rises to 83 percent among Filipinos and 84 percent among the Chinese, precisely the minorities most affected by perceived outside discrimination. Thus, immigrant groups that feel most threatened by external prejudice adopt a more defensive stance, falling back on their families and community resources.

Repeating the pattern found for parental ambition, perceptions of discrimination among immigrant parents in the United States were also minimal, with over 80 percent indicating that their children would experience no difficulty in joining white clubs, moving into white neigh-

TABLE 27    PERCEPTIONS OF DISCRIMINATION AND RELATED VARIABLES
BY NATIONALITY OF IMMIGRANT PARENTS IN SPAIN[1]

| Nationality[2] | Has been discriminated against (sometimes or often) (%) | Co-nationals in Spain help each other a lot (%) | It is important our children know the country we came from (%) |
|---|---|---|---|
| Total | 26.21 | 61.06 | 95.30 |
| Ecuador | 25.22 | 58.60 | 97.19 |
| Morocco | 22.56 | 64.92 | 95.29 |
| Colombia | 36.55 | 59.03 | 95.83 |
| Peru | 24.00 | 58.06 | 96.00 |
| Dominican Republic | 18.63 | 81.37 | 99.02 |
| Romania | 24.21 | 52.69 | 95.74 |
| Bolivia | 30.43 | 61.96 | 98.91 |
| China | 75.00 | 84.15 | 91.46 |
| Pakistan | 11.11 | 68.89 | 75.56 |
| Philippines | 34.88 | 82.93 | 95.12 |
| Argentina | 26.32 | 52.63 | 81.58 |
| Bulgaria | 14.81 | 40.74 | 96.30 |
| Chile | 14.81 | 24.00 | 81.48 |
| Ukraine | 12.00 | 70.83 | 100.00 |
| Venezuela | 16.00 | 60.01 | 80.00 |
| Other | 17.92 | 52.07 | 97.65 |
| Pearson chi square | 141.23*** | 78.73*** | 96.47*** |
| Cramer's V | .276 | .208 | .230 |
| N | 1,858 | 1,818 | 1,829 |

SOURCE: ILSEG parental survey, 2010.

1. Missing data excluded.

2. Listed by number of cases in the parental sample; nationalities with fewer than twenty-five cases are grouped in the "Other" category.

*** Probability of a chance effect less than 1 in 1,000.

borhoods, or marrying whites.[22] Levels of co-ethnic solidarity were also high, but, as in Spain, there were significant differences among different nationalities. Over 80 percent of Southeast Asian refugees (Cambodian, Laotian, and Vietnamese) and Cubans reported strong levels of support from people of their own country. As in Spain, the figure for Filipino parents was also quite high (79 percent), but then it dropped to 54 percent among Mexicans and only to about one-third among Colombians, Nicaraguans, and other Latin Americans.[23]

On the basis of combined CILS and ILSEG results, it is possible to construct a typology of immigrant nationalities by joining their relative

**Economic achievement**

|  | Less successful | More successful |
|---|---|---|
| **Less solidary** | -A-<br><br>U.S.: Mexicans, Nicaraguans<br><br>Spain: Ecuadoreans, Peruvians, Romanians | -B-<br><br>U.S.: West Europeans, Chinese/other Asians<br><br>Spain: Argentinians, Chileans |
| **More solidary** | -C-<br><br>U.S.: Cambodians, Laotians, Vietnamese<br><br>Spain: Dominicans, Filipinos | -D-<br><br>U.S.: Cubans, Filipinos<br><br>Spain: Chinese, Venezuelans |

**Internal cohesion** (row label, left side spanning both rows)

FIGURE 6. A Typology of Economic Success and Internal Solidarity among Immigrant Communities in Two Countries. Sources: Portes and Rumbaut, *Legacies*, figure 5.2, based on data from CILS; ILSEG parental survey, 2010. See also Tables 23, 24, and 27.

levels of economic success with their reported levels of co-ethnic solidarity. The resulting typology is presented in Figure 6. Obviously, the more desirable situations is found in cell D, where economic success combines with strong co-ethnic support, with the least desirable being cell A. Even among less economically successful nationalities, however, internal solidarity can be found and can make a significant difference in their adaptation process. In America, this situation was typified by Southeast Asian refugees in the 1990s; in Spain, it corresponds to the condition of Dominicans, Filipinos, and, to a lesser extent, Moroccans.

Table 28 models Spanish parental perceptions of discrimination on the same set of variables used to predict aspirations and expectations previously. Binary logistic regression coefficients are estimated, with positive ones indicating greater perceptions of discrimination. As in Table 24, we transform coefficients into average marginal effects for greater ease of interpretation.[24] The first model presents effects of parental characteristics, and the second one adds those of national origins. Among parental traits, only socioeconomic status has a strong effect on perceptions of discrimination. Contrary to what may be expected, this effect is positive, indicating *higher* perceptions of discrimination among

TABLE 28    DETERMINANTS OF REPORTED EXPERIENCES OF DISCRIMINATION
AMONG IMMIGRANT PARENTS IN SPAIN

| Predictor | I | | | II | | |
|---|---|---|---|---|---|---|
| | Coeff.[1] | AME[2] | z-ratio | Coeff.[1] | AME[2] | z-ratio |
| Age | .000 | — | -.05 | .006 | — | .62 |
| Gender (male) | -.071 | — | -.60 | -.199 | — | -1.59 |
| Civil status (married) | .071 | — | .58 | .090 | — | .71 |
| Length of Spanish residence | -.015 | -.004 | -1.78# | -.015 | -.003 | -1.65# |
| Knowledge of Spanish | -.151 | -.036 | -1.81# | .050 | — | 0.44 |
| Has Spanish nationality | .015 | — | 0.14 | -.011 | — | -.09 |
| Family socio-economic status | .314 | .075 | 4.26*** | .361 | .081 | 4.40*** |
| National origins:[3] | | | | | | |
| Bulgaria | | | | -1.329 | -.205 | -2.90** |
| Colombia | | | | .673 | .156 | 2.58* |
| China | | | | 2.971 | .580 | 6.85** |
| Ecuador | | | | .546 | .125 | 2.67* |
| Wald chi square | | 23.06** | | | 96.70*** | |
| Pseudo-R[2] | | .011 | | | .062 | |
| N | | 1,541 | | | 1,541 | |

SOURCE: ILSEG parental survey, 2010.

1. Binary logistic regression coefficients.

2. Average marginal effects. Only significant ones are reported.

3. Other nationalities is the reference category. Only significant nationality effects are presented.

# p < .10

* p < .05

** p < .01

*** p < .001

better educated and more affluent parents. While in principle surprising, similar effects have been reported by past research in the United States, where they have been interpreted as indicating higher levels of awareness of externally hostile attitudes among better informed immigrant adults than among their less educated peers.[25] Knowledge of Spanish and length of residence in the country marginally reduce perceptions of discrimination, but their effects do not compare in strength to those of socioeconomic status.

The introduction of national origins increases the pseudo-$R^2$ coefficient sixfold, indicating a better fit to the data. Colombian, Ecuadorean, and Chinese parents tend to report many more experiences of discrimination. Again, the Chinese are in a category by themselves, displaying a much higher propensity of such reports than other parents. No other nationality comes even close to this critical stance. The introduction of national origins in the model does not affect prior results, with family socioeconomic status continuing to have a significant and positive effect on the dependent variable. Thus, higher socioeconomic status appears to increase awareness of external hostility or discrimination; such awareness reaches the highest levels among the Chinese.

Contrary to these differences, there is much greater consensus among all parents that it is important for their children to know the country that they came from. Ninety-five percent of the total sample expressed such views, and no nationality fell below 75 percent. This near-unanimous attitude is reflective of the strong feeling among adult immigrants in favor of selective acculturation. As seen previously and in the next table, such desires do not imply alienation from Spanish society but rather the desire to combine learning its culture and language with preserving elements of the culture of countries left behind. Contrary to nativists views, immigrants perceive this combination of the old and the new not as a zero-sum game but as a positive addition, strengthening their children's chances for social and economic success.[26] The desire of most parents for their children to remain in Spain, seen previously, runs in the same direction.

Table 29 presents the distribution of responses to three final attitudinal items, reflecting perceptions of equality of opportunities in Spain, openness to acculturation, and satisfaction with the schooling received by the children so far. With the single exception of the Chinese, the vast majority of parents view opportunities for their children in Spain as the same as for native youths. For the sample as a whole, 91 percent holds this opinion. The strong positive stance toward the host society is again reflected in high levels of satisfaction with the schooling received by children and with the desire that they be educated according to Spanish customs. More than four-fifths of the parental sample expressed satisfaction with Spanish schools as well as a positive view of acculturation.

These results may be objected to on the grounds that they reflect a desirability bias in which respondents answered questions according to what they thought interviewers expected of them. Such objection is countered by three facts. First, parental interviews were conducted by telephone, a methodology that reduces the capacity or possibility of interviewers influencing respondents. Second, interviews were conducted independently of each other and with parents of multiple cultural backgrounds; it is unlikely that immigrants from so many different nationalities would all be equally affected by a "desirability" syndrome.

TABLE 29   ATTITUDES TOWARD SPAIN AMONG IMMIGRANT PARENTS[1]

| Nationality[2] | Satisfied with my children's education in Spain so far (%) | My children will have the same opportunities in in the future as Spaniards (%) | My children should be educated according to Spanish customs (%) |
|---|---|---|---|
| Ecuador | 86.89 | 90.37 | 85.49 |
| Morocco | 92.51 | 91.58 | 74.09 |
| Colombia | 89.58 | 91.61 | 88.97 |
| Peru | 82.11 | 91.94 | 82.40 |
| Dominican Rep. | 97.03 | 95.05 | 88.00 |
| Romania | 93.68 | 93.65 | 85.11 |
| Bolivia | 92.39 | 95.60 | 86.96 |
| China | 60.98 | 63.86 | 65.48 |
| Pakistan | 82.22 | 88.89 | 71.11 |
| Philippines | 92.68 | 100.00 | 92.68 |
| Argentina | 83.78 | 97.30 | 86.84 |
| Bulgaria | 92.59 | 100.00 | 100.00 |
| Chile | 62.96 | 80.77 | 92.59 |
| Ukraine | 70.83 | 87.50 | 84.00 |
| Venezuela | 100.00 | 92.00 | 95.83 |
| Other | 90.06 | 93.49 | 81.07 |
| Total | 87.40 | 90.85 | 83.56 |
| Pearson chi square | 103.20*** | 93.13*** | 58.64*** |
| Cramer's V | .237 | .226 | .179 |
| N | 1,834 | 1,815 | 1,837 |

SOURCE: ILSEG parental survey, 2010.

1. Missing data excluded.

2. Nationalities listed by sample size.

*** = p < .001

Third, the notable case of the Chinese indicates that respondents could have taken a far more skeptical view about the receiving country, as these parents did. Reflecting the inward-looking character of their own community, Chinese parents were much less likely to give positive replies to all three items, as well as reporting high levels of external discrimination.

Overall, and with the partial exception of the Chinese case, it is possible to conclude that the general outlook of immigrant parents in Spain was both positive and optimistic, at least at the time that the ILSEG survey was conducted. This is reflected in their high educational ambition for their offspring, the desire that their children remain in Spain, and the limited extent of perceived discrimination. Coming from relatively modest origins and occupying low-to-middling positions in the Spanish labor market, immigrants still hold high hopes that their children will justify the many sacrifices made on their behalf by moving ahead educationally and economically. It remains to be seen to what extent the severe and protracted economic recession suffered by Spain in recent years has affected or reversed these positive outlooks. We reserve for subsequent chapters a discussion of this possibility and move on to consider the orientations and achievements of our second-generation respondents.

# SIX

# The Psychosocial Adaptation of the Second Generation

*Self-Identities, Self-Esteem,
and Related Variables*

A first important family of outcomes has to do with the psychosocial adaptation of children of immigrants. The issue of self-identity has received a great deal of attention in the immigration literature. As seen in Chapter 2, self-identities are "soft" variables that can change over time, especially in adolescence. Nevertheless, they can be subjectively important and, under certain circumstances, can lead to political mobilizations and even public upheavals.[1]

In the case of the second generation, a great deal can be inferred about the progress or lack thereof of the process of integration from the extent to which these youths identify with the host society or, on the contrary, re-affirm foreign origins and pride. Reactive ethnic identities are often associated with the perception of being treated as second-class persons by the native population and of being deprived of opportunities for educational and occupational mobility because of race or national origin.[2] Comparing results from the CILS and ILSEG surveys in this chapter tells us something significant about differences in the process of adaptation to host societies.

## SELF-IDENTIFICATION IN COMPARATIVE PERSPECTIVE

As shown in Table 30, the second generation in Spain is about evenly divided among those who call themselves Spanish and those who do not. There are no significant differences by gender, school type, or city of

| | Do you call yourself Spanish? | | |
|---|---|---|---|
| | *Yes* | *No* | *Totals* |
| Gender:[1] | | | |
| Female | 47.1 | 52.9 | 100.0 (2,663) |
| Male | 49.4 | 50.6 | 100.0 (2,626) |
| Chi square: 2.90 (n.s.)[2] | | | |
| City of Residence:[1] | | | |
| Madrid | 49.5 | 50.5 | 100.0 (2,809) |
| Barcelona | 46.9 | 53.1 | 100.0 (2,485) |
| Chi square: 3.37 (n.s.) | | | |
| School:[3] | | | |
| Private | 47.4 | 52.6 | 100.0 (1,765) |
| Public | 52.4 | 47.6 | 100.0 (1,997) |
| Chi square 9.61** | V = .05[4] | | |
| Country of birth:[1] | | | |
| Spain | 81.5 | 18.6 | 100.0 (1,032) |
| Abroad | 40.2 | 59.8 | 100.0 (4,249) |
| Chi square: 569.69*** | V = .35 | | |
| Total, joint sample | 48.3 | 51.7 | 100.0 (5,294) |
| Total, follow-up sample | 50.1 | 49.9 | 100.0 (3,784) |

1. Joint follow-up and replacement samples.
2. n.s. = Difference not significant statistically.
3. Follow-up sample only.
4. Cramer's V coefficient of strength of association.
** $p < .01$
*** $p < .001$

TABLE 31   NATIONAL SELF-IDENTIFICATION OVER TIME

| | Do you call yourself Spanish? | | |
| --- | --- | --- | --- |
| | Yes | No | Totals |
| Born in Spain, 2008 | 77.7 | 22.3 | 100.0 (963) |
| Born in Spain, 2012[1] | 81.4 | 18.6 | 100.0 (657) |
| Born abroad, 2008 | 22.1 | 77.9 | 100.0 (5,494) |
| Born abroad, 2012[1] | 43.6 | 56.4 | 100.0 (3,127) |

| | How important to you is your nationality? Important or very important |
| --- | --- |
| Born in Spain, 2008 | 82.2 |
| Born in Spain, 2012[1] | 62.7 |
| Born abroad, 2008 | 90.1 |
| Born abroad, 2012[1] | 74.5 |

1. Follow-up sample.

residence. The number of second-generation youths identifying themselves as Spanish in Barcelona is only slightly lower than in Madrid. Predictably, this identification is far more common among those who were born in Spain, the second generation "proper." Among them, identification with the host country exceeds 80 percent. However, even among the foreign-born, this orientation is on the increase. Again, the longitudinal character of the ILSEG data allows us to examine variations over time. These are shown in Table 31. Thus, less than 25 percent of the foreign-born in our sample identified themselves with Spain in 2008, but the number increased to almost half four years later. This is an indication of a gradual but significant advance in the process of integration.

The results obtained by CILS in the United States were quite different. Ninety percent of respondents identifying themselves as unhyphenated Americans were U.S.-born, confirming the strong influence of place of birth on self-identification. However, these unhyphenated identities represented only 3.5 percent of the total and actually *declined* from early to late adolescence. Those identifying themselves as plain American went down by almost 10 percent; even those identifying themselves with a hyphenated label (such as Mexican-American or Chinese-American) declined from 41 to 31 percent in the four years between both CILS

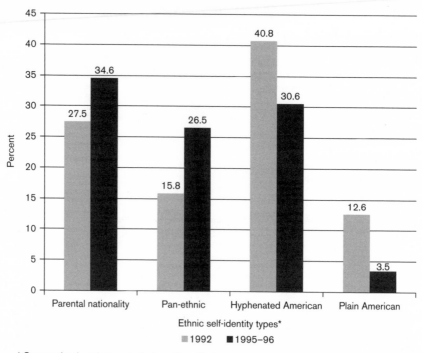

* See text for description of ethnic self-identity types.
N = 4,288

FIGURE 7. Ethnic Self-identity Shifts among Children of Immigrants in the United States, 1992 and 1995–96. Source: Portes and Rumbaut, *Legacies,* 155.

surveys. In contrast, respondents identifying with a pan-ethnic label (such as Hispanic, Latino, or Asian) rose from 16 to 27 percent of the sample, and those re-affirming their parental country-of-origin identification increased from 27 to 35 percent.[3]

Hence, in America, the process of psychosocial integration into mainstream society *reversed itself* during adolescence, giving rise to either ethnic-national re-affirmations, generally associated with parents' home countries, or embracement of the pan-ethnic categories under which foreign youths are commonly classified. Figures 7 and 8 portray this evolution. In contrast to Spain, where second-generation youngsters increasingly identify with the host country as a whole, in the United States they were subjected to an increasing process of ethnicization and even "racialization."[4]

This process actually had two strands. The first entailed mainly acculturation to the ethnic/racial hierarchy of American society and

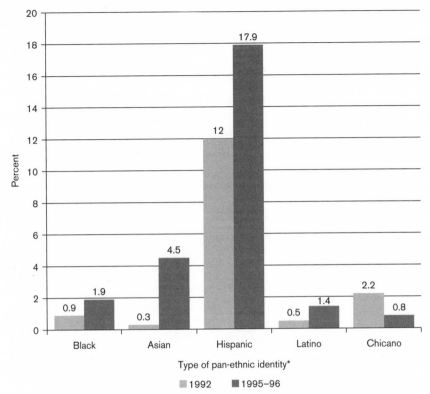

FIGURE 8. Percent of Children of Immigrants Selecting Various Types of Pan-ethnic Identities in the United States, 1992 and 1995–96. Source: Portes and Rumbaut, *Legacies*, 156.

acceptance of the label under which it classifies different nationalities. The growth of pan-ethnic identities represents, in this case, essentially an adaptation to the dominant culture of the receiving society. The second strand is more poignant because it represents a reactive assertion of foreign nationalities in opposition to what is perceived as American racism. In this instance, children of immigrants are not so much integrating into the host society as creating distance from it and seeking to defend their own separate, autonomous identities.[5]

From this comparative perspective, integration to Spanish society appears to be less traumatic since it does not confront foreign youths with a rigid ethno-racial framework into which they are perforce classified, even against their desires or original self-images. How these self-images relate to perceptions of discrimination by natives is examined next.

## PERCEPTIONS OF DISCRIMINATION

Results for the questions measuring perceptions of discrimination in Spain tell us the same story. Just 5 percent of the original sample and just 8.5 percent of our replacement sample reported experiencing discrimination frequently or repeatedly during the preceding three years. As seen in Table 32, these perceptions did not vary much by gender or sample type. These low perceptions of discrimination can also be taken as a *prima facie* indicator of a successful integration process. Most of the ethnographic interviews conducted during the CILS qualitative module strongly reinforce this conclusion. As seen in Chapter 1, the majority of respondents seldom felt discriminated against in Spain, and, when this did happen, the instances were random and isolated.

Overall, the second generation in late adolescence does not appear defensive in its relationship with Spanish society, nor is there evidence of widespread ethnic reactivity. This conclusion is given additional weight by the fact that the proportion who felt rejected or discriminated against among *children of Spaniards* (the native-parentage sample) is about the same, 6.1 percent. It seems evident that children of immigrants and children of natives partake of the same sociocultural world.

The outcomes obtained by CILS on this psychosocial outcome were quite different. Perceptions of discrimination among second-generation youths in the United States were much higher, more than quintupling the levels registered by ILSEG in Spain. More importantly, such perceptions *increased* over time, including almost two-thirds of respondents (62 percent) by average age 17. Although the timing of both studies and the composition of their samples in terms of national origins were different, the question asked to respondents was the same, thereby increasing the feasibility of this cross-national comparison. They highlight, once again, the strength of ethno-racial hierarchies in the United States and their profound effect on second-generation youths. These differences in experiences of discrimination are congruent with the observed patterns of ethno-national self-identifications in Figures 7 and 8.

Supporting this line of argument, perceptions of discrimination increased for the entire CILS sample in the United States, but they

TABLE 32    PERCEPTIONS OF DISCRIMINATION IN THE SPANISH SECOND
GENERATION, 2012

| | During the last three years, have you felt rejected or discriminated against? | | |
|---|---|---|---|
| | Never or only a few times % | Frequently or many times % | Total % (N) |
| Follow-up sample:[1] | | | |
| Female | 94.6 | 5.4 | 100.0 |
| Male | 95.2 | 4.8 | 100.0 |
| Total | 94.9 | 5.1 | 100.0 |
| | | | (3,811) |
| Replacement sample:[1] | | | |
| Female | 90.6 | 9.4 | 100.0 |
| Male | 92.5 | 7.5 | 100.0 |
| Total | 91.6 | 8.4 | 100.0 |
| | | | (1,581) |
| Native-parentage sample:[1] | | | |
| Female | 93.0 | 7.0 | 100.0 |
| Male | 94.6 | 5.4 | 100.0 |
| Total | 93.9 | 6.1 | 100.0 |
| | | | (1,905) |

1. None of the differences between sexes are statistically significant.

increased most among youths who embraced a reactive identity, labeling themselves by the nationality of parents rather than as Americans. For the total sample, perceptions of discrimination rose from 55.2 percent in the baseline survey to 62.2 percent in the follow-up three years later; however, among those who self-identified with their parents' nationality, such perceptions increased from 62.3 to 66.4 percent.[6]

By contrast, perceptions of discrimination in Spain were uniformly low and did not increase over time. Thus, children of immigrants in Spain face a rather different and seemingly more benign context of reception, where the absence of entrenched ethno-racial hierarchies among the native population translates into a relative scarcity of racist slurs or other hostile actions addressed to them. The consequence is an apparently smooth process of integration, in contrast with the more difficult and contested environment encountered by foreign-groups in America.

## LANGUAGE KNOWLEDGE AND USE

As shown in Table 33, 70 percent of the original ILSEG sample reported speaking Spanish at home, a proportion that did not vary significantly by gender but did so, to a limited extent, by school type and city of residence. Youths attending private ("concerted") schools and those growing up in Barcelona were less likely to speak Spanish at home. The large sample size makes these differences statistically significant but, substantially, they are not sizable, as they do not exceed 10 percent of the sample.

The very large proportion who speak Spanish at home is not surprising since it is a direct reflection of the composition of the sample, made up primarily of children of Latin American immigrants. Nor is the difference in favor of Madrid unexpected, given the emphasis placed by school authorities in Barcelona on the use of Catalan, and the stronger presence of non-Spanish speaking nationalities in that city. In general, however, widespread knowledge and use of the language of the host society can be interpreted as an additional indicator of an overall positive integration of second-generation youths in the Spanish context.

In contrast, whereas over 90 percent of children of immigrants in the CILS survey were fluent in English, over 60 percent spoke a language other than English at home. Use, knowledge, and preference for non-English languages were also the overwhelming choices among immigrant parents. Given the decisive importance of English as a marker of "Americanization," the resilient and widespread presence of foreign languages in immigrant homes in the United States had a direct bearing on the ethnicization of many of their members by the native majority.[7]

## INTERGENERATIONAL RELATIONS

In both the original and the follow-up ILSEG samples, we included an index of intergenerational relations between children and their parents. The index, described in Chapter 4, is an internally consistent and reliable measure, with scores ranging from 1 to 4. Higher scores indicate better relations with parents. As shown in Table 34, the average score in the 2012 survey was 3.1, indicating a generally positive profile on this measure of integration. There is a significant difference in favor of males in both the follow-up and replacement samples, and Madrid residents did somewhat better in the follow-up. In absolute terms, neither difference is sizable. Scores in this index for both second-generation samples are practically identical to that found among native-parentage Spaniards, again reflecting the close similarity of both universes.

TABLE 33    LANGUAGE SPOKEN AT HOME

| | Original sample, 2008 | | | Joint sample, 2012[1] | | |
|---|---|---|---|---|---|---|
| | *Spanish* | *Other* | *Total % (N)* | *Spanish* | *Other* | *Total % (N)* |
| **Gender:** | | | | | | |
| Female | 70.1 | 29.9 | 100.0 (3,297) | 68.5 | 31.5 | 100.0 (2,672) |
| Male | 69.5 | 30.5 | 100.0 3,464) | 70.1 | 29.9 | 100.0 (2,626) |
| Chi square: 0.29 (n.s.) | | | | Chi square: 1.55 (n.s.) | | |
| **City:** | | | | | | |
| Madrid | 73.8 | 26.5 | 100.0 (3,338) | 74.1 | 25.9 | 100.0 (2,813) |
| Barcelona | 65.3 | 34.7 | 100.0 (3,479) | 63.8 | 36.2 | 100.0 (2,948) |
| Chi square: 58.22*** | V = .092[2] | | | Chi square: 65.5*** V=.111[2] | | |
| **School Type:** | | | | | | |
| Private | 67.5 | 32.5 | 100.0 (3,272) | 67.8 | 32.2 | 100.0 (730) |
| Public | 71.4 | 28.6 | 100.0 (3,549) | 69.5 | 30.5 | 100.0 (3,992) |
| Chi square: 12.15*** | V= .042 | | | Chi square: 0.79 (n.s.) | | |
| Total | 69.5 | 30.5 | 100.0 (6,817) | 69.2 | 30.8 | 100.0 (5,311) |

n.s. = Not statistically significant difference.

1. Follow-up and replacement samples.

2. Cramer's V coefficient of strength of association.

*** $p < .001$

It is possible with the data at hand to compare responses to individual questions over time. Since item components of the index were the same as those used by the CILS follow-up survey in the United States, it is also feasible to compare results between countries. Table 35 presents the relevant figures. In Spain, there is a slight but notable improvement over time in several items, especially in the decline of youths who felt embarrassed by their parents or who declared that parents "do not like me much." More significant, however, is the similarity of results despite major gaps in time and contexts of reception.

In both the United States and Spain, only a small minority—less than 15 percent—reported themselves embarrassed by their parents, and

TABLE 34   INTERGENERATIONAL RELATIONS IN LATE ADOLESCENCE, 2012[1]

|  | Follow-up sample | Replacement sample | Native-parentage sample |
|---|---|---|---|
| Gender: |  |  |  |
| Females | 3.064 | 2.986 | 3.078 |
| Males | 3.137 | 3.049 | 3.051 |
|  | F = 16.82*** | F = 4.29* | F = 1.27 (n.s.) |
| City: |  |  |  |
| Madrid | 3.116 | 3.019 | 3.058 |
| Barcelona | 3.082 | 3.019 | 3.066 |
|  | F = 3.59* | F = 0.00 (n.s.) | F = .10 (n.s.) |
| School type: |  |  |  |
| Private | 3.094 | 3.091 | 3.006 |
| Public | 3.106 | 3.009 | 3.067 |
|  | F = .49 (n.s.) | F = 3.42# | F = 1.80 (n.s.) |
| Totals | 3.100 | 3.019 | 3.061 |
| N | 3,783 | 1,500 | 1,956 |

n.s. = Not statistically significant difference.

1. Scores in the Intergenerational Relations Index. Range 1 (lowest) to 4 (highest).

# $p < .10$

* $p < .05$

*** $p < .001$

similarly low percentages complained about not being liked by them. In both countries, figures climbed to about 20 percent reporting parental lack of interest in what they had to say, and to about half (39 percent in CILS) indicating that they argued frequently with parents because of different ways of viewing the world. This convergence suggests that relations between immigrants and their offspring moved along parallel tracks in both societies, with most children asserting pride in their parents' cultural ways but also indicating a growing generational gap in attitudes and values. Paradoxically, affirming one's own ethnic origins and putting distance from parents' "old country" ways appear to run in tandem during adolescence, a process observable in both countries.

SELF-ESTEEM

As we saw in Chapter 2, a final important psychosocial dimension is self-esteem. We measured this variable in the first ILSEG survey with Rosenberg's Self-esteem Scale, which is the most commonly employed

TABLE 35    INDICATORS OF INTERGENERATIONAL RELATIONS IN THE UNITED
STATES AND SPAIN, 1996–2012

| Indicators | United States CILS-2 (Average age = 17) % | Spain ILSEG-1 (Av. age = 14) % | ILSEG-2 (Av. age = 17) % | ILSEG replacement (Av. age = 17) % |
|---|---|---|---|---|
| 1. "Embarrassed by parents' cultural ways." | 12.8 | 12.4 | 8.6 | 11.1 |
| 2. "My parents don't like me very much." | 8.2 | 18.0 | 9.7 | 11.4 |
| 3. "My parents and I argue frequently due to different ways of viewing the world." | 38.8 | 50.0 | 53.8 | 51.1 |
| 4. "My parents are not very interested in what I have to say." | 23.4 | 20.0 | 18.0 | 19.0 |
| $N^1$ | 4,262 | 6,474 | 5,323[2] | 1,522 |

1. Percentages computed on valid cases only.

2. Joint second-wave sample.

way to measure this dimension among adolescents. A factor analysis of the ten items composing this index yielded a clear unidimensional structure, with almost all items loading highly on the first factor. Internal consistency reliability was satisfactory in both cities—Cronbach's alpha reached .732 in Madrid and .694 in Barcelona. These results support the scale as a cross-nationally reliable indicator of self-esteem.

Rosenberg's scale ranges from 1 to 4, with higher scores indicating better self-images. The average for the total sample in Spain was 2.97, suggesting a moderately positive profile. This average did not vary much by city (3.01 for Madrid, 2.93 for Barcelona), by type of school (2.94 for private schools, 3.00 for public ones), or by birthplace (2.96 for foreign-born, 3.07 for native-born). It did vary significantly by sex, however. Corresponding to predictions advanced in Chapter 2, females had significantly lower self-esteem than males.

The same scale was used to measure self-esteem by CILS in the United States, and, in this instance, results favor the American sample. The average Rosenberg score in early adolescence was 3.3, significantly ahead of the Spanish sample of the same age and any of its subcategories. Self-esteem in CILS actually increased over time so that, by late adolescence, almost half of the sample (47.8 percent) had scores exceeding 3.5. Yet a common result in the United States and Spain was the gender gap favoring males.[8] The absolute gaps in levels of self-esteem between both countries must be interpreted with caution, given the different timing and cultural contexts where the surveys took place. They should be read as general tendencies that stand in need of further investigation.

## MULTIVARIATE RESULTS: DETERMINANTS
*Barcelona, March 2014*

*Interviewer:* Hello, Sheng. Thanks for agreeing to be re-interviewed for our study. Please tell me again your age and where you were born.

*Sheng:* I was born in Barcelona and am 18 years old.

*Int.:* What are you studying and what are your future plans?

*Sheng:* I am in the second year of high school (*bachillerato*) and I would like to follow a career in engineering, mechanical or industrial. I do much better with numbers than with letters.

*Int.:* Have you received help from your professors?

*Sheng:* Yes, at the Salles (name of school), they have been great. Especially those of physics and math . . . they always find time to help me with difficult problems.

*Int.:* And by age 40, how do you see yourself?

*Sheng:* I would like to have an important job in a large firm in the United States, Germany, or China . . .

*Int.:* Not in Spain?

*Sheng:* I have visited those countries and I like them, their ambiance more. . . . If possible, I would like to go live in China.

*Int.:* You were born in Spain, do you consider yourself Spanish?

*Sheng:* No, I consider myself Chinese. I speak Chinese with my parents at home and am learning the language. The written characters are difficult, but I keep trying.

*Int.:* Have you felt discriminated against in Spain?

*Sheng:* No, never, because I was born here and speak the language, but I know many Chinese who are made fun of because they don't know how to speak Spanish well.

*Int.:* Is there anything that you like about life here?

*Sheng:* Yes, many. The cultural sites, the literature is quite good, both Spanish and Catalan. . . . The cuisine is great.

*Int.:* And those you like least?

*Sheng:* People here give too much importance to football and, for me, there are many things that are far more important than football. People here waste a lot of time.

*Int.:* Let's talk a bit about your parents: When did they arrive? How have they done here?

*Sheng:* They arrived twenty years ago. . . . They now have a restaurant. My father is the cook and my mother is the waitress. . . . They are doing quite well right now.

*Int.:* But if your parents are doing well economically and you are pleased with your school and doing well in it, why do you want to go live in China?

*Sheng:* Because of the ambiance, the culture. For example, for the Chinese it's very normal that children help in house chores from a young age; that's not normal in Spain. I would like to raise my children according to my roots that are really Chinese . . .

*Int.:* And what would you like to improve about yourself in the future?

*Sheng:* About myself? Well, I would like to become more hardworking. Living in Barcelona, I have become rather lazy . . . helping less at home; studying less. Having time, I postpone things—I start chatting online or watching TV, and then leave studying and important things for tomorrow. I need to move out of this mind-set if I'm going to move ahead.

This story serves well to introduce the analysis of determinants of psychosocial outcomes in the Spanish second generation, *not* because it is representative of average trends in the sample but precisely the opposite. Sheng's resilient Chinese identity, despite a Spanish birth and the perceived absence of discrimination, is exceptional—arguably the exception that confirms the rule and points to the very diverse outcomes that the process of adaptation can take.

In this section, we present results of multivariate models predicting each of the outcomes examined previously. Determinants were all measured in the original ILSEG survey, thereby establishing a clear temporal order between hypothesized causes and effects. We nest the models, beginning with dummy variables corresponding to nationalities with at least fifty cases in the original survey; this is followed by objective predictors and, finally, by psychosocial variables. For the latter, in particular, the issue of time order is paramount since it is not usually possible to untangle cause from effect in cross-sectional surveys employing this kind of subjective dimensions. For clarity of presentation, only significant results are discussed. We transform binary logistic coefficients into average marginal effects (AMEs). For dichotomous predictors, AMEs estimate the net probability of occurrence of the outcome associated with the presence of the predictor.[9]

## National Self-Identification

Table 36 presents results of a binary logistic regression of Spanish self-identification on selected predictors. The first model shows that a number of foreign nationalities are associated with resistance to identify as Spanish, while only a few lean significantly in the opposite direction. The model is statistically significant, but a pseudo-$R^2$ coefficient of only .025 shows that it fits the data poorly.

The next models indicate that most of these nationality effects merely conceal the influence of more powerful predictors. When these enter the equation, only the positive effect of Filipino national origin remains. The strongest effect is associated with years of Spanish residence that exceeds seven times its standard error. Each additional year of residence in the country increases the probability of Spanish self-identification by 3 percent. Despite Sheng's resistance to embrace his country of birth, the general trend runs in the opposite direction: being born in the country raises the probability of Spanish identification by a net 8 percent. Family socioeconomic status completes the set of significant predictors, with each standard deviation in the index of this status increasing the probability of identification with the country by about 4 percent.

The final model does an acceptable job of fitting the data. The pseudo-$R^2$ coefficient increases to close to .09, and the Wald chi square is 2.5 times higher than that corresponding to the first model, despite an increase of 11 degrees of freedom. Results generally agree with theoretical expectations, with the only unexpected ones being the higher likelihood of Filipinos identifying with Spain and the higher tendency of males to do so. Neither effect was originally predicted, and it would be risky to advance *ad hoc* explanations here.

TABLE 36   DETERMINANTS OF SPANISH SELF-IDENTIFICATION IN THE SECOND
GENERATION, 2012

| Predictors[1] | I[2] | | II[3] | | III[4] | |
|---|---|---|---|---|---|---|
| | AMEs[5] | z-ratio | AMEs | z-ratio | AMEs | z-ratio |
| National origins: | | | | | | |
| Argentina | | | | | | |
| Bolivia | −.262 | −5.17*** | | | | |
| Bulgaria | | | | | | |
| Chile | | | | | | |
| China | −.147 | −2.31* | | | | |
| Colombia | −.134 | −3.51** | | | | |
| Dominican Republic | −.117 | −2.48* | | | | |
| Ecuador | −.174 | −6.66*** | | | | |
| Equatorial Guinea | | | | | | |
| Morocco | | | | | | |
| Peru | −.174 | −4.30*** | | | | |
| Philippines | .208 | 2.85** | .300 | 4.13*** | .306 | 4.15*** |
| Romania | −.566 | −3.62*** | | | | |
| Venezuela | | | | | | |
| Objective traits: | | | | | | |
| Age | | | | | | |
| Male | | | .045 | 2.52* | .045 | 2.45* |
| Spanish-born | | | .078 | 1.84# | .078 | 1.82# |
| Length of Spanish residence | | | .030 | 8.17*** | .030 | 8.08*** |
| Year in school | | | | | | |
| Knowledge of Spanish | | | | | | |
| Hours of school homework | | | | | | |
| Family socio-economic status | | | .038 | 2.78** | .039 | 2.77** |
| Both parents present | | | | | | |
| Lives in Madrid | | | | | | |
| Attended public school | | | | | | |
| Psychosocial traits: | | | | | | |
| Educational expectations | | | | | | |
| Familism | | | | | | |
| Intergenerational relations | | | | | | |

(continued)

TABLE 36 *(continued)*

| Predictors[1] | I[2] | | II[3] | | III[4] | |
|---|---|---|---|---|---|---|
| | AMEs[5] | z-ratio | AMEs | z-ratio | AMEs | z-ratio |
| Perceptions of discrimination | | | | | | |
| Self-esteem | | | | | | |
| Wald chi square | 86.67*** | 260.66*** | | 261.60*** | | |
| Pseudo-R$^2$ | .025 | | .088 | | .088 | |
| N | 2,700 | | | | | |

1. All predictors measured during the original survey (2008).
2. Predictors limited to national origins. Only groups numbering at least fifty cases in the original survey and twenty-five in the follow-up are included. The rest forms the reference category ($N$ = 1,055).
3. Predictors include national origins and objective variables.
4. Predictors include national origins, objective and psychosocial variables.
5. Average marginal effects. Significant effects only are presented.
# $p < .10$
* $p < .05$
** $p < .01$
*** $p < .001$

Nevertheless, results are similar to those obtained by CILS in the United States, where country of birth and length of residence in the host country also played decisive roles in adopting an "American" (hyphenated or not) self-identification.[10] In both countries, self-esteem had *no* relationship with ethno-national identifications. This is compatible with the argument, spelled out in Chapter 2, that second-generation youths adjust their identities in order to protect their self-esteem, a process that reduces the association between both variables.[11]

*Perceptions of Discrimination*

This variable is categorized as an ordinal scale—from "never or almost never" through "occasionally" to "frequently." Accordingly, we use an ordered logistic regression routine and nest models, as done previously. Positive coefficients indicate greater likelihood of reporting discrimination by the time of the ILSEG follow-up survey. Table 37 presents the results. There are practically no differences among nationalities in this variable, a pattern that reflects the uniformly low perceptions of discrimination in our sample. The only significant nationality effects are those of Equatorial Guinea and the Philippines. They are relatively weak and disappear when other predictors are added to the equation. A marginally significant effect for Bulgarian-origin children emerges in the final regressions.

Among other predictors, the most noteworthy effects are those of intergenerational relations at the time of the original survey, family socioeconomic status, and family composition. Good relations with parents significantly reduced reported experiences of discrimination four years later. This effect more than quadruples its standard error. Higher family status and having been raised by both parents also reduce later episodes of discrimination or hostility. This trio of findings strongly supports the predictions of segmented assimilation theory regarding the protective effects of intact families, parental human capital, and selective acculturation. The latter in particular, as reflected in positive intergenerational relations, effectively shields children from instances of outside hostility.

The last model includes perceptions of discrimination lagged four years. As expected, this lagged variable becomes a significant predictor of itself in later life. In addition, the meaning of other effects is altered to indicate their influence on *change* over time in the dependent variable. In this case, however, coefficients remain basically the same: two-parent families, family socioeconomic status, and good intergenerational relations in early adolescence reduce the probability of experiencing or reporting discrimination later on. As seen previously, reports of discrimination were much less frequent than those recorded in the United States a decade earlier. In Spain, such reports are not only infrequent but are further lowered by the influence of this trio of causal effects.

*Intergenerational Relations*

These results naturally lead to the question of what factors account for positive relations between children and their parents. The Intergenerational Relations Index is a continuous variable available in both the original and the follow-up surveys. It is thus possible with these data to answer the questions of what factors lead to good relations between generations and what predictors affect *change* in such relations. For this purpose, we nest models but add a final iteration, as done with the prior dependent variable, where intergenerational relations in early adolescence are allowed to enter the model. We also include early perceptions of discrimination to address the question of a possible causal loop between both variables. The Intergenerational Relations Index is a highly skewed variable; to adjust for

TABLE 37 DETERMINANTS OF PERCEPTIONS OF DISCRIMINATION IN LATE
ADOLESCENCE. THE SECOND GENERATION IN SPAIN, 2012

| Predictors[1] | I[2] Coefficient[5] | z-ratio | II[3] Coefficient[5] | z-ratio | III[4] Coefficient[5] | z-ratio |
|---|---|---|---|---|---|---|
| National origins: | | | | | | |
| Argentina | | | | | | |
| Bolivia | | | | | | |
| Bulgaria | | | .619 | 1.73# | .621 | 1.75# |
| Chile | | | | | | |
| China | | | | | | |
| Colombia | | | | | | |
| Dominican Republic | | | | | | |
| Ecuador | | | | | | |
| Equatorial Guinea | .765 | 1.79# | .752 | 1.73# | | |
| Morocco | | | | | | |
| Peru | | | | | | |
| Philippines | .570 | 2.21* | | | | |
| Romania | | | | | | |
| Venezuela | | | | | | |
| Objective traits: | | | | | | |
| Age | | | | | | |
| Male | | | −.164 | −1.94# | | |
| Spanish-born | | | | | | |
| Length of Spanish residence | | | | | | |
| Year in school | | | | | | |
| Knowledge of Spanish | | | | | | |
| Hours of school homework | | | | | | |
| Family socio economic status | | | −.148 | −2.30* | −.150 | −2.35* |
| Both parents present | | | −.224 | −2.34* | −.218 | −2.28* |
| Lives in Madrid | | | | | | |
| Attended public school | | | | | | |
| Psychosocial traits: | | | | | | |
| Educational expectations | | | −.067 | −1.73# | −. 065 | 1.66# |
| Familism | | | | | | |
| Intergenerational relations | | | −.334 | −4.68*** | −.325 | −4.55*** |

*(continued)*

| | | | |
|---|---|---|---|
| Perceptions of discrimination | | | .416   2.14* |
| Self-esteem | | | |
| Cut 1 | .940 | –.865 | –.763 |
| Cut 2 | 3.013 | 1.240 | 1.339 |
| Cut 3 | 4.667 | 2.901 | 3.002 |
| Wald chi square | 19.19 (n.s.) | 77.90*** | 81.84*** |
| Pseudo-R² | .004 | .018 | .020 |
| N | | 2,705 | |

1. All predictors measured during the original survey (2008).

2. Predictors limited to national origins. Only groups numbering at least fifty cases in the original survey and twenty-five in the follow-up are included. The rest forms the reference category ($N = 1,055$).

3. Predictors include national origins and objective and psychosocial variables, except perception of discrimination in the first study.

4. Predictors include all variables.

5. Ordered multinomial logistic coefficients. Positive coefficients indicate higher perceptions of discrimination; negative ones, the opposite. Only significant effects are presented.

n.s. = Not significant.

\# = p < .10

\* = $p$ < .05

\*\* = p < .01

\*\*\* = p < .001

this, we transformed it logarithmically before modeling it with ordinary least squares. The transformation has the effect of rendering coefficients interpretable as percent changes in this dependent variable.

The first column of Table 38 shows significantly positive parent-child relations in Chilean and Moroccan families and negative ones among the Chinese. The complex integration process of the latter group, marked by a strong entrepreneurial drive in the midst of a foreign Western culture, is now reflected in significant tensions between generations. This effect endures when other predictors enter the equation and only vanishes in the third model when the lagged effect of the dependent variable is included.[12]

The second model, including all objective and psychosocial predictors, shows that higher self-esteem in early adolescence has a significant influence on subsequent parent-child relations. Each point increase in the Self-esteem scale raises intergenerational relations scores by about 5 percent four years later. Two unexpected results are that males get along with their parents significantly better than females and that the Spanish-born are more conflict-driven than the foreign-born. Unlike the strong positive effects of self-esteem, which are in line with findings in the research

TABLE 38 DETERMINANTS OF INTERGENERATIONAL RELATIONS IN THE SPANISH
SECOND GENERATION, 2012

| Predictors[1] | I[2] | | II[3] | | III[4] | |
|---|---|---|---|---|---|---|
| | Coefficient[5] | z-ratio | Coefficient | z-ratio | Coefficient | z-ratio |
| National origins: | | | | | | |
| Argentina | | | | | | |
| Bolivia | | | | | | |
| Bulgaria | | | | | | |
| Chile | .063 | 2.91** | | | | |
| China | −.065 | −2.30* | −.062 | −2.13* | | |
| Colombia | | | | | | |
| Dominican Republic | | | | | | |
| Ecuador | | | | | | |
| Equatorial Guinea | | | | | | |
| Morocco | . 037 | 2.09* | .037 | 2.09* | .036 | 2.03* |
| Peru | | | | | | |
| Philippines | | | | | | |
| Romania | | | | | | |
| Venezuela | | | | | | |
| Objective traits: | | | | | | |
| Age | | | | | | |
| Male | | | .025 | 3.18** | .024 | 3.09** |
| Spanish-born | | | −.050 | −2.85** | −.048 | −2.73** |
| Length of Spanish residence | | | | | | |
| Year in school | | | | | | |
| Knowledge of Spanish | | | | | | |
| Hours of school homework | | | | | | |
| Family socioeconomic status | | | | | | |
| Both parents present | | | .022 | 2.54*. | 020 | 2.22* |
| Lives in Madrid | | | | | | |
| Attended public school | | | | | | |
| Psychosocial traits: | | | | | | |
| Educational expectations | | | | | | |
| Familism | | | | | | |

(continued)

| | Model 1 | Model 2 | | Model 3 | |
|---|---|---|---|---|---|
| Intergenerational relations (2008) | | | | .064 | 8.75*** |
| Perceptions of discrimination | | −.059 | −2.71** | −.048 | −2.28* |
| Self-esteem | | .047 | 4.59*** | .023 | 2.33* |
| Constant | 1.104 | .921 | | .788 | |
| F-test | 1.62 (n.s.) | 3.36*** | | 6.19*** | |
| R² | .008 | .038 | | .075 | |
| N | 2,695 | | | | |

1. All predictors measured during the original survey (2008).

2. Predictors limited to national origins. Only groups numbering at least fifty cases in the original survey and twenty-five in the follow-up are included. The rest forms the reference category (N = 1,055).

3. Predictors include all variables, except intergenerational relations in the first survey.

4. Predictors include all variables.

5. Ordinary least squares coefficients. Significant effects only.

n.s. = Not significant.

# = p < .10

* = p < .05

** = p < .01

*** = p < .001

literature, these last two effects were not anticipated. It is possible that the cultural gap between parents and their young is greater among children born in Spain than among those born in the same country as the parents. In the latter case, selective acculturation would be greater, thereby facilitating better communications between generations. Several of the life stories presented in Chapter 1 support and illustrate this finding. The importance of family stability is also reflected in the positive and significant effect of growing up with both biological parents.

When intergenerational relations in early adolescence enters the equation, several things happen. First, as expected, this lagged variable becomes the strongest predictor, significantly raising explained variance. Second, the positive influence of self-esteem and the previously noted effects of gender, Spanish birth, and family composition remain significant, and the latter three are unaltered in size. This result implies that these variables influence not only the absolute level of intergenerational relations but also their evolution over time: being male and foreign-born bear positively on this outcome, as does having been raised by both parents. It is thus possible to conclude that intact families who have migrated together have a greater chance of maintaining a selective pattern of acculturation marked by non-conflictive relations between parents and children.

Lastly, reported experiences of discrimination earlier in life have a negative influence on intergenerational relations, confirming the existence of a causal loop. The two variables thus appear intimately related, with good family relations protecting youngsters against the negative effects of external discrimination, but discrimination experiences in early adolescence leading to a significant deterioration of parent-child relations later on. This result is important because it points to the existence of both vicious and virtuous circles of integration: for some second-generation youths, a strong and positive family life effectively shields them from the impact of outside discrimination; for others, such experiences actually undermine their own domestic sphere. Several stories presented in Chapter 1 illustrate both trends.

### Language Spoken at Home

A fourth dimension of interest is linguistic usage. Use of Spanish at home virtually guarantees fluency in the language—which represents, as seen previously, another positive indicator of integration. As in other outcomes of adaptation, there is variation in this, and the question thus becomes what its determinants are. The answer is provided by the set of regressions presented in Table 39. Home language use is a dichotomy with Spanish coded *1* and others *0*. We model this outcome with a logistic regression routine and present the corresponding average marginal effects and significance levels.

As seen in the table, national origins are the overwhelming determinant of this outcome. Predictably, Latin American nationalities register very strong positive effects, whereas East European, North African, and Asian origins are uniformly negative. Being Dominican, for example, increases the net probability of speaking Spanish at home by approximately 40 percent; for Ecuadoreans, the increase is about 30 percent with a predicted effect that exceeds 15 times its standard error. In contrast, being Chinese decreases the probability of Spanish home usage by about 35 percent, and coming from Morocco by 19 percent. These coefficients are very strong. By themselves, the array of dummy variables representing national origins explains 41 percent of the variance in linguistic usage, a figure far above those obtained for all prior indicators of psychosocial adaptation.

The addition of objective predictors increases explained variance by 4 percent. The strongest effects are associated with the Knowledge of Spanish Index (KSI) and city of residence. On the one hand, the associa-

| Predictors[1] | I[2] | | II[3] | | III[4] | |
|---|---|---|---|---|---|---|
| | AMEs[5] | z-ratio | AMEs[5] | z-ratio | AMEs[5] | z-ratio |
| National Origins:[6] | | | | | | |
| Argentina | .346 | 5.28*** | .375 | 6.14*** | .373 | 6.23*** |
| Bolivia | .273 | 6.60*** | .305 | 7.56*** | .302 | 7.52*** |
| Bulgaria | -.187 | -3.72 | -.141 | -2.92** | -.143 | -2.97** |
| Chile | .263 | 3.94*** | .291 | 4.51*** | .294 | 4.58*** |
| China | -.348 | -5.28*** | -.307 | -4.65*** | -.311 | -4.72*** |
| Colombia | .312 | 8.84*** | .321 | 9.80*** | .318 | 9.77*** |
| Dominican Republic | .399 | 6.13*** | .399 | 6.52*** | .393 | 6.45*** |
| Ecuador | .300 | 15.30*** | .305 | 17.86*** | .301 | 15.20*** |
| Equatorial Guinea | .101 | 1.72# | | | | |
| Morocco | -.186 | -8.30*** | -.182 | -8.20*** | .183 | -8.25*** |
| Peru | .331 | 8.08*** | .344 | 9.08*** | .342 | 9.02*** |
| Philippines | -127 | -4.10*** | -.061 | -2.00* | -.064 | -2.02* |
| Romania | -.164 | -6.55*** | -.129 | -5.06*** | .132 | -5.17*** |
| Venezuela | .251 | 3.74*** | .274 | 4.31*** | .274 | 4.27*** |
| Objective traits: | | | | | | |
| Age | | | | | | |
| Male | | | | | | |
| Spanish-born | | | .077 | 3.02** | .079 | 3.09** |
| Length of Spanish residence | | | | | | |
| Year in School | | | | | | |
| Knowledge of Spanish | | | .072 | 5.10*** | .077 | 5.33*** |
| Hours of school homework | | | | | | |
| Family socioeconomic status | | | -.021 | -2.48* | -0.19 | -2.10* |
| Both parents present | | | .009 | 2.91* | .009 | 2.76** |
| Lives in Madrid | | | .098 | 5.82*** | .098 | 5.80*** |
| Attended public school | | | -.049 | -3.16** | -.050 | -3.19** |
| Psychosocial traits: | | | | | | |
| Educational expectations | | | | | | |
| Familism | | | | | | |
| Intergenerational relations | | | | | | |

(continued)

TABLE 39 *(continued)*

| Predictors[1] | $I^2$ AMEs[5] | z-ratio | $II^3$ AMEs[5] | z-ratio | $III^4$ AMEs[5] | z-ratio |
|---|---|---|---|---|---|---|
| Perceptions of discrimination Self-esteem | | | | | | |
| Constant | 1.130 | | .199 | | .559 | |
| Wald chi square | 758.29*** | | 746.79*** | | 748.68*** | |
| Pseudo-R² | .406 | | .447 | | .449 | |
| N = 2,701 | | | | | | |

1. All predictors measured during the original survey (2008).

2. Predictors limited to national origins. Only groups numbering at least fifty cases in the original survey and twenty-five in the follow-up are included. The rest forms the reference category (N = 1,055).

3. Predictors include national origins and objective variables.

4. Predictors include national origins, objective and psychosocial variables.

5. Average marginal effects. Significant effects only.

\* = p < .05

\*\* = p < .01

\*\*\* = p < .001

tion between KSI and Spanish home-language use is not really causal because the two variables are intimately connected. This coefficient is best interpreted as an indicator of validity of results, as it fully corresponds to expectations of the relationship between knowing a language and using it at home. On the other hand, the causal effect of city of residence is important because it indicates a significantly stronger probability of Madrid residents using Spanish at home, net of other factors. The probability of doing so increases by 10 percent relative to residents of Barcelona. As noted previously, this effect is attributable to the emphasis that Catalan authorities place on use of their language in school and the greater presence of non-Spanish-speaking immigrant groups in that city.

As may be expected, determinants of fluency and use of the host country language are quite different in the United States. Whereas, as just seen, Latin American origins strongly determine this outcome in Spain, it has the opposite effect in North America. According to CILS results, only 28 percent of children of Latin American parents were fluent English monolinguals at average age 17, as opposed to 55 percent of children from other national origins.[13] In both countries, the second generation "proper" is significantly more likely to speak the host country language at home. Two other important effects are, however, at odds: In the CILS sample, higher parental status and attending a public school (as opposed to private bilingual school) led to significantly higher levels of English knowledge and use.[14] In Spain, the opposite happens.

In the Spanish case, the negative family socioeconomic effect is likely due to the presence of higher-status families in the "other nationalities" category used as the reference point in these regressions. Most of these families come from non-Spanish-speaking countries in Eastern and Western Europe and the Middle East. Such families are also less likely to send their children to predominantly Catholic private schools, a pattern that would partially account for the net negative influence of public school attendance in Spain. Latin American parents tend to come from lower status origins, but they are also more likely to send their children to private Catholic schools if given the opportunity. No psychosocial predictor has a significant effect on this outcome, leaving the principal story unchanged: national origins (first) and city of residence (second) are the major determinants of language spoken at home by second-generation youths in Spain.

## Self-Esteem

Because of the large number of items in Rosenberg's Self-esteem Scale, it was omitted from the ILSEG follow-up. We still have, however, the scores obtained in the original survey and reported above. On the basis of these data, it is possible to investigate determinants of self-esteem in the second generation. In this instance, we use a somewhat different set of predictors, also drawn from the original survey, inverting their order by presenting first a model including objective and psychosocial predictors and adding national origins next. The order of causality between objective variables such as age, sex, and length of Spanish residence and self-esteem is unambiguous. In the case of psychosocial predictors, and given the cross-sectional nature of the available data, causality is more problematic. Nevertheless, we include these predictors in order to examine their association with this key dependent variable. Since this variable is continuous and normally distributed, we model it with ordinary least squares regression using listwise deletion of missing data. Table 40 presents the results.

As shown in the table, older respondents and males display higher self-esteem. The gender effect was hypothesized in Chapter 2. Not

| Predictors | I | | II | |
|---|---|---|---|---|
| | Coeff.[1] | t-ratio | Coeff.[1] | t-ratio |
| Age | 0.011 | 2.0* | 0.010 | 1.9* |
| Sex (female) | –0.034 | –2.9** | –0.033 | –2.9** |
| City of residence (Barcelona) | –0.051 | –4.00*** | –0.046 | –3.6*** |
| Birthplace (Spain) | | | | |
| Length of Spanish residence | | | | |
| Father's birthplace (Spain) | | | | |
| Mother's birthplace (Spain) | | | | |
| Family socioeconomic status | 0.047 | 5.9*** | 0.041 | 5.0*** |
| Knowledge of Spanish (KSI) | 0.148 | 12.5*** | 0.146 | 11.3*** |
| Intergenerational relations | 0.255 | 21.6*** | 0.253 | 21.4*** |
| Experiences of discrimination | –0.091 | –8.6*** | –0.094 | –8.8*** |
| Self-identity (Spanish) | | | | |
| National origin: | | | | |
|   Argentina | | | | |
|   Bolivia | | | –0.073 | –2.5* |
|   China | | | | |
|   Colombia | | | | |
|   Dominican Republic | | | | |
|   Ecuador | | | | |
|   Morocco | | | | |
|   Pakistan | | | | |
|   Peru | | | | |
|   Philippines | | | –0.125 | –3.5*** |
|   Romania | | | | |
|   Other Western Europe | | | | |
| Constant | 1.638 | 16.8*** | 1.676 | 16.5*** |
| $R^2 = 0.201$ | | | $R^2 = 0.205$ | |
| $N = 4,704$ | | | $N = 4,700$ | |

1. Ordinary least squares regression coefficients (unstandardized). Only significant effects are presented.

* $p < .05$

** $p < .01$

*** $p < .001$

expected, however, is the significantly lower level of self-esteem among Barcelona respondents, a finding for which we have no ready explanation at present. As predicted, family socioeconomic status and knowledge of Spanish bear positively and strongly on students' sense of self-worth. The order of causality is unambiguous in both cases since it is implausible that adolescents' views would determine family status or linguistic ability.

The strongest effect, however, corresponds to intergenerational relations, which exceeds 21 times its standard error. In this case, causality is ambiguous since it is as plausible that good relations with parents affect self-esteem as vice versa. The safest conclusion is that both variables are intimately related. The previous finding in Table 38 showing self-esteem in early adolescence to be a significant and positive determinant of intergenerational relations four years later supports this conclusion. As in the case of the mutual influence of experiences of discrimination and intergenerational relations over time, we appear to be in the presence of a causal loop.

A comparison with results obtained by CILS in the United States is especially appropriate because both studies used the same self-esteem scale and because CILS did measure self-esteem in the follow-up survey. By restricting predictors to those present in the original sample, it is possible in this case to establish a clear temporal order between hypothesized causes and effects. In the event, results from both studies are remarkably similar. Those from CILS are reproduced in Table 41.

As in Spain, females in the United States displayed significantly lower self-esteem. Family socioeconomic status and fluency in the host country language increased the sense of self-worth in both countries. Equally important, items measuring intergenerational relations had similar effects in both surveys. In the CILS case, the temporal order is unambiguous, supporting the above-noted causal loop: bad parent-child relations in early adolescence reduce self-esteem, whereas high early self-esteem leads to positive intergenerational relations later on in life.

Similarities continue: perceptions of discrimination have a significant negative influence on self-esteem in both countries, and, again, the order of causality is unambiguous in the American case. These results confirm the general finding in the literature that external discrimination hurts children's self-image, leading to a series of negative consequences later on. As was shown in Table 37, the opposite effect does *not* hold in the Spanish case, as earlier self-esteem has no effect on subsequent experiences of discrimination. When national origins enter the equation,

TABLE 41   DETERMINANTS OF SELF-ESTEEM AMONG CHILDREN
OF IMMIGRANTS IN THE UNITED STATES

| Predictors[1] | I[2] | II[3] |
|---|---|---|
| Age | | |
| Female | −1.93** | −1.97** |
| So. California | −5.14*** | |
| Parental socioeconomic status | .88* | .81* |
| Two-parent family | | |
| U.S.-born | 1.58* | 1.25* |
| Long-term U.S. resident[4] | 1.57* | 1.16* |
| Limited bilingual | −2.63** | −2.13* |
| Fluent bilingual | 4.51*** | 4.20*** |
| Parent-child conflict | −1.14** | −1.07* |
| Embarrassed by parents | −1.48** | −1.35** |
| Experienced discrimination | −1.08* | −1.09* |
| National Origins: | | |
|   Filipino | | −3.37* |
|   Laotian/Cambodian | | −4.43** |
|   Vietnamese | | −6.45*** |
| Constant | 40.48 | 35.34 |
| $R^2$ | .11 | .12 |
| N | 4,321 | |

SOURCE: Portes and Rumbaut, *Legacies*, table 8.6.

1. All predictors measured in the baseline CILS survey, at average age 14. Self-esteem measured in the follow-up survey, at average age 17.

2. Ordinary least squares regression coefficients. Positive scores indicate higher self-esteem; negative ones, the opposite. Model excludes national origins. All effects presented.

3. Ordinary least squares regression coefficients. National origins included. Only statistically significant effects are presented.

4. Ten or more years of U.S. residence.

* p < .05
** p < .01
*** p < .001

another unexpected finding emerges: despite differences in time and place, Filipino origins have a significant net negative influence on self-worth in both countries. In Spain, the effect is quite strong, exceeding three times its standard error. Other Asian nationalities, not present in Spain, also displayed significantly lower levels of self-esteem in the American case.

In both CILS and ILSEG, as well as in other studies reviewed in Chapter 2, self-esteem proves to be an important psychosocial dimension affecting a range of subsequent outcomes. The very similar causal profiles present in both countries represent an important finding. They indicate that, despite different national contexts of reception, the same set of factors appear to determine children of immigrants' sense of self-worth—with gender, family status, relations with parents, and early experiences of discrimination being paramount.

## CONCLUSION

This analysis of linguistic and psychosocial dimensions yields a rather positive prognosis for the integration of children of immigrants in Spain. We observe no evidence of mass reactive ethnicity or alienation and, on the contrary, note a sustained increase in self-identification with the country and widespread knowledge and use of its language. These trends were adumbrated by several of the life stories presented in Chapter 1. Levels of self-esteem and the quality of intergenerational relations are generally high, further supporting the conclusion of positive adaptation. The similar profile of our second-generation sample to that of native-parentage Spaniards leads to the conclusion that both form part of the same universe of young people, thereby re-affirming the reality of integration.

A systematic comparison with results obtained in the United States demonstrates a number of similarities in determinants of national identity, intergenerational relations, and self-esteem, but also several telling differences. Unlike the situation in Spain, children of immigrants in America are more challenged by a racialized social system that makes their integration into the native white mainstream problematic. This situation fosters, instead, higher perceptions of discrimination and the internalization of the pan-ethnic labels under which these children are routinely classified by American institutions as well as by the general public. In the worst case, the process leads to reactive ethnicity, with youngsters refusing to abandon their parents' nationalities as markers of self-identification. Little of this occurs in Spain.

Concerning the bearing of these results on theories and hypotheses reviewed in Chapter 2, we find support for predictions concerning the positive effects of native birth and length of residence on identification with Spanish society. There are similarly positive effects of family socioeconomic status and family composition in protecting youths against the effects of discrimination, and corresponding negative effects of early experiences of discrimination on both intergenerational relations and self-esteem. We identified two causal loops between these psychosocial variables. As predicted, girls have significantly lower self-esteem, a result similar to that found in the United States and elsewhere. Less expected, girls are also less likely to identify with Spain, a pattern possibly due to their greater emotional attachment to their own immigrant families.

Our analysis finds no support for blanket predictions of second-generation "advantage," but neither does it show evidence of a uniform process of racialization or exclusion. As just seen, there is also little support for the hypothesis of reactive ethnicity. Overall, results favor the neo-assimilationist expectation of a gradual process of psychosocial integration into the host society, as well as segmented assimilation predictions concerning the protective effects of selective acculturation and the intimate association between parent-child relations and children's self-esteem. As we saw in Chapter 5, there are major differences in modes of incorporation affecting immigrant parents' labor market outcomes, but there is little evidence that such differences systematically affect the psychosocial profile of adolescents from different national origins. With the exception of a few resilient nationality effects, of which those for the Chinese and Filipinos are paramount, the process of incorporation into Spanish society appears to have been relatively uniform. As a consequence, second-generation youths find themselves partaking of the same sociocultural world as their native-parentage peers.

# SEVEN

# The Educational Goals and Achievements of the Second Generation

## STAYING IN SCHOOL

The principal questions concerning the future of the second generation are, by age 18, whether its members have stayed in school and how well they are doing in it. Both questions are answerable by results from our follow-up sample. Table 42 presents a breakdown of the sample by country of birth and by whether respondents continued to be enrolled in school. Three observations are worth making. First, over four-fifths of respondents originally interviewed in 2007–8 continued to be enrolled in school. Second, the second generation "proper" (that is, those born in Spain) has one of the highest levels of enrollment, with almost nine out of ten still in school. Only Argentinean and Filipino students and those from several Andean countries exhibit comparable levels. Third, two nationalities fall significantly below the average: Dominicans and Chinese. The low Dominican retention is attributable to the modest average socioeconomic background of the parents; Chinese school abandonment reflects the entrepreneurial "bet" of these families as an alternative mobility path, as discussed in Chapter 5.

Table 43 presents similar tabulations by gender, city, and type of school (public versus private). These results indicate slight differences in favor of females and residents of Barcelona that attain statistical significance because of the large sample size; the difference in favor of private school students does not attain significance. The relatively low levels of school abandonment by late adolescence are congruent

TABLE 42 ENROLLED IN SCHOOL AT AVERAGE AGE 18. THE SECOND GENERATION IN SPAIN, 2012

| Country of Birth[1] | N | Enrolled in school (%) |
|---|---|---|
| Born in Spain (of foreign parentage) | 590 | 89.7 |
| Ecuador | 1,030 | 83.0 |
| Colombia | 280 | 83.2 |
| Morocco | 238 | 84.9 |
| Peru | 218 | 89.5 |
| Romania | 177 | 84.2 |
| Dominican Republic | 171 | 77.2 |
| Bolivia | 168 | 83.9 |
| Argentina | 91 | 90.1 |
| China | 79 | 68.4 |
| Philippines | 69 | 89.9 |
| Bulgaria | 52 | 78.9 |
| Chile | 52 | 92.3 |
| Venezuela | 47 | 91.5 |
| Equatorial Guinea | 37 | 83.8 |
| Other countries | 465 | 82.8 |
| Total | 3,764 | 84.5 |
| Pearson chi square = 51.23** | Cramer's V = 0.117 | |

SOURCE: ILSEG original and follow-up samples.

1. Countries ordered by size after the Spanish-born. Only individual countries numbering at least forty cases in the follow-up sample are listed (Equatorial Guinea is exceptionally included for its importance, as seen below). Missing data are excluded.

** $p < .01$

with the more optimistic perspectives on second-generation acceptance, predicting a paced process of advancement by children of immigrants.[1]

Equally or more important are the type of studies that these youths pursue. At average age 18, the key difference is between respondents still attempting to complete basic secondary education (ESO in the Spanish acronym) or enrolled in remedial studies (PCPI) and those who have advanced to academic senior high school, superior technical studies, or even a university career. Table 44 presents the relevant information, broken down by country of birth and gender. Overall, about one-third of the sample originally interviewed in 2008 is still struggling in basic secondary or remedial studies. Moroccans, Bolivians, and Chileans are most commonly represented in this category. At the other end, Bulgarians, Romanians, Argentineans, Colombians, Venezuelans, and the Chinese who have persisted in staying in school are most strongly present in advanced secondary studies. Over half of each of these groups have reached that level, as compared with 45 percent for the sample as a whole.

TABLE 43  ENROLLED IN SCHOOL BY GENDER, SCHOOL TYPE, AND CITY
OF RESIDENCE. THE SECOND GENERATION IN SPAIN, 2012[1]

|  | $N$[2] | Enrolled in school (%) |
|---|---|---|
| Gender: |  |  |
| Male | 1,852 | 82.7 |
| Female | 1,955 | 86.3 |
| Total | 3,807 | 84.6 |
| Pearson chi square = 9.28* | Cramer's V = -.049 |  |
| City: |  |  |
| Madrid | 1,910 | 81.5 |
| Barcelona | 1,897 | 87.7 |
| Pearson chi square = 28.00*** | Cramer's V = 0.096 |  |
| School Type: |  |  |
| Public | 2,001 | 83.0 |
| Private | 1,779 | 86.1 |
| Pearson chi square = 6.93 n.s.[3] | Cramer's V = -0.04 |  |

1. Missing data excluded.
2. Follow-up sample.
3. Not significant difference.
* $p < .05$
*** $p < .001$

The small minority who have reached the university is composed mainly of the Spanish native-born, Bulgarians, Romanians, and Venezuelans. Strong educational progress in the latter group corresponds to the high level of human capital observed among their parents previously. Disparities in educational performance across nationalities offer *prima facie* evidence in support of segmented assimilation, insofar as it points to a non-uniform adaptation process affected by characteristics of immigrant families and communities.

The bottom of Table 44 breaks down the samples by gender. In this case, there is a definite advantage in favor of females. Boys are overrepresented in the bottom educational categories; girls are more numerous in academic senior high school and among the minority who have reached the university. The male disadvantage is even more apparent if we focus on respondents enrolled in remedial studies. Only 1 percent of females in the follow-up sample were enrolled in that program, whereas the figure reached close to 5 percent among males.

To avoid clutter, we omit figures for the second-generation replacement sample. They closely parallel those presented above, with Bolivians, Dominicans, and Moroccans overrepresented in the bottom educational

TABLE 44 TYPE OF SCHOOL ATTENDED BY SECOND-GENERATION YOUTHS, 2012

| | School type[2] | | | | | |
|---|---|---|---|---|---|---|
| | Basic secondary (ESO) % | Remedial (PCPI) % | Vocational, medium level % | Advanced secondary and technical[3] % | University[4] % | N[5] |
| Country of birth:[1] | | | | | | |
| Spain (of foreign parentage) | 30.6 | 1.7 | 12.0 | 46.2 | 8.1 | 532 |
| Ecuador | 30.4 | 3.6 | 16.5 | 44.5 | 3.9 | 856 |
| Colombia | 28.6 | 2.1 | 12.8 | 52.1 | 4.3 | 234 |
| Morocco | 41.1 | 5.9 | 15.8 | 33.7 | 3.5 | 202 |
| Peru | 34.9 | 1.0 | 11.8 | 46.2 | 5.6 | 195 |
| Romania | 27.5 | 0.7 | 11.4 | 50.3 | 8.1 | 149 |
| Bolivia | 39.7 | 2.1 | 13.5 | 41.8 | 2.1 | 141 |
| Dominican Republic | 32.8 | 4.5 | 17.2 | 38.8 | 4.5 | 134 |
| Argentina | 28.1 | 2.4 | 12.2 | 54.9 | 2.4 | 82 |
| Philippines | 30.2 | 0.0 | 23.8 | 38.1 | 6.4 | 63 |
| China | 25.9 | 0.0 | 11.1 | 57.4 | 5.6 | 54 |
| Chile | 45.8 | 2.1 | 12.5 | 33.3 | 4.2 | 48 |
| Venezuela | 25.6 | 2.3 | 2.3 | 53.5 | 11.6 | 43 |
| Bulgaria | 12.2 | 0.0 | 26.8 | 51.2 | 9.8 | 41 |
| Equatorial Guinea | 16.1 | 6.5 | 29.0 | 41.9 | 6.5 | 31 |
| Other countries | 37.1 | 2.3 | 11.3 | 45.9 | 2.1 | 388 |

Pearson chi square = 149.26***      Cramer's V = 0.097

| | | | | | | |
|---|---|---|---|---|---|---|
| **Gender:** | | | | | | |
| Male | 35.7 | 4.6 | 15.1 | 39.3 | 3.9 | 1,532 |
| Female | 29.7 | 1.1 | 13.2 | 49.7 | 6.0 | 1,700 |
| Totals | 32.5 | 2.7 | 14.1 | 44.7 | 4.8 | |
| N | 1,051 | 88 | 456 | 1,446 | 155 | 3,232 |

Pearson chi square = 73.50\*\*\*          Cramer's V = 0.151

1. Ordered by numerical size after the Spanish-born except for "Other" category. Only countries with at least forty cases in the follow-up sample are listed. (Equatorial Guinea is exceptionally included). Drop-outs excluded.

2. Percentages do not add to 100 because of omission of the "Other" category. Missing data excluded.

3. Senior high school and vocational-technical, superior level.

4. Includes bridge/preparatory year.

5. Follow-up sample (excluding school drop-outs).

\*\*\* p < .00

categories, and Argentineans, Venezuelans, East Europeans, and the Spanish-born in the top academic tracks. The male disadvantage in schooling is even more apparent in this new sample, as the number of male second-generation youths in remedial studies exceeds 16 percent, tripling the corresponding figures for females.

## ACADEMIC GRADES

There are significant differences as well in objective indicators of academic performance, as indexed by average school grades, both in the original and in the replacement samples. In both cases, the average grade fluctuates around 6.00 out of a possible maximum of 10.00. Nationalities falling below the average include youths of Bolivian and Dominican origin in the follow-up sample; to these are added Moroccans and Peruvians in the replacement sample. The coefficients of strength of association attain statistical significance in both cases, indicating wide variation across countries in levels of school performance. Table 45 presents the relevant data.

As shown in the bottom rows of Table 45, there are no major differences in average grades, either by city of residence or type of school. Noteworthy differences are present, however, by gender, and girls once more display a significant advantage. This is apparent in both samples, confirming a definite trend in favor of females in every indicator of educational achievement. High diversity in academic performance between genders and across immigrant nationalities question uniform theories of "exclusion," "advantage," or "convergence" in the second generation. The source of these disparities requires additional investigation, a task to which we will turn in the following sections.

## ATTITUDES TOWARD SCHOOL

In contrast with grades, we detect no significant differences among nationalities concerning attitudes toward school. As explained in Chapter 4, this is a constructed index of high internal consistency, reflecting critical versus positive opinions of the schools that respondents attended at the time of the second survey. With a range of 1 to 4, higher scores indicate a more positive attitude. The sample averages were 3.2 in the follow-up sample and 3.15 in the replacement sample, reflecting an overall positive orientation. As shown in Table 46, there were no major differences among nationalities in both samples, and girls and boys

TABLE 45   AVERAGE GRADES BY SAMPLE, COUNTRY OF BIRTH, GENDER, SCHOOL
TYPE, AND CITY OF RESIDENCE. THE SECOND GENERATION IN SPAIN, 2012

| | Follow-up sample | | Replacement sample | |
|---|---|---|---|---|
| | Av. grade | N[2] | Av. grade | N[2] |
| Country of birth:[1] | | | | |
| Spain (of foreign parentage) | 6.40 | 582 | 6.48 | 366 |
| Ecuador | 6.02 | 1,014 | 6.04 | 372 |
| Colombia | 6.07 | 275 | 6.23 | 89 |
| Morocco | 6.08 | 232 | 5.92 | 85 |
| Peru | 6.00 | 214 | 5.89 | 108 |
| Romania | 6.45 | 176 | 6.38 | 72 |
| Dominican Republic | 5.96 | 168 | 6.02 | 55 |
| Bolivia | 5.90 | 165 | 5.86 | 61 |
| Argentina | 6.01 | 90 | 6.58 | 26 |
| China | 6.08 | 76 | 6.62 | 31 |
| Philippines | 6.48 | 69 | 6.11 | 8 |
| Bulgaria | 6.38 | 52 | – | – |
| Chile | 6.08 | 52 | 6.35 | 10 |
| Venezuela | 6.28 | 47 | 6.44 | 17 |
| Equatorial Guinea | 5.90 | 37 | – | – |
| Other countries | 6.30 | 459 | 6.11 | 192 |
| Bartlett's Test of Equal Variance | 43.98*** | | 31.37*** | |
| Gender: | | | | |
| Male | 5.99 | 1,830 | 6.02 | 720 |
| Female | 6.30 | 1,921 | 6.37 | 772 |
| t-ratio | 7.37*** | | 4.84*** | |
| School type:[3] | | | | |
| Public | 6.18 | 1,978 | — | — |
| Private | 6.12 | 1,746 | — | — |
| t-ratio | 1.41 (n.s.)[4] | | | |
| City of residence: | | | | |
| Madrid | 6.16 | 1,888 | 6.19 | 896 |
| Barcelona | 6.14 | 1,863 | 6.19 | 596 |
| t-ratio | 0.56 (n.s.)[4] | | .09 (n.s.)[4] | |
| Totals | 6.15 | 3,751 | 6.19 | 1,492 |

1. Countries ordered by sample size in the follow-up sample after the Spanish-born. Only countries with at least forty cases in the follow-up sample are included (Equatorial Guinea is exceptionally included).

2. Excludes missing data.

3. School type ascertained during the original 2008 survey and thus absent from the replacement sample.

4. Coefficient not significant at the .001 level.

*** p < .001

TABLE 46   ATTITUDES TOWARD SCHOOL BY SAMPLE, COUNTRY OF BIRTH,
GENDER, SCHOOL TYPE, AND CITY OF RESIDENCE. THE SECOND GENERATION
IN SPAIN, 2012

| | Follow-up sample | | Replacement sample | |
|---|---|---|---|---|
| | *Index score* | N[2] | *Index score* | N[2] |
| Country of birth:[1] | | | | |
| Spain (of foreign parentage) | 3.28 | 488 | 3.14 | 345 |
| Ecuador | 3.22 | 776 | 3.11 | 333 |
| Colombia | 3.31 | 216 | 3.22 | 82 |
| Morocco | 3.23 | 191 | 3.29 | 80 |
| Peru | 3.20 | 171 | 3.13 | 100 |
| Romania | 3.22 | 139 | 3.11 | 66 |
| Bolivia | 3.10 | 126 | 3.09 | 50 |
| Dominican Republic | 3.31 | 119 | 3.25 | 55 |
| Argentina | 3.29 | 65 | 3.17 | 24 |
| China | 3.06 | 43 | 3.02 | 25 |
| Philippines | 3.22 | 56 | 3.23 | 7 |
| Chile | 3.12 | 46 | 3.20 | 10 |
| Bulgaria | 3.22 | 39 | – | – |
| Venezuela | 3.27 | 38 | 3.00 | 12 |
| Equatorial Guinea | 3.19 | 30 | – | – |
| Other countries | 3.21 | 355 | 3.16 | 176 |
| Bartlett's Test of Equal Variance | 24.60 (n.s.)[3] | | 11.39 (n.s.)[3] | |
| Gender: | | | | |
| Male | 3.22 | 1,399 | 3.12 | 709 |
| Female | 3.23 | 1,529 | 3.17 | 656 |
| t-ratio | 0.55 (n.s)[3] | | 2.01 (n.s.)[3] | |
| School type:[4] | | | | |
| Public | 3.26 | 1,497 | – | – |
| Private | 3.20 | 1,410 | – | – |
| t-ratio | 3.19*** | | | |
| City of residence: | | | | |
| Madrid | 3.27 | 1,406 | 3.16 | 806 |
| Barcelona | 3.19 | 1,522 | 3.13 | 559 |
| t-ratio | 4.23*** | | 1.34 (n.s.)[3] | |
| Totals | 3.23 | 2,928 | 3.15 | 1,365 |

1. Countries ordered by sample size in the follow-up sample after the Spanish-born. Only countries with at least forty cases in the follow-up are included (Equatorial Guinea is exceptionally included).

2. Excludes missing data.

3. Not significant difference.

4. School type ascertained during the original 2008 survey and thus absent from the replacement sample.

\*\*\* $p < .001$

evaluated their schools equally well. Interesting differences are observable, however, by city of residence and school type. Madrid respondents judged their schools more positively than residents of Barcelona, the difference being statistically significant in the follow-up sample. Contrary to general expectations, public school students tended to have a somewhat more positive orientation toward their centers than those attending private or "concerted" schools.

## EDUCATIONAL AMBITION

A final dimension deserving consideration is ambition toward the future. As noted in Chapter 2, aspirations are a significant predictor of academic performance and are affected, in turn, by it. Our surveys provide data on ideal goals ("aspirations") and realistic ones ("expectations") for both the follow-up and the replacement samples. Table 47 presents the relevant data for the proportions aspiring to high educational achievement (that is, a university degree or higher). Table 48 presents the corresponding data for expectations, broken down by country of birth, gender, school type, and city of residence.

In both samples, about 65 percent aspires to a university degree. Higher-than-average aspirations are associated with the Spanish-born and certain South American nationalities such as Argentineans, Colombians, Peruvians, and Venezuelans. Lower levels of aspirations are found among Dominicans, Moroccans, Guineans, and the Chinese, to which are added, in the replacement sample, Filipinos and Chileans. Differences across countries are highly significant statistically, although this is primarily due to large sample sizes. The Cramer's V coefficient of strength of association indicates a weak-to-moderate correlation between country of birth and levels of aspirations. The same is the case for differences between types of schools and cities of residence, none of which reaches statistical significance. Females, however, display significantly higher educational goals. The difference in their favor is highly significant in both samples, confirming the patterns observed earlier.

Realistic expectations drop by 10 percent in the follow-up and 15 percent in the replacement sample relative to aspirations, but the general tendencies noted previously hold. Consistently high expectations are found among the Spanish-born and certain South American nationalities, particularly Venezuelans. Lower expectations are again more common among Dominicans, Moroccans, and Guineans, as well as Filipinos in the replacement sample. The association between expecta-

TABLE 47 EDUCATIONAL ASPIRATIONS BY SAMPLE, COUNTRY OF BIRTH, SCHOOL
TYPE, AND CITY OF RESIDENCE. THE SECOND GENERATION IN SPAIN, 2012

| | Follow-up sample | | Replacement sample | |
|---|---|---|---|---|
| | High aspirations[2] | | High aspirations[2] | |
| | (%) | N[3] | (%) | N[3] |
| Country of birth:[1] | | | | |
| Spain (of foreign parentage) | 70.2 | 530 | 74.6 | 374 |
| Ecuador | 60.1 | 855 | 61.9 | 378 |
| Colombia | 70.1 | 234 | 63.3 | 90 |
| Morocco | 59.2 | 201 | 45.4 | 88 |
| Peru | 74.4 | 195 | 75.8 | 108 |
| Romania | 61.6 | 151 | 57.4 | 73 |
| Bolivia | 65.0 | 140 | 60.7 | 61 |
| Dominican Republic | 55.6 | 133 | 50.0 | 58 |
| Argentina | 71.6 | 81 | 80.8 | 26 |
| Philippines | 69.8 | 63 | 33.3 | 9 |
| China | 59.3 | 54 | 58.8 | 34 |
| Chile | 62.5 | 48 | 54.6 | 11 |
| Venezuela | 81.4 | 43 | 76.5 | 17 |
| Bulgaria | 65.8 | 41 | – | – |
| Equatorial Guinea | 56.7 | 30 | – | – |
| Other countries | 67.7 | 387 | 62.0 | 200 |
| Chi square: | 44.69*** | | 53.66*** | |
| Cramer's V: | .118 | | .188 | |
| Gender: | | | | |
| Male | 55.6 | 1,535 | 54.9 | 792 |
| Female | 73.7 | 1,690 | 75.0 | 735 |
| Chi square: | 115.90*** | | 66.93*** | |
| Cramer's V: | −.19 | | −.21 | |
| School type:[4] | | | | |
| Public | 66.3 | 1,666 | — | — |
| Private | 63.8 | 1,533 | — | — |
| Chi square: | 2.14 (n.s.)[5] | | | |
| Cramer's V: | .03 | | | |
| City of residence: | | | | |
| Madrid | 67.5 | 1,562 | 62.6 | 911 |
| Barcelona | 62.8 | 1,663 | 67.4 | 613 |
| Chi square: | 7.82 (n.s.)[5] | | 3.69 (n.s.)[5] | |
| Cramer's V: | .05 | | .05 | |
| Totals | 65.2 | 3,225 | 64.5 | 1,524 |

1. Countries ordered by sample size in the follow-up sample after the Spanish-born. Only countries with at least forty cases in the follow-up are included (Equatorial Guinea is exceptionally included).

2. University title or postgraduate degree.

3. Excludes missing data.

4. School type ascertained during the original survey and thus not available for replacement sample.

5. Not significant difference.

*** p < .001

TABLE 48   EDUCATIONAL EXPECTATIONS BY SAMPLE, COUNTRY OF BIRTH,
SCHOOL TYPE, AND CITY OF RESIDENCE. THE SECOND GENERATION IN SPAIN, 2012

| | Follow-up sample | | Replacement sample | |
|---|---|---|---|---|
| | High educational expectations[2] | | High educational expectations[2] | |
| | (%) | N[3] | (%) | N[3] |
| Country of birth:[1] | | | | |
| Spain (of foreign parentage) | 64.1 | 529 | 63.1 | 374 |
| Ecuador | 48.9 | 855 | 42.7 | 377 |
| Colombia | 62.4 | 234 | 44.9 | 89 |
| Morocco | 46.0 | 202 | 29.2 | 89 |
| Peru | 60.5 | 195 | 62.0 | 108 |
| Romania | 53.6 | 151 | 38.4 | 73 |
| Bolivia | 50.0 | 140 | 39.3 | 61 |
| Dominican Republic | 41.0 | 134 | 36.2 | 58 |
| Argentina | 56.8 | 81 | 80.8 | 26 |
| Philippines | 52.4 | 63 | 22.2 | 9 |
| China | 51.8 | 54 | 39.4 | 33 |
| Chile | 52.1 | 48 | 36.4 | 11 |
| Venezuela | 69.8 | 43 | 58.8 | 17 |
| Bulgaria | 58.5 | 41 | – | – |
| Equatorial Guinea | 41.9 | 31 | – | – |
| Other countries | 55.3 | 385 | 51.8 | 199 |
| Chi square: | 62.86*** | | 83.01*** | |
| Cramer's V: | .14 | | .23 | |
| Gender: | | | | |
| Male | 45.7 | 1,534 | 41.7 | 791 |
| Female | 61.9 | 1,691 | 58.2 | 733 |
| Chi square: | 84.60*** | | 40.92*** | |
| Cramer's V: | –.16 | | –.16 | |
| School type:[4] | | | | |
| Public | 55.9 | 1,666 | – | – |
| Private | 52.4 | 1,533 | – | – |
| Chi square: | 4.08 (n.s.)[5] | | | |
| Cramer's V: | .04 | | | |
| City of residence: | | | | |
| Madrid | 57.4 | 1,562 | 48.9 | 910 |
| Barcelona | 51.2 | 1,663 | 50.4 | 611 |
| Chi square: | 12.43*** | | 0.33 (n.s.)[5] | |
| Cramer's V: | .06 | | .01 | |
| Totals | 54.2 | 3,225 | 49.5 | 1,521 |

1. Countries ordered by sample size in the follow-up sample after the Spanish-born. Only countries with at least forty cases in the follow-up are included (Equatorial Guinea is exceptionally included).

2. University graduate and/or postgraduate degree.

3. Excludes missing data.

4. School type ascertained during the original survey and thus not available for replacement sample.

5. Not significant difference.

*** p < .001

tions and country of birth is statistically significant in both samples, reaching moderate strength among replacements. Associations with city of residence or school type are, as is the case of aspirations, either non-significant or statistically weak. Once again, the difference in realistic goals in favor of females is highly significant, being the strongest association detected in the analysis.

## CHANGES OVER TIME

The sizable proportions of "high" educational goals (university degree or higher) run contrary to negative predictions of marginalization or exclusion of second-generation youths. The relatively homogenous character of these goals point toward convergence, although visible differences exist among nationalities, and they correspond closely to the known characteristics of various immigrant nationalities. These traits will be investigated further in the following sections. For the moment, it suffices to note that, on the basis of the study's longitudinal data, it is possible to examine the evolution of aspirations and expectations over time. This is done by comparing the original sample with the follow-up sample four years later. The relevant results, broken down by gender, are presented in Table 49.

The major observed difference is the rise of both aspirations and expectations, especially at the highest level. Although realistic expectations trail ideal aspirations and girls maintain the consistent advantage noted earlier, both genders raised their goals significantly. Hence, only 10 percent of the total sample aspired to a postgraduate degree at age 14, but 26 percent did so four years later. For females, the figures were 11 and 30 percent, respectively. A similar trend is observable in expectations, leading to the conclusion that, as the educational process advanced and respondents matured, higher educational goals became both more desirable and more reachable.

Note that these figures include the full follow-up sample—composed of respondents who stayed in school and the 15 percent who had left it. Even for the latter, educational goals did not drop drastically, as the majority planned to return to school at some point. These figures omit "don't know" answers, which reached a sizable 20 percent in the follow-up. This level of uncertainty is noteworthy, but it does not negate the general rise in ambition: even after taking these answers into account, the numbers expressing high educational goals rose significantly from the early school years. This evolution of educational ambition over time clearly favors an assimilationist account predicting a

TABLE 49   EDUCATIONAL ASPIRATIONS AND EXPECTATIONS OVER TIME
IN THE SPANISH SECOND GENERATION

| | Basic secondary and lower vocational (%) | Advanced secondary and technical (%) | University degree (%) | Post-graduate degree (%) |
|---|---|---|---|---|
| | | Aspirations | | |
| Original sample, 2008 (Mean age, 14) | 22.1 | 23.3 | 45.0 | 9.6 |
| Follow-up sample, 2012 (Mean age, 18) | 6.7 | 25.5 | 41.8 | 26.0 |
| Males, 2008 | 25.2 | 26.1 | 39.9 | 8.8 |
| Males, 2012 | 9.5 | 32.2 | 36.7 | 21.6 |
| Females, 2008 | 18.9 | 20.3 | 50.3 | 10.5 |
| Females, 2012 | 4.0 | 19.2 | 46.6 | 30.2 |
| | | Expectations | | |
| Original sample, 2008 | 33.1 | 31.6 | 29.7 | 5.6 |
| Follow-up sample, 2012 | 11.1 | 32.1 | 40.6 | 16.2 |
| Males, 2008 | 35.8 | 32.4 | 26.8 | 5.00 |
| Males, 2012 | 14.9 | 37.3 | 34.8 | 13.00 |
| Females, 2008 | 30.3 | 30.8 | 32.7 | 6.2 |
| Females, 2012 | 7.5 | 27.3 | 46.2 | 19.0 |

paced process of integration. By the same token, it negates theories of marginalization or lack of integration of immigrant youths. It remains to be seen how these goals and other aspects of educational attainment relate to those of children in the Spanish mainstream.

## COMPARISONS WITH SPANISH-PARENTAGE YOUTHS

As noted previously, another advantage of the ILSEG survey is the inclusion of a large native-parentage sample. Table 50 presents this evidence by placing side-by-side results from the original, replacement, and native-parentage samples over all the educational outcomes discussed previously. There are no major differences in types of school enrollment, especially if we focus on the superior educational levels. About 50 percent of our original sample was pursuing advanced studies in 2012, including university courses; the figure rises slightly to 54 percent in the replacement sample and 57 percent among native-parentage respondents. The slight advantage in favor of the latter is also apparent

TABLE 50   EDUCATIONAL OUTCOMES BY GENERATION IN SPAIN, 2012

| Outcome | Children of immigrants (second generation) | | Children of natives (third generation or higher) | | |
|---|---|---|---|---|---|
| | Original sample (%) | Replacement sample (%) | Boys (%) | Girls (%) | Total (%) |
| School enrollment: | | | | | |
|   Basic secondary (ESO) | 32.5 | 18.7 | 19.9 | 19.6 | 19.7 |
|   Remedial studies (PCPI) | 2.7 | 11.0 | 5.8 | 2.5 | 4.3 |
|   Advanced secondary and university | 49.6 | 54.0 | 53.3 | 62.3 | 57.4 |
| Educational aspirations: | | | | | |
|   Low (secondary or less) | 44.9 | 35.8 | 40.3 | 23.9 | 32.79 |
|   High (university degree and postgraduate studies) | 55.1 | 64.2 | 59.7 | 76.1 | 67.2 |
| Educational expectations: | | | | | |
|   Low (secondary or less) | 54.1 | 50.8 | 52.3 | 38.1 | 45.7 |
|   High (university degree and postgraduate studies) | 45.9 | 49.2 | 47.7 | 61.9 | 54.3 |
| Average school grade (1–10) | 6.15 | 6.19 | 6.39 | 6.71 | 6.54 |
| Attitudes toward school (1–4) | 3.23 | 3.15 | 3.16 | 3.17 | 3.17 |
| N | 3,807 | 1,528 | 888 | 1,062 | 1,950 |

in the bottom educational categories, but the association between type of sample and schooling is weak.

Similar results are apparent in levels of ambition. Ideal educational aspirations are about 12 percentage points higher among native-parentage youths than among the original second-generation respondents; realistic expectations drop by 10 to 15 percent in both samples. Thus, when it comes to assessing their real chances for high educational achievement, both groups are less optimistic, with only about half of all youths thinking that it is feasible. The difference between native-parentage respondents and the two second-generation samples combined reaches statistical significance, but again the association is not strong. As among children of immigrants, many more native-parentage girls expected to achieve a university degree, 62 percent, as opposed to just 48 percent of boys.

In terms of grades, native-parentage students display an advantage of about .4 points relative to the second generation as a whole. The difference is sizable and statistically significant. It confirms results from the OECD-sponsored Program for International Student Assessment (PISA) surveys of academic achievement in the advanced countries that consistently show a pattern of disadvantage for children of immigrants as a whole.[2] Spanish-parentage girls exhibit the best performance, as indexed by grades, but the natives' advantage holds across both sexes. Although the lag in grades is not overwhelming, it indicates that the second generation as a whole still has some distance to catch up with their Spanish peers.

The disparity in grades does not translate into different assessments of the schools that these youths attend. Consistently, children of immigrants and of natives evaluate their educational centers in the same favorable terms. The difference between both samples is statistically insignificant. Overall, this set of comparisons does not support a second-generation "advantage" perspective, but neither does it lend credibility to pessimistic predictions of non-integration or exclusion. Instead, it is in line with neo-assimilationist views predicting convergence between children of immigrants and those of natives. These averages may conceal, however, significant differences among the various immigrant nationalities. We will consider them after comparing these results with those obtained in the United States.

CROSS-NATIONAL COMPARISONS

School abandonment was measured in CILS by two variables supplied by the Miami/Ft. Lauderdale and San Diego educational districts: "inactive," meaning that the student was no longer attending school; and "drop out," meaning that the student was officially registered as having abandoned his/her studies. By the first indicator, the proportion of second-generation students leaving school in late adolescence was about the same in the United States as in Spain.[3] Figure 9 presents the U.S. results, broken down by nationality. As shown in the figure, inactivity ranged from a high of 25 percent among Mexican origin students to 13 percent among Chinese and Koreans.

Official dropout rates were much lower, averaging about 7 percent, although the rank order among nationalities was about the same: highest for Mexicans (8.5 percent) and lowest for Chinese and Koreans (2.5 percent). Comparing nationalities with a sizable number of cases in

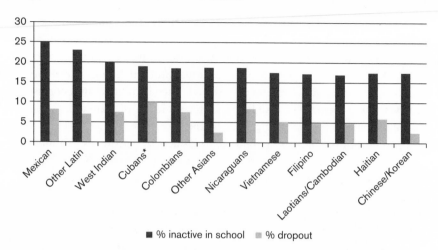

% inactive in school ▣ % dropout

*Cuban students in public schools only; no data for those attending private schools.

FIGURE 9. Indicators of School Attrition in the United States by Nationality, 1995.
Source: Miami/Ft. Lauderdale and San Diego Public School Systems, 1996.

both Spain and the United States, Colombian-origin students register about the same inactivity rates (18 percent) in both countries; however, the Filipino rate was almost double in the United States (18 versus 10 percent). By contrast, the Chinese were much more likely to leave school in Spain (22 versus 13 percent), a pattern that supports the previously noted entrepreneurial orientation among youngsters of this nationality.

Comparisons of grade-point averages are made difficult by the different grade scales used in both countries: 0–10 in Spain, and 0–4 in the United States. To explore possible similarities and differences, we transformed average grades reported in CILS, multiplying them by a factor of 2.5 (10/4). The average transformed grade in the CILS sample was 6.3; this is very close to the ILSEG average of 6.15.[4] Figure 10 presents grade averages for the total sample in both countries and for the five largest nationalities represented in each. For the Latin American groups, the comparison yields a notable similarity in average performance—all below the mean of their respective national samples. The total average is pushed upward in both countries by the Chinese, Filipinos, and other Asian groups, but the achievement gap in favor of these groups is much greater in the United States. Despite differences in time and grading scales, the gap illustrates again the greater selectivity of Asian flows coming to America. A large proportion of these nationalities is com-

Educational Goals and Achievements | 155

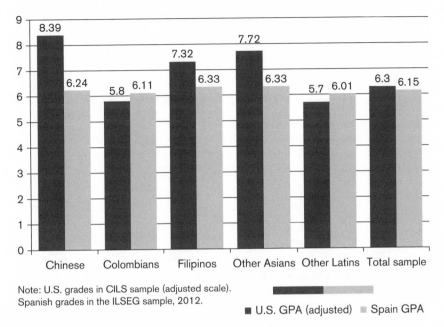

Note: U.S. grades in CILS sample (adjusted scale).
Spanish grades in the ILSEG sample, 2012.

 ■ U.S. GPA (adjusted) ▨ Spain GPA

FIGURE 10. Average Grades in Spain and in the United States.

posed of professionals and other high-level immigrants. Their children perform accordingly.[5]

Similarities cease when we consider the topic of educational ambition. In principle, the 68 percent who aspired to graduate from college or attain a postgraduate degree among second-generation youths in Spain appears high (see Table 49), but it pales by comparison with the 90.1 percent who did so in the United States a decade earlier. In both countries, women held a considerable advantage over their male peers; however, in Spain, female high aspirations (university degree or more) reached 77 percent, whereas the parallel CILS figure was 93 percent.[6]

Comparable data for realistic expectations yield the same conclusion. As noted before, high expectations drop 10 percentage points to 57 percent of the total second-generation sample in Spain and to 65 percent among females. In the United States, the corresponding figures also declined to 82 percent in the full sample and 85 percent among females. Thus, *realistic* expectations for a university degree were actually higher in the United States than *idealistic* aspirations in Spain a decade later. Since, as shown by the literature reviewed in Chapter 2, ambition plays a decisive role in attainment, the observed gap points to a likely more modest educational profile of the Spanish second generation in years to come.

## DETERMINANTS OF EDUCATIONAL OUTCOMES

*Ali, Spanish-born from Moroccan parents, Madrid (Alcorcón), April 2014.*[7] Ali's parents came to Spain twenty-five years ago. His father came from the Rif mountains in northern Morocco, and his mother was born in Tangier. Neither had an education. They met in Spain and married. His father worked in construction, and his mother worked cleaning houses. They have five children; Ali is the oldest. He is completing his second year of chemical engineering at the elite Carlos Tercero University of Madrid. He chose sciences in the last year of basic secondary and then the same subject in senior high school (*bachillerato en Ciencias*). He passed the high school examinations on the first try and obtained a high enough score in the national university entrance examinations (*Selectividad*) to be able to enter his chosen career at a top university.

Ali is a devout Muslim and still identifies himself as Moroccan, although he plans to live in Spain. He attributes his achievements to his early ambition and the help of his professors in elementary and early secondary school. "I always wanted to go to the university; I wanted to be different, ahead of the pack," he says. He is the only Moroccan among the fifty students in the second year of engineering at his university. By age forty, he would like to be a manager or chief of operations at a large chemical plant, but he would not disdain becoming a college professor. For that, he would need a doctorate—though, for the time being, he is focused on completing his engineering master's degree.

Ali has three brothers and a sister still attending elementary or basic secondary school. He says that he helps them all the time in their studies, "so they have the support that I did not have because my parents could not give it." In his opinion, the main problem of Moroccans in Spain is that they have not achieved enough. "In other countries, like France and Belgium, you find Moroccans who are police officers and even city councilors, but not in Spain." By his own efforts, Ali is seeking to change that situation.

Ali's story provides a suitable entry point into the analysis of determinants of educational outcomes among children of immigrants in Spain, not because he is representative of the mainstream but just the opposite: he is an outlier. As we will see, Moroccans on average do not show exceptional outcomes and indeed suffer from several educational handicaps. But in this immigrant community, as in all others, there are individuals who find a way to move ahead, riding on their own ambition and whatever support they can garner in their environment. For Ali, it was enough to have the support of a few professors in elementary and secondary school to set him on his way.

### School Retention

In this section, we examine determinants of four educational outcomes in late adolescence on the basis of predictors measured in the first survey. Of these outcomes, none was more important than staying in school. As seen previously, about 15 percent of the original ILSEG sample abandoned their studies. To examine determinants of this key result, we ran a series of logistic regressions with school retention as a binary dependent variable and positive coefficients indicating school enrollment. We begin with nationalities of origin, adding objective characteristics of respondents and, then, psychosocial traits. This set of predictors correspond to those advanced by all theoretical models discussed in Chapter 2, with the advantage that they are lagged four years so that causal order can be clearly established. Table 51 lists the full array of predictors used in this series of regressions—though, to avoid clutter, only statistically significant effects are presented. All models use robust standard errors to correct for the school-clustered nature of the sample and list-wise deletion of missing data.[8]

To facilitate interpretation, we present average marginal effects (AMEs) rather than actual coefficients. National origins enter the model as a series of dummy variables for groups who numbered at least fifty cases in the original 2007–8 survey and twenty-five cases in the follow-up; the rest of the sample serves as the reference category. National origins were assigned according to the country of birth of the respondent and, if Spanish-born, according to the country of birth of the parents.[9] Thus, all respondents, including the second generation "proper" (i.e., those born in Spain), were assigned a nationality. The first column of Table 51 shows that, relative to a large and diversified reference category ($N = 1,105$), only three nationality effects are statistically significant. Among the Chinese, the net probability of staying in schools is about 10 percent lower than the rest of the sample; among Dominicans, it is 7 percent less; Peruvian students, on the contrary, display a significant advantage.

TABLE 51  DETERMINANTS OF SCHOOL RETENTION IN THE SPANISH SECOND GENERATION, 2012

| Predictors[1] | I[2] AMEs[5] | I[2] z-ratio | II[3] AMEs[5] | II[3] z-ratio | III[4] AMEs[5] | III[4] z-ratio |
|---|---|---|---|---|---|---|
| National origins: | | | | | | |
| Argentina | | | | | | |
| Bolivia | | | | | .045 | 1.7# |
| Bulgaria | | | | | | |
| Chile | | | | | | |
| China | −.094 | −1.9# | | | | |
| Colombia | | | | | | |
| Dominican Republic | −.067 | −1.8# | | | | |
| Ecuador | | | | | .037 | 2.4* |
| Equatorial Guinea | | | | | | |
| Morocco | | | | | | |
| Peru | .062 | 2.2* | .087 | 2.7** | .088 | 3.2** |
| Philippines | | | | | | |
| Romania | | | | | | |
| Venezuela | | | | | | |
| Objective traits: | | | | | | |
| Age | | | −.062 | −8.0*** | −.048 | −6.3*** |
| Male | | | | | | |
| Spanish-born | | | .088 | 2.6** | .084 | 2.8** |
| Length of Spanish residence | | | | | | |
| Year in school | | | | | | |
| Knowledge of Spanish | | | .029 | 2.0* | | |
| Hours of school homework | | | .036 | 3.4** | .025 | 2.4* |
| Lives in Barcelona | | | | | | |
| Attended public school | | | | | | |
| Family socioeconomic status | | | .025 | 2.5* | | |
| Both parents present | | | | | | |
| Psychosocial traits: | | | | | | |
| Educational expectations:[6] | | | | | | |
| Secondary complete/tech school | | | | | .097 | 5.4*** |
| University degree | | | | | .117 | 5.7*** |
| Post-university title | | | | | .165 | 3.6*** |
| Familism | | | | | −.021 | −1.9# |

*(continued)*

Intergenerational
   relations
Perceptions of
   discrimination
Self-esteem

| | | | |
|---|---|---|---|
| Wald chi square | 22.54# | 211.34*** | 258.15*** |
| Pseudo-$R^2$ | .012 | .110 | .140 |
| N = 2,488 | | | |

1. All predictors measured during the original 2008 survey.

2. National origins only. Limited to nationalities numbering at least fifty cases in the original sample and twenty-five in the follow-up. Other nationalities form the reference category.

3. National origins plus objective predictors.

4. National origins plus objective and psychosocial predictors.

5. Average marginal effects. Only significant effects are presented.

6. Secondary school or lower is the reference category.

\# p < .10

\* p < .05

\*\* p < .01

\*\*\* p < .001

When objective predictors enter the equation, only the Peruvian effect remains significant. With year in school controlled, students older than their respective age cohorts were much less likely to stay in school. Their probability of doing so declined by 6 percent per additional age year. The second generation "proper" are 9 percent more likely to remain in school. As expected, family socioeconomic status, knowledge of Spanish, and hours of homework in early adolescence bear significantly and positively on subsequent retention.

Most of these effects remain unchanged when psychosocial predictors enter the equation, but the final model highlights the decisive role of educational expectations. Each step up in expectations in the 2008 survey yielded a strong improvement in the probability of remaining in school four years later. For example, those expecting a postgraduate degree in basic secondary were 16 percent more likely to have remained in school relative to the rest of the sample. The inclusion of all predictors improves the fit of the model, producing a respectable pseudo-$R^2$ of .140. Peruvian and Ecuadorean youths now register significantly greater probabilities of remaining in school. The Ecuadorian effect is weak, but the Peruvian one remains highly significant even when all other predictors are controlled.

The analysis of school attrition among children of immigrants in the United States yielded similar results, again pointing to a pattern of cross-national convergence. In the United States, older students relative to their respective class cohorts were also at much greater risk of abandoning their studies—each additional year reducing the likelihood of school retention by 4 percent. As in Spain, being native-born significantly increased school retention (by 4 percent), and each additional year of U.S. residence did so by a net 3 percent. Most importantly, educational ambition, measured by expectations in early adolescence, had the same key role in both countries: each additional step in the CILS four-level educational expectations scale reduced school attrition by a net 2 percent, even after controlling for grade-point average in early adolescence.[10]

## School Placement

Before discussing the theoretical implications of these findings, we examine the type of schooling that second-generation youths are enrolled in. As noted previously, it makes a great deal of difference if they are still trying to complete basic secondary or enrolled in remedial courses, as opposed to pursuing advanced secondary education or university studies. For this analysis, we first used ordered multinomial regression, defining basic secondary and remedial studies as the base category and estimating models for the higher levels of enrollment. We then combined the two highest levels (advanced secondary and university) and estimated the model with logistic regression. Table 52 presents results of this analysis plus the final results of the multinomial model predicting the highest (university) enrollment.[11] As before, missing data are deleted list-wise, and all non-significant coefficients are excluded.

Chilean children, plus Filipinos and Moroccans, are much less likely to be enrolled in advanced secondary or university studies. This result confirms the exceptional character of Ali's story. Only Chinese students significantly exceed the sample average, with a 24 percent higher probability of doing so. This implies that the minority of second-generation Chinese who persisted in their studies have advanced well ahead of other nationalities. When other predictors enter the equation, the Moroccan negative effect declines and the Filipino effect disappears, but the Chinese positive coefficient remains highly significant.

Other significant predictors of educational placement are age, gender, family status, family composition, and early educational expectations. The strong effect of school year is a straightforward function of the greater likelihood that students originally interviewed in the last (third) year of basic secondary schooling were more likely to reach higher grades later on. This predictor functions only as a control, with-

| Predictors | Binary logistic regression[1] | | | | Ordered multinomial regression[2] | |
| | I[3] | | II[4] | | III[5] | |
| | AMEs | z-ratio | AMEs | z-ratio | Coeff. | z-ratio |
|---|---|---|---|---|---|---|
| National origins:[6] | | | | | | |
| Argentina | | | | | | |
| Bolivia | | | | | | |
| Bulgaria | | | | | | |
| Chile | −.256 | −2.8** | −.250 | −3.4** | | |
| China | .242 | 3.0** | .223 | 3.4** | 3.00 | 4.2*** |
| Colombia | | | | | | |
| Dominican Republic | | | | | | |
| Ecuador | | | −.045 | −1.8# | | |
| Equatorial Guinea | | | | | | |
| Morocco | −.186 | −3.8*** | −.073 | −1.9# | | |
| Peru | | | | | | |
| Philippines | −.136 | −2.0# | | | 1.89 | 2.2* |
| Romania | | | | | | |
| Venezuela | | | | | | |
| Objective traits: | | | | | | |
| Age | | | −.049 | −3.6*** | | |
| Male | | | −.072 | −3.9*** | −.90 | −3.3** |
| Spanish-born | | | | | | |
| Length of Spanish residence | | | | | | |
| Year in school | | | .282 | 13.8*** | 4.74 | 12.0*** |
| Knowledge of Spanish | | | .038 | 1.7# | 0.87 | 2.6* |
| Hours of school homework | | | | | | |
| Lives in Barcelona | | | −.225 | −8.3*** | −3.11 | −7.0*** |
| Attended public school | | | | | | |
| Family socioeconomic status | | | .033 | 2.5* | .41 | 2.3* |
| Both parents present | | | .083 | 3.8*** | .97 | 2.9** |
| Psychosocial traits: | | | | | | |
| Educational expectations:[7] | | | | | | |
| Secondary complete/tech school | | | .125 | 4.8*** | | |
| University degree | | | .190 | 7.0*** | .95 | 2.5* |
| Post-university title | | | .248 | 5.9*** | 1.24 | 2.3* |

(continued)

TABLE 52 *(continued)*

| Predictors | Binary logistic regression[1] | | | | Ordered multino-mial regression[2] | |
|---|---|---|---|---|---|---|
| | I[3] | | II[4] | | III[5] | |
| | AMEs | z-ratio | AMEs | z-ratio | Coeff. | z-ratio |
| Familism | | | −.041 | −2.8** | | |
| Intergenerational relations | | | | | | |
| Perceptions of discrimination | | | | | −.53 | 1.9# |
| Self-esteem | | | | | | |
| Wald chi square | 49.58*** | | 497.21*** | | 596.36*** | |
| Pseudo-R[2] | .018 | | .248 | | .367 | |
| N = 2,130 | | | | | | |

1. Probability of attending advanced secondary, superior technical school or university.

2. University only. Multinomial logistic coefficients.

3. National origins only. Non-significant effects excluded.

4. National origins plus all other predictors. Non-significant effects excluded.

5. National origins plus all other predictors. Non-significant effects excluded.

6. Limited to nationalities numbering at least fifty cases in the original survey and twenty-five cases in the follow-up. Other nationalities form the reference category.

7. Basic secondary or lower is the reference category.

\# = p < .10

\* = p < .05

\*\* = p < .01

\*\*\* = p < .001

out any theoretical implication. With that control in place, age has a significant negative effect, implying that students older than their respective cohort back in basic secondary school are much less likely to reach an advanced education. Gender functions the same way, as seen previously with females being 7 percent more likely to reach advanced secondary schooling or the university. As expected, families with both parents present and those of higher socioeconomic status have positive and strong effects on educational placement. According to results in the final model, children with both parents at home improve their probability of advanced placement by 8 percent, and each additional unit in the family socioeconomic status index increases that probability by 3 percent.

Educational expectations in early adolescence again have an extraordinary positive effect on school placement. Each step up in expectations translates into a significantly higher probability of subsequent achievement. For example, the probability of students who aspired to a post-university degree in 2008 to be enrolled in advanced schooling in 2012 is 25 percent higher than others, net of all other predictors. Results also indicate a significant negative effect for residents of Barcelona. We do not believe that this reflects a substantial disadvantage for students in that city but, rather, that it is a function of the way the sample was drawn. Many more first-year secondary students were included in the original 2008 sample in Barcelona than in Madrid. As also indicated by the school year coefficient, those attending earlier secondary years during the original survey were less likely to have reached advanced schooling by the second. As such, this result carries no meaningful substantive implications.

If we focus on the small minority who have reached the university (col. III), results are similar with a few differences. The Chinese educational advantage persists, and now they are joined by Filipinos, though that effect is weaker. The age effect disappears, but others remain, including the positive coefficients associated with educational expectations. In this final model, experiences of discrimination in early adolescence has a negative effect on educational placement four years later, a result in line with past theoretical predictions.[12]

## Grades

A third major educational outcome are school grades. We asked for top and average grades, and we model the latter in this section. To neutralize for a highly skewed grade distribution, we logged this variable. Since the resulting scale is continuous, we modeled it with ordinary least squares and robust standard errors. In logged form, coefficients indicate the approximate net percent gain or loss associated with a unit change in each predictor. Results are presented in Table 53. Relative to the reference category, a number of Latin American nationalities, such as Bolivians, Colombians, Dominicans, and Ecuadoreans, receive significantly lower grades. Equatorial Guineans display the greatest disadvantage, with grades 14 percent lower than others in the sample.

The large reference category for this analysis is composed of smaller European, Middle Eastern, and Asian nationalities that tend to perform better in school. This explains the relative disadvantage of Latin American and African youths. On the opposite side, Romanians exhibit a significant positive net effect. This effect persists and actually increases

TABLE 53   DETERMINANTS OF AVERAGE SECONDARY SCHOOL GRADES (LOGGED) AMONG CHILDREN OF IMMIGRANTS IN SPAIN, 2012

| Predictors[1] | I[2] Coeff.[5] | t-ratio | II[3] Coeff.[5] | t-ratio | III[4] Coeff.[5] | t-ratio |
|---|---|---|---|---|---|---|
| National origins:[6] | | | | | | |
| Argentina | | | | | | |
| Bolivia | −.075 | −3.1** | −.059 | −2.4* | −.052 | −2.1* |
| Bulgaria | | | | | | |
| Chile | | | | | | |
| China | | | .066 | 2.4* | .076 | 2.9** |
| Colombia | −.048 | −2.1* | | | | |
| Dominican Republic | −.075 | −3.0** | −.061 | −2.3* | −.045 | −1.7# |
| Ecuador | −.044 | −3.0** | | | | |
| Equatorial Guinea | −.145 | −2.5* | −.121 | −2.0* | −.112 | −1.9# |
| Morocco | | | | | | |
| Peru | −.039 | −1.8# | −.039 | −1.9# | | |
| Philippines | | | | | | |
| Romania | .038 | 1.8# | .046 | 2.1* | .053 | 2.5* |
| Venezuela | | | | | | |
| Objective traits: | | | | | | |
| Age | | | −.017 | −3.0** | | |
| Male | | | −.043 | −4.4*** | −.038 | −3.9*** |
| Spanish-born | | | | | | |
| Length of Spanish residence | | | −.003 | −2.1* | | |
| Year in school | | | | | | |
| Knowledge of Spanish | | | .046 | 4.2*** | .030 | 2.7** |
| Hours of school homework | | | .024 | 3.9***. | 017 | 2.9** |
| Lives in Barcelona | | | −.022 | −1.8# | | |
| Attended public school | | | | | | |
| Family socioeconomic status | | | .029 | 4.2*** | .022 | 3.1** |
| Both parents present | | | | | | |
| Psychosocial traits: | | | | | | |
| Educational expectations:[7] | | | | | | |
| Secondary complete/tech school | | | | | | |
| University degree | | | | | .057 | 4.3*** |
| Post-university title | | | | | .106 | 5.4*** |
| Familism | | | | | −.020 | −2.8** |
| Intergenerational relations | | | | | .014 | 1.7# |
| Perceptions of discrimination | | | | | | |
| Self-esteem | | | | | | |

TABLE 53   *(continued)*

| | | | |
|---|---|---|---|
| Constant | 1.83 | 1.88 | 1.76 |
| F-test | 3.61*** | 7.38*** | 8.40*** |
| $R^2$ | .018 | .060 | .082 |
| N = 2,447 | | | |

1. All predictors measured during the original survey.

2. Predictors limited to national origins.

3. Predictors include national origins and objective characteristics.

4. Predictors include national origins and all objective and psychosocial characteristics.

5. Unstandardized ordinary least squares regression coefficients. Non-significant effects excluded.

6. Limited to nationalities numbering at least fifty cases in the original survey and twenty-five cases in the follow-up. Other nationalities form the reference category.

7. Basic secondary or lower is the reference category.

# = p < .10

* = p < .05

** = p < .01

*** = p < .001

when other predictors enter the equation. In the next models, Romanians are joined by the Chinese in displaying higher relative grades. As already noted, Chinese youths who have persisted in their studies tend to perform significantly better than others.

In the final model, major effects on grades are associated with several objective predictors (gender, knowledge of Spanish, school homework, and family socioeconomic status) as well as two subjective variables (early educational expectations and familism). In the familiar pattern, females continue to have a significant academic advantage equivalent to about 4 percent net of other predictors. Better knowledge of Spanish significantly improves grades, as do more hours spent on academic homework in early adolescence. Both effects are predictable and point to a patterned process of academic achievement; equally expected is the positive effect of family status.

No other variable, however, has a stronger effect on grades than early ambition. Expectations of a university degree in 2008 raised grades four years later by 6 percent on average. Aiming at a postgraduate degree increased that figure to 11 percent. The story of Ali above illustrates well this key effect. Yet familism has a significant negative effect on grades, again indicating that a particularistic preference for family members over others does not bode well for academic performance. With other predictors controlled, negative grade effects persist for youths of Bolivian and Dominican origin, as well as Guineans. The size of the Guineans' net handicap, equivalent to 11 percent lower grades, is worthy of additional future investigation.[13]

These results can also be compared with those obtained by CILS in the United States. Again, we observe a number of notable similarities. In the American case, grades (in the original 0–4 U.S. scale) were not logged but were directly modeled with least squares regression. As in Spain, girls displayed a highly significant advantage, equivalent to a net 0.3 higher grade; older students also suffered a significant handicap equivalent to .05 lower grade for each additional age year. Family socioeconomic status again had a positive bearing on academic performance, which in the American case was reinforced by family structure: two-parent families raised average grades by a net .19.[14]

In both countries, knowledge of the host country language had a significant positive influence. The most important common effect, however, corresponds to ambition. Next to gender, educational expectations in early adolescence had the strongest influence on late high school grades in the United States: each additional step in the four-level expectations scale used in CILS increased net grades by .20. With other predictors in the equation controlled, children of Chinese and Korean origin in America excelled, displaying a net gain equivalent to .88 higher grades. They were followed by the Vietnamese, also with a strong positive effect. Mexican-origin students, however, suffered a handicap comparable to Equatorial Guineans in Spain, a net -.23 grades.[15]

These comparative results again indicate strong commonalities in determinants of educational achievement despite differences in time, social context, and measurement of the dependent variable. Such differences, in fact, reinforce the validity of these conclusions by showing that they are not linked to a particular context or measurement model. In both countries, differences in human capital and modes of incorporation of immigrant nationalities had significant and consistent effects on children's performance, reinforcing the major effects of children's gender and their own ambition.

## Attitudes toward School

Finally, we considered determinants of school attitudes on the assumption that a more positive outlook toward academic centers should generally reflect better adaptation outcomes in the second generation. Since the dependent variable is also continuous, we modeled it with ordinary least squares and robust standard errors. Results are presented in

Table 54. Few nationalities differ significantly in this variable, reflecting the rather homogenous and generally positive approach toward schools in the sample. Bolivian and Chinese students display the most critical attitudes, these effects being of comparable size.

Few individual predictors have any influence on this outcome, but those that do are revealing. Among objective predictors, positive influences on school attitudes are associated with length of residence in Spain, school year, and family socioeconomic status. Students with longer residence in the country and those in later school years in the original 2008 survey have more favorable orientations toward their academic centers. As seen previously, respondents originally interviewed in the third year of basic secondary school were more likely to have moved toward advanced secondary or the university by the time of the follow-up. Enrollment in these more select institutions, away from those that dispense basic secondary instruction, may plausibly account for their more favorable orientations.

Among psychosocial predictors in the final model, intergenerational relations and early experiences of discrimination have sizable effects running in opposite directions: better relations with parents in early adolescence lead to more favorable school attitudes, arguably reflecting the influence of the principal institution in adolescent life—the family— on the second—the school. Early experiences of discrimination lead, on the contrary, to a more critical stance.

This pattern of effects is similar to that found for other psychosocial dimensions of adaptation in the preceding chapter. It is also congruent with predictions of segmented assimilation theory concerning the positive and protective role of good intergenerational relations and the negative one of external discrimination. In Chapter 6, we saw how the trials of adaptation to a foreign land had a negative bearing on relations between Chinese adolescents and their parents. Now, we see that this pattern also bears negatively on Chinese school attitudes. Hence, despite having advanced most academically, Chinese students join Bolivians, one of the least advantaged nationalities, in being the most critical of their educational experiences in Spain.

Taking stock of results so far, we note that they do not support any general tendency toward second-generation "advantage," but neither do they reflect a trend toward exclusion. In support of assimilationist views, there is a clear convergence of educational outcomes between second-generation and native-parentage youths, with premature abandonment of school being exceptional in both cases. However, as we

TABLE 54   DETERMINANTS OF SCHOOL ATTITUDES AMONG SECOND-GENERATION
YOUTHS IN SPAIN, 2012

| Predictors[1] | I[2] | | II[3] | | III[4] | |
|---|---|---|---|---|---|---|
| | Coeff.[5] | t-ratio | Coeff.[5] | t-ratio | Coeff.[5] | t-ratio |
| National origins:[6] | | | | | | |
| Argentina | | | | | | |
| Bolivia | −.171 | −3.2** | −.137 | −2.4* | −.137 | −2.4* |
| Bulgaria | | | | | | |
| Chile | | | | | | |
| China | −.204 | −2.6* | −.201 | −2.6** | −.181 | −2.3* |
| Colombia | | | | | | |
| Dominican Republic | | | | | | |
| Ecuador | | | | | | |
| Equatorial Guinea | | | | | | |
| Morocco | | | | | | |
| Peru | | | | | | |
| Philippines | | | | | | |
| Romania | | | | | | |
| Venezuela | | | | | | |
| Objective traits: | | | | | | |
| Age | | | | | | |
| Male | | | | | | |
| Spanish-born | | | | | | |
| Length of Spanish residence | | | .009 | 2.7** | .009 | 2.8** |
| Year in school | | | .038 | 1.9# | | |
| Knowledge of Spanish | | | | | | |
| Hours of school homework | | | | | | |
| Lives in Barcelona | | | | | | |
| Attended public school | | | | | | |
| Family socioeconomic status | | | .030 | 2.1* | | |
| Both parents present | | | | | | |
| Psychosocial traits: | | | | | | |
| Educational expectations:[7] | | | | | | |
| Secondary complete/tech school | | | | | | |
| University degree | | | | | | |
| Post-university title | | | | | | |
| Familism | | | | | | |
| Intergenerational relations | | | | | .039 | 2.1* |
| Perceptions of discrimination | | | | | −.050 | −2.2* |

TABLE 54 *(continued)*

| | | | |
|---|---|---|---|
| Constant | 3.26 | 3.15 | 3.08 |
| F-test | 1.99* | 2.85*** | 2.70*** |
| $R^2$ | .015 | .034 | .044 |
| N = 1,944 | | | |

1. All predictors measured during the original survey, 2007–8.

2. Predictors limited to national origins.

3. Predictors include national origins and objective characteristics.

4. Predictors include national origins and all objective and psychosocial characteristics.

5. Unstandardized ordinary least squares regression coefficients. Non-significant effects excluded.

6. Limited to nationalities numbering at least fifty cases in the original sample and twenty-five in the follow-up. Other nationalities form the reference category.

7. Basic secondary or lower is the reference category.

\# = p < .10

\* = p < .05

\*\* = p < .01

\*\*\* = p < .001

focus on the more demanding indicators of attainment—grades and enrollment in advanced courses—differences start to emerge that reflect the role of core background factors, in particular family socioeconomic status, family composition, and parental modes of incorporation. These effects, made clear by patterned differences among various nationalities, are congruent with the predictions of segmented assimilation.

Worth noting are the numerous convergencies between the findings of ILSEG in Spain and those of CILS in the United States a decade earlier. These range from indicators of school attrition to academic grades and determinants of these outcomes. In both countries, females display a consistent advantage, and students older than their class peers experience a significant handicap. In both, the Chinese who stay in school and other Asian groups perform better academically, whereas nationalities characterized by a negative mode of incorporation—Mexicans in the United States; Bolivians, Dominicans, and sub-Saharan Africans in Spain—do significantly worse. These similarities point to the common influence of key determinants of educational adaptation in the second generation and, by extension, the cross-national validity of specific theories.

## PARENTAL INFLUENCES ON EDUCATIONAL OUTCOMES

As seen in Chapter 2, a strong and consistent finding in the research literature is that parental human capital and, for immigrants, the educational levels brought from the home country play a decisive role in molding children's aspirations.[16] The same literature predicts that a good portion of the family status influence on adolescent aspirations will be mediated by the parents' own ambition. Claudia Buchman and Ben Dalton compared the effects of parents' educational aspirations on their children's orientation in twelve countries. Their findings support the prediction advanced in Chapter 2 of significant effects of parental goals in countries with "relatively undifferentiated" secondary school systems. In those with strong tracking systems, parents' influence made less of a difference because of the decisive role of the type of school attended in adolescence.[17]

Overwhelmingly, studies of youths' aspirations and their determinants have depended on students' reports of their families' characteristics, including parental goals. However, student reports are subject to the danger of endogeneity, as the students' own orientations can color their reports of their parents' views. As seen previously, ILSEG included an independent parental survey that provides a decisive advantage in allowing us to examine parental effects on their children's ambition and educational attainment independently of students' own reports. Furthermore, unlike other European countries, Spain does not track students at an early age.[18] It is thus possible for youths to plan alternative career paths for themselves and for parents to affect these plans.

In Chapter 5, we examined levels of ambition and their determinants in the parental sample. Here we wish to investigate how they affect their children's own goals. Further, we wish to examine the extent to which parental characteristics affect educational outcomes in late adolescence before and after controlling for their offspring's own characteristics. Table 55 answers the first question by presenting the influence of parental predictors on children's educational aspirations and expectations before and after controlling for the child's own traits. The sample is restricted to matched cases containing data from the original student survey and the independent parental sample. Figures in the table come from a series of ordered logistic regressions.[19]

Results confirm the strong influence of family socioeconomic status and parental ambition on the students' own goals. As shown in the table, parents' realistic expectations are consistently more important than idealistic goals in affecting those of their children. Figure 11 summarizes these findings by presenting a synthetic structural equations model based on the same analysis. For this model, we constructed two latent variables: "parents' ambition" as a function of parents' own educational aspirations and expectations, and "child's ambition" as a function of their future educational and occupational goals.

TABLE 55  DETERMINANTS OF EDUCATIONAL ASPIRATIONS AND EXPECTATIONS
AMONG SECOND-GENERATION YOUTHS IN SPAIN, 2009–10

| Predictors[1] | I | | II | |
|---|---|---|---|---|
| | Coeff.[2] | z-ratio | Coeff.[2] | z-ratio |
| | Aspirations | | | |
| **Parents:** | | | | |
| Age | | | | |
| Gender (female) | | | | |
| Years of Spanish residence | | | | |
| Nationality (Spanish) | | | | |
| Both parents present | | | −.233 | −1.99* |
| Socioeconomic status (PSES) | .473 | 6.43* | .373 | 4.40*** |
| Knowledge of Spanish (PKSI) | | | | |
| School involvement (PSII) | | | | |
| Educational aspirations | .205 | 2.63** | .145 | 1.72# |
| Educational expectations | .607 | 9.93*** | .479 | 7.18*** |
| **Children:** | | | | |
| Age | | | −.505 | −7.21*** |
| Gender (Male) | | | −.390 | −3.82*** |
| Birthplace (Spain) | | | | |
| School type (private) | | | | |
| Year in school | | | .310 | 3.11** |
| Knowledge of Spanish (KSI) | | | .608 | 5.93*** |
| City of residence (Barcelona) | | | | |
| **National origin:[3]** | | | | |
| Argentina | | | | |
| Ecuador | | | | |
| Peru | | | −.442 | −2.35* |
| Wald chi square | 263.80 | | 391.07 | |
| Pseudo-R² | .065 | | .106 | |
| N | 1,636 | | 1,576 | |
| | Expectations | | | |
| **Parents:** | | | | |
| Age | | | | |
| Gender (female) | | | | |
| Years of Spanish residence | −.001 | 1.80# | | |
| Nationality (Spanish) | | | | |
| Both parents present | | | | |
| Socioeconomic status (PSES) | .005 | 4.70*** | .259 | 3.23*** |
| Knowledge of Spanish (PKSI) | | | | |
| School involvement (PSII) | | | | |
| Educational aspirations | .208 | 2.54* | | |
| Educational expectations | .611 | 9.93*** | .506 | 7.58*** |

*(continued)*

TABLE 55 *(continued)*

| Predictors[1] | I | | II | |
|---|---|---|---|---|
| | *Coeff.*[2] | *z-ratio* | *Coeff.*[2] | *z-ratio* |
| Children: | | | | |
| Age | | | −.438 | 6.39*** |
| Gender (male) | | | | |
| Birthplace (Spain) | | | | |
| School type (private) | | | | |
| Year in school | | | .311 | 3.08*** |
| Knowledge of Spanish (KSI) | | | .603 | 5.97*** |
| City of residence (Barcelona) | | | | |
| National origin:[3] | | | | |
| Argentina | | | −.710 | −2.09* |
| Ecuador | | | −.522 | −2.91** |
| Peru | | | −.527 | −2.38* |
| Wald chi square | 78.80*** | | 348.52*** | |
| Pseudo-R² | .018 | | .089 | |
| N | 1,651 | | 1,563 | |

1. All predictors measured in the original student and parental surveys.

2. Ordered logistic regression coefficients. Only significant effects presented.

3. Dummy variables for fourteen different nationalities were included in Step II; only significant coefficients are presented.

\# p < .10

\* p < .05

\*\* p < .01

\*\*\* p < .001

The model provides a good fit to the data indicating that the parents' ambition has the strongest influence on children's own goals exceeding those of all other significant predictors—child's age, gender, and knowledge of Spanish.[20] The model accords with predictions of the Wisconsin Status Attainment theory and may actually be interpreted as a Spanish re-actualization of that model. Results are also in line with one of the basic predictions of segmented assimilation concerning the positive roles of parental human capital and positive intergenerational relations.

To answer the second question—the extent to which parental characteristics affect educational outcomes in late adolescence—we re-ran models of determinants of three key outcomes (school retention, type of school attended, and academic grades) on parental as well as children's predictors. As before, the first two outcomes are dichotomies and are modeled with logistic regression; the third is a continuous variable

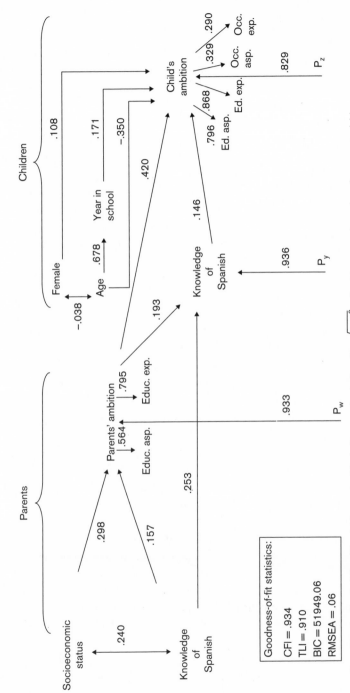

Note: Standardized effects. P variables are residual effects, estimated as $P_i = \sqrt{1-R^2_{.i}}$, where i represents each endogenous variable.

FIGURE 11. A Structural Model of Ambition in the Spanish Second Generation.
Source: Portes et al., "Dreaming in Spain", fig. 1.

(logged grades) and is modeled with ordinary least squares. Only cases with full information in the original survey, the parental survey, and the follow-up are included. The first column of each nested model includes parental predictors only; the second adds children's variables, including national origin. Results are presented in Table 56. To avoid clutter, only significant effects are included.

The first model for each outcome makes clear that parental ambition has the predicted positive and significant effect on all indicators of academic achievement. To avoid co-linearity, only parental educational expectations—shown previously to be the stronger predictor—are included. Children of parents who expected them to reach at least a university degree are 14 percent more likely to remain in school, net of other variables. Further, children of parents who expected them to achieve a postgraduate education have a 27 percent greater probability to be enrolled in advanced secondary or university courses. These children's academic grades at the time of the follow-up survey were 10 percent higher than their peers.

Parental socioeconomic status also displays the predicted positive effects on type of school attended and grades, although the latter effect disappears when children's predictors enter the equation. This is not the case for parental expectations whose effects, albeit reduced, remain positive and significant in all dependent variables even when children's own ambition level and other variables are included.

Two other findings deserve mention. First, parental knowledge of Spanish has a *negative* effect on grades. This result is partially due to the superior command of the language by Latin American parents, many of whom come from lower socioeconomic origins. When national origins enter the equation, this negative effect is significantly reduced. As predicted, the net influence of children's own command of Spanish on grades is both positive and significant. Second, with all parental and children's predictors controlled, several Andean nationalities display a positive effect on remaining in school. These effects disappear, however, when advanced school enrollment or grades are considered. In these last models, the only sizable national origin effect corresponds to the Chinese. Once more, Chinese youths who have persisted in their studies are significantly more likely to be enrolled in advanced courses and to receive higher grades than their peers.

National differences aside, the principal story in Table 56 is the resilient effects of parental ambition on academic achievement. Children's own expectations have a consistently stronger influence, a predictable

TABLE 56  PARENTAL AND CHILDREN'S INFLUENCES ON INDICATORS OF ACADEMIC ACHIEVEMENT, SECOND-GENERATION YOUTHS IN SPAIN, 2010

| Predictors[1] | Enrolled in school | | | | Enrolled in advanced secondary or university | | | | Average academic grades (logged) | | | |
|---|---|---|---|---|---|---|---|---|---|---|---|---|
| | I[2] | | II[3] | | I[2] | | II[3] | | I[4] | | II[5] | |
| | AMEs | z-ratio | AMEs | z-ratio | AMEs | z-ratio | AMEs | z-ratio | Coeff. | t-ratio | Coeff. | t-ratio |
| **Parents** | | | | | | | | | | | | |
| Age | | | | | .007 | 2.5* | | | | | | |
| Male | | | | | | | | | .003 | 1.8# | | |
| Years of Spanish res. | | | | | | | | | | | | |
| Spanish nationality | | | | | | | | | | | | |
| Married | | | | | | | | | | | | |
| Knowledge of Spanish | | | | | .074 | 2.8** | -.041 | 2.0* | -.032 | -2.0* | | |
| Socioeconomic status | | | | | | | .045 | | .028 | 2.0* | | |
| Educ. expectations: | | | | | | | | | | | | |
| Univ. degree | .136 | 4.6*** | | | .228 | 6.0*** | .180 | 5.2*** | .027 | 1.7# | | |
| Post-college title | .172 | 3.4** | | | .272 | 4.7*** | .163 | 3.1** | .100 | 3.3** | .061 | 2.0* |
| **Children** | | | | | | | | | | | | |
| Objective traits: | | | | | | | | | | | | |
| Age | | | -.054 | -3.25** | | | -.051 | -2.7** | | | | |
| Male | | | | | | | -.048 | -1.7# | | | -.024 | -1.8# |
| School year | | | | | | | 2.78 | 10.7*** | | | | |
| Years of Spanish residence | | | | | | | | | | | | |
| Knowledge of Spanish | | | | | | | | | | | .041 | 2.7** |
| Barcelona residence | | | -.071 | -1.8# | | | -.224 | -6.3*** | | | | |
| Public school | | | | | | | | | | | | |
| Psychosocial traits: | | | | | | | | | | | | |
| Self-esteem | | | .070 | 2.3* | | | | | | | .035 | 2.0* |

TABLE 56 (continued)

| Predictors[1] | Enrolled in school | | | | Enrolled in advanced secondary or university | | | | Average academic grades (logged) | | | |
|---|---|---|---|---|---|---|---|---|---|---|---|---|
| | $I^2$ | | $II^3$ | | $I^2$ | | $II^3$ | | $I^4$ | | $II^5$ | |
| | AMEs | z-ratio | AMEs | z-ratio | AMEs | z-ratio | AMEs | z-ratio | Coeff. | t-ratio | Coeff. | t-ratio |
| Familism | | | | | | | | | | | −.035 | −2.9* |
| Educational expectations: | | | | | | | | | | | | |
| Advanced secondary | | | .072 | 2.0* | | | .159 | 4.1*** | | | | |
| University degree | | | .128 | 3.4** | | | .199 | 4.6*** | | | | |
| Postgraduate title | | | .153 | 2.6* | | | .258 | 4.8*** | | | .081 | 2.4* |
| National origin:[6] | | | | | | | | | | | | |
| Ecuador | | | .099 | 2.2* | | | | | | | | |
| Chile | | | .251 | 2.9** | | | | | | | | |
| Peru | | | .143 | 2.3* | | | | | | | | |
| China | | | | | | | .356 | 5.7*** | | | .071 | 1.7# |
| Wald chi square | 36.20*** | | 96.93*** | | 68.74*** | | 195.07*** | | | | | |
| Pseudo-$R^2$ | .027 | | .081 | | .069 | | .306 | | | | | |
| F | | | | | | | | | 4.55*** | | 3.22*** | |
| $R^2$ | | | | | | | | | .037 | | .101 | |
| N | 1,130 | | | | 799 | | | | 925 | | | |

1. All predictors measured in the original student survey or parental survey.

2. Logistic average marginal effects. Regression limited to parental predictors. Only significant effects are presented.

3. Logistic average marginal effects. Parental and child predictors included. Only significant effects included.

4. Ordinary least squares coefficients with robust standard error. Regression limited to parental predictors. Only significant effects are presented.

5. Ordinary least squares coefficients with robust standard error. Parental and children predictors included. Only significant effects are presented.

6. Dummy variables for all national origins with at least twenty-five cases in the joint sample were included. Only significant effects are presented.

# = p < .10

* = p < .05

** = p < .01

result. However, the key finding is that the effect of parental ambition is not entirely "filtered" by children's own, but it continues to be resilient in late adolescence. This result supports the Wisconsin Status Attainment model concerning the decisive influence of significant others, in particular parents, on children's educational achievement.

## A SYNTHETIC MODEL OF EDUCATIONAL ATTAINMENT

To conclude the analysis, we estimated a synthetic model of educational attainment that makes use of the full information provided by the original and follow-up children's surveys. Having established the continuing influence of parental expectations, we omit parental predictors from this final model because they would drastically reduce sample size, eliminating a large number of otherwise valid cases. We limit the model to objective and psychosocial predictors measured in the original survey that were found to have reliable effects on outcomes in late adolescence. We measured these outcomes on the basis of two latent variables: *ambition,* indicated by four-point scales of educational aspirations and expectations;[21] and *attainment,* indicated by average grades and by a five-point scale of school attendance from "no enrollment" to "university."[22]

All theory requires simplification and, for reasons of clarity and parsimony, we omit several significant but weaker predictors in favor of those shown to have the largest consistent influence on both dependent variables. For the sake of generality, we also exclude national origins in search of a causal model applicable to all children of immigrants.

The model, estimated with the MPLUS routine, includes five objective exogenous variables: age, gender, place of birth, school year in 2007–8, and family socioeconomic status. These predictors affect, in different ways, a first set of endogenous variables that includes knowledge of Spanish, self-esteem, and friends' educational plans. These variables were also measured in the original 2008 survey: knowledge of Spanish and self-esteem are composite indices, described in Chapter 4. Friends' plans is a three-point scale shown in a prior analysis to be a strong correlate of respondents' own level of ambition in early adolescence.[23] With cross-sectional data from the original survey, it was impossible to establish causal order between respondents' own and friends' plans. With the longitudinal data available from the follow-up, it is possible to test unambiguously the hypothesis that friends' educational plans bear on respondents' subsequent ambition level. The hypothesis also draws on the Wisconsin model concerning the influence of friends, as significant others, on both aspirations and attainment.

This array of predictors is then set to bear on the two latent variables measured four years later. The first version of the model adds a causal path from *ambition* to *attainment* corresponding to predictions from the research literature, as well as findings presented earlier. Other predictors of *attainment* include gender, family socioeconomic status, and school year. The model is presented in Figure 12. It is recursive, positing no causal loops and assuming uncorrelated errors among residuals.

Model estimation by the MPLUS routine converged normally and yielded acceptable goodness-of-fit statistics (RMSEA = .064; CFI = .992; TLI = .987). Part of the reason for these positive results is the model's parsimony, since it employs only 36 of the available 56 degrees of freedom in the data.[24] In substantive terms, the model succeeds in accounting for 81 percent of variance in the key dependent variable—*attainment*. Not surprisingly, the strongest predictor by far is *ambition*, whose effect is twelve times its standard error. It is followed by family socioeconomic status and gender. Males, as shown previously, are at a significant educational disadvantage. This effect is also strong, reaching five times its standard error. Early school year also has a strong influence, but this is a straightforward consequence of the greater likelihood that students originally interviewed in later basic secondary years reached advanced placement later on.

The model also succeeds in explaining almost 20 percent of the variance in *ambition*. In this instance, the strongest positive effect corresponds to friends' educational plans. It is followed by positive and sizable effects of knowledge of Spanish and self-esteem, both of which quintuple their respective standard errors. Negative influences are associated with age and gender (male). As shown previously, older students relative to their class cohort tend to adjust their educational expectations downward, with deleterious consequences later in life; males trail females in academic ambition as well as in attainment.

The model provides a good synthesis of causal forces leading to educational achievement in the second generation with one exception: because the two latent variables were measured contemporaneously, there is the real possibility that they influence each other. The theoretical literature that predicts a decisive influence of ambition on academic attainment also points to a reverse effect: success in school tends to encourages higher goals, whereas failure leads to their downward adjustment.[25] This implies a causal loop.

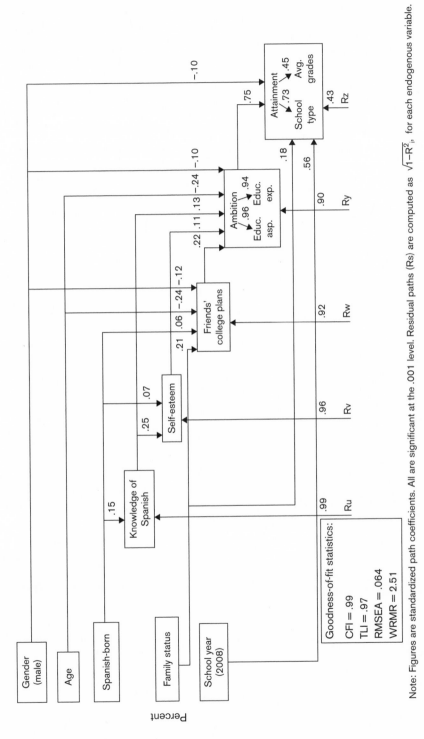

FIGURE 12. A Recursive Causal Model of Educational Attainment in the Spanish Second Generation.

Note: Figures are standardized path coefficients. All are significant at the .001 level. Residual paths (Rs) are computed as $\sqrt{1-R^2_{in}}$, for each endogenous variable.

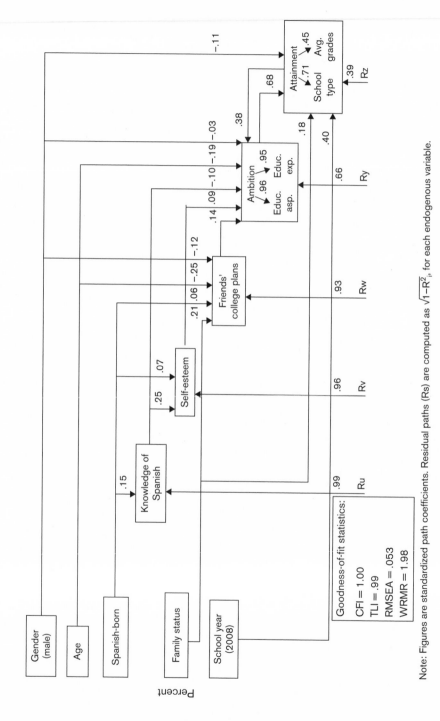

FIGURE 13. A Non-recursive Causal Model of Educational Attainment in the Spanish Second Generation, 2012.

Note: Figures are standardized path coefficients. Residual paths (Rs) are computed as $\sqrt{1-R_i^2}$, for each endogenous variable.

MPLUS allows for estimation of this revised model by adding a reverse path from *attainment* to *ambition*. The estimation routine converged and actually improved the diagnostic tests relative to the first model. This final model is presented in Figure 13. The original causal path from *ambition* to *attainment* continues to be very strong, exceeding twelve times its standard error, but the reverse path is also positive and significant. All other causal paths noted previously remain similar in direction and strength. The CFI and TLI goodness-of-fit tests remain about the same but, crucially, the root mean square error of approximation (RMSEA) that incorporates both the model's fit and its parsimony declines to .05, indicating a fully satisfactory fit.[26] For this reason, this model is adopted as the final synthesis of results of this analysis. It is interpretable as a summary statement of the main causal paths leading to educational achievement in the Spanish second generation.

## CONCLUSION

Xiaojing Li came to Spain at age 9 with no knowledge of the country or its language. Her parents came first to improve their economic situation and succeeded in establishing their own dry goods store. Then, they brought their children. At age 23, Xiaojing is pursuing advanced finance and administration studies in the European University of Madrid. She works part-time as a Spanish-Chinese translator in a L'Oreal luxury outlet in downtown Madrid; she earns 900 euros per month. Occasionally, she has felt discriminated against: "Sometimes they tell you something in the street; these are silly people." Rather than paying attention, she has gone on with her life and her studies. By now, most of her friends are Spanish and she feels "half Spanish, half Chinese." In the future, she plans to work as a bank executive. She is confident to achieve that goal given her success at the university, "and I am also improving my English," she reports.

For Xiaojing, the main problem for Chinese youths like herself in Spain is that many parents force them to quit their studies to work in the family business. "Many Chinese kids quit school and then they are stuck, working in a restaurant or in their parents' stores." Fortunately for Xiaojing, her parents were supportive of her continuing in school. She is quite proud of herself and closes the interview by saying that she has "nothing more to improve, nothing more to ask of life."[27]

Having estimated a synthetic model of second-generation educational ambition and attainment in Spain, it is time to take stock of how these findings bear on theories of adaptation and on the future of the principal nationalities represented in the Spanish immigrant population and in the ILSEG sample. Overall, the second generation in Spain has not delivered an exceptional performance, but neither has it been a failure. We found no evidence in support of pessimistic theories of exclusion or alienation from the mainstream; instead, results provide general support for assimilationist predictions of convergence. Of concern, however, are the 15 percent of respondents who abandoned their studies and the additional 3 percent or so struggling in remedial courses.

Causes of school abandonment and low performance were examined at length, providing an empirical basis to address problems confronted by these youths in the future. At the other end, however, about half of our second-generation sample managed to reach advanced secondary schooling or even the university and are doing well. These divergent paths support the expectations of segmented assimilation theory, both in their presence and in their determinants.

Despite such differences, the general tendency toward convergence is strong. In terms of ambition and school attitudes, children of immigrants do not differ significantly from children of natives; they lag somewhat in academic grades, but the gap is neither insurmountable nor as high as that observed in other European countries. The consistent advantage in all indicators of performance shown by females is not an exclusive feature of Spain, since it has been repeatedly observed among both immigrant and native-parentage youths in other countries.

Children from certain nationalities, particularly Bolivians, Dominicans, and sub-Saharan Africans, trail in several indicators of achievement. These results are attributable to the modest socioeconomic background of their families and a negative parental mode of incorporation associated with race. Along with older-than-average students, these national groups appear most at risk of falling behind and, hence, should be the focus of attention by educational and governmental authorities in the future. At the opposite end, Chinese youths display a notable trajectory that combines significant school attrition (to join their family businesses) with exceptional performance among those who stay in the educational system. The story of Xiaojing Li above reflects these contradictory trends. They also deserve further investigation in the future.

A notable finding is the convergent trends in educational attainment between children of immigrants in the United States and those in Spain. By taking advantage of the common research design employed to study the second generation in both countries, it was possible to compare systematically key educational outcomes. Similarities include comparable levels of school attrition and its determinants, as well as average grades and their predictors. Family composition and socioeconomic status, but especially early ambition, play decisive roles in educational attainment in both countries. Important as well are the residual negative effects associated with specific nationalities. Such results consistently support the predictions of segmented assimilation concerning the significance of parental modes of incorporation. The lower average levels of ambition detected among both children of immigrants and children of natives in Spain, relative to America, point to a less bifurcated future. For the most part, these youths are all part of a common universe aiming at good (but not extraordinary) goals. As another ILSEG respondent concluded: "We are all in this together, trying as best we can to get out of the crisis." Although the case of Ali indicates that outliers exist, for the majority of children of immigrants as well as children of natives that statement summarizes well their present outlook.

# EIGHT

# The Entry into the Real World

*Labor Market Participation and*
*Downward Assimilation*

This final empirical chapter supplements previous ones with an examination of economic variables, including family income, labor market entry, personal income, and occupational aspirations and expectations. The first set of results complements and updates those presented in Chapter 5 concerning parental economic conditions, both by presenting more current figures and comparing them with native parents. The relevant data are presented in Tables 57 and 58. The first shows again the modest economic circumstances of immigrant families. Since the overwhelming majority of respondents still live with their parents, these figures are interpretable as family incomes. More than one-third of these families must make ends meet with less than a thousand euros per month, and more than half earn 1,500 euros or less. At the other end, those families having an income that exceeds 2,000 euros per mnth represent only 15 percent of the sample.

There are no significant differences by gender or by city of residence in this variable. A slight, predictable advantage can be seen for children who attended private (concerted) schools over public ones, though it is not large, as indicated by a V coefficient of strength of association of less than .10.[1] The truly significant difference is with native Spanish families. Almost 40 percent of native-parentage youths live in families enjoying monthly incomes of 2,000 euros or more, over twice the proportion than among immigrant families. Only 13 percent of Spanish families survive with less than 1,000 euros per month.[2]

TABLE 57   MONTHLY FAMILY INCOME IN SPAIN, 2012

| | Less than €1,000 (%) | Between €1,000 and €1,500 (%) | Between €1,500 and €2,000 (%) | More than €2,000 (%) | Total $N^1$ |
|---|---|---|---|---|---|
| Second generation[2] | | | | | |
| Total | 36.99 | 28.63 | 19.20 | 15.18 | 4,603 |
| Gender: | | | | | |
| Girls | 41.13 | 27.58 | 17.88 | 13.41 | 2,300 |
| Boys | 32.80 | 29.70 | 20.54 | 16.96 | 2,293 |
| V = .075 | Chi square = 8.13 (n.s.)[3] | | | | |
| School: | | | | | |
| Public | 38.23 | 29.47 | 18.85 | 13.45 | 3,539 |
| Private | 26.47 | 25.52 | 21.55 | 26.47 | 631 |
| V = .142 | Chi square = 84.11*** | | | | |
| City: | | | | | |
| Madrid | 36.27 | 28.62 | 20.43 | 14.68 | 2,501 |
| Barcelona | 37.83 | 28.62 | 17.70 | 15.85 | 2,107 |
| V = .037 | Chi square = 6.23 (n.s.) | | | | |
| Native parentage[4] | | | | | |
| Total | 13.03 | 25.01 | 24.41 | 37.55 | 1,811 |
| Gender: | | | | | |
| Boys >Girls | | | | | |
| V = .129* | Chi square = 30.37*** | | | | |
| School: | | | | | |
| n.s.[3] | | | | | |
| City: | | | | | |
| n.s. | | | | | |

1. Missing data excluded.

2. Joint second-generation sample.

3. Not statistically significant.

4. Detailed breakdowns omitted to avoid clutter. Available upon request.

** p < .01

*** p < .001

TABLE 58   HOME OWNERSHIP IN SPAIN, 2012

| | Rents (%) | Owns (%) | Other (%) | Total $N^1$ |
|---|---|---|---|---|
| Second generation[2] | | | | |
| Total | 53.55 | 40.24 | 6.21 | 5,312 |
| Gender: | | | | |
| Girls | 52.49 | 40.51 | 7.00 | 2,671 |
| Boys | 54.61 | 39.96 | 5.43 | 2,633 |
| V = .039 | Chi square = 8.11 (n.s.)[3] | | | |
| School: | | | | |
| Public | 54.94 | 39.19 | 5.87 | 3,988 |
| Private | 43.25 | 51.98 | 4.77 | 733 |
| V = .094 | Chi square = 41.81*** | | | |
| City: | | | | |
| Madrid | 52.20 | 40.98 | 6.82 | 1,906 |
| Barcelona | 55.03 | 38.78 | 6.19 | 1,890 |
| V = .053 | Chi square = 10.58* | | | |
| Native parentage[4] | | | | |
| Total | 8.33 | 86.22 | 5.45 | 1,945 |
| Gender | n.s.[3] | | | |
| School | n.s. | | | |
| City | n.s. | | | |

1. Missing data excluded.
2. Joint second-generation sample.
3. Not statistically significant.
4. Detailed breakdowns omitted. Available upon request.
* $p < .05$
*** $p < .001$

The same story is told by the data on home ownership. More than half of immigrant families rent their premises, and there are no significant differences by sex or city of residence, according to the criterion indicated in note 1. There is, however, a significant difference in favor of respondents who attended private schools. This reflects the higher economic position of immigrant families able to afford this type of education. Such differences pale, however, when we compare immigrant and native Spanish families. Less than 10 percent of the latter rent their homes, and almost 90 percent own them. The strong bent in Spanish culture toward owning one's own home is well reflected in these data.[3]

LABOR MARKET OUTCOMES

The economic crisis still affecting Spain at the time of the follow-up survey in 2012 appeared to have had an unexpected, favorable consequence in keeping many second-generation students in school. A consensus among school personnel at the time of the original survey (2008) was that many adolescents, immigrants and natives alike, abandoned school prematurely because of the ready availability of jobs. The deep economic recession after 2009 led to the disappearance of these labor market opportunities, prompting young people to remain in school.[4] As Table 59 shows, only 12 percent of our sample was employed at the time of the follow-up survey. This figure is in line with—and provides additional validation for—the finding of a low dropout rate, as reported in Chapter 7.

The table also indicates that, among those working, more than four-fifths did so part-time, a result also reflecting a feeble labor market insertion. There is a visibly higher proportion of boys employed full-time, though, by the statistical standard noted earlier, the difference is not significant. However, sizable differences are apparent between the two cities: Madrid residents are more likely to be employed, and to be employed full-time, than those living in Barcelona. This is a noteworthy finding, indicating greater labor market opportunities in the capital.

The more significant gap in labor market insertion occurs, however, between second-generation youths and those of Spanish parentage, not so much in the numbers declaring employment as in the proportion working part-time—which is far higher among the natives. Almost all respondents reporting employment in the native-parentage sample do so on a part-time basis. This suggests that, for these youngsters, work is mainly a supplementary activity to school attendance. Adolescents engaged in full-time employment are much more often found among children of immigrants.

The impression of weak labor market engagement is reinforced by figures in Table 60 showing that, in both samples, over half of those employed do so without a contract (that is, informally). In comparison, less than 15 percent of both children of natives and of immigrants have received a permanent labor contract. In both samples, there is a significant tendency for boys to have at least a temporary labor contract, whereas the majority of girls work informally. Madrid residents are not only more likely to work full-time but also to do so with some type of contract, a difference also present among both second-generation and native-parentage youths. Among all of them, informal employment appears to be more common in Barcelona.

TABLE 59   EMPLOYMENT AND ITS TYPES IN SPAIN, 2012

| | Currently working(%) | Type of employment (if working) | | |
| --- | --- | --- | --- | --- |
| | | *Full-time* (%) | *Part-time* (%) | Total $N^1$ |
| Second generation[2] | | | | |
| Total | 11.9 | 22.5 | 77.5 | 5,323 |
| Gender: | | | | |
| Girls | 13.0 | 19.3 | 80.7 | 2,679 |
| Boys | 10.8 | 26.3 | 73.7 | 2,644 |
| V = .033 | Chi square = 5.97* | V = .083 | Chi square = 4.43* | |
| School: | | | | |
| Public | 13.0 | 30.6 | 69.4 | 3,149 |
| Private | 11.8 | 19.5 | 80.5 | 651 |
| V = .013 | Chi square = 0.62 (n.s.)[3] | V = .090 | Chi square = 3.91* | |
| City: | | | | |
| Madrid | 13.4 | 26.6 | 73.4 | 2,822 |
| Barcelona | 10.3 | 16.5 | 83.5 | 2,509 |
| V = .048 | Chi square = 12.17*** | V = .119 | Chi square = 9.07** | |
| Native parentage[4] | | | | |
| Total | 9.1 | 4.9 | 95.1 | 1,951 |
| Gender | n.s. | n.s. | | |
| School | n.s. | Full-time: Private > Public | | |
| | | V = .200 | Chi square = 7.27** | |
| City | n.s. | n.s. | | |

1. Missing data excluded.
2. Joint second-generation sample.
3. Not statistically significant.
4. Detailed breakdowns omitted. Available upon request.
* p < .05
** p < .01
*** p < .001

About three-fourths of employed youths earned less than 600 euros per month, whereas less than 5 percent attained remunerations exceeding 1,000 euros. Girls were significantly less likely to earn that much. The proportion of low-earners among native- parentage youths exceeded 85 percent. These results confirm the conclusion that, among that population, labor market participation is mostly a supplementary activity.

TABLE 60  JOB CONTRACT AND EARNINGS (IF WORKING) IN SPAIN, 2012

| | Contract | | | Earnings per month | | | Total |
|---|---|---|---|---|---|---|---|
| | Works without contract (%) | Has indefinite contract (%) | Other contract (%) | Less than €600 (%) | €600 to €1,000 (%) | More than €1,000 (%) | N[1] |
| Second generation[2] | | | | | | | |
| Total | 52.2 | 11.3 | 36.5 | 73.6 | 21.9 | 4.5 | 640 |
| Gender: | | | | | | | |
|   Girls | 56.3 | 12.7 | 31.0 | 77.6 | 19.5 | 2.9 | 343 |
|   Boys | 47.2 | 10.0 | 42.8 | 68.7 | 25.0 | 6.3 | 284 |
| | V = .119 | Chi square = 9.05[#] | | V = .130 | Chi square = 10.56# | | |
| School: | | | | | | | |
|   Public | 47.4 | 10.5 | 42.1 | 86.3 | 10.9 | 2.9 | 409 |
|   Private | 55.8 | 10.4 | 33.8 | 88.5 | 6.6 | 4.9 | 77 |
| | V = .092 | Chi square = 4.12 (n.s.) | | V = .064 | Chi square = 1.66 (n.s.) | | |
| City: | | | | | | | |
|   Madrid | 50.4 | 13.5 | 36.1 | 69.4 | 25.3 | 5.3 | 379 |
|   Barcelona | 54.8 | 7.7 | 37.5 | 80.0 | 16.8 | 3.2 | 250 |
| | V = .142 | Chi square = 12.94* | | V = .136 | Chi square = 11.61# | | |
| Native parentage[4] | | | | | | | |
| Total | 53.7 | 14.7 | 31.6 | 85.7 | 10.3 | 4.0 | 177 |
| Gender: | Some type of contract: Boys > Girls V = .223  Chi square = 9.20# | | | | n.s.[3] | | |
| School: | Some type of contract: Private > Public V = .292  Chi square = 15.14** | | | | n.s. | | |
| City: | Some type of contract: Madrid > Barcelona V = .259  Chi square = 11.70* | | | | n.s. | | |

1. Missing data excluded.
2. Follow-up and replacement joint sample.
3. Not statistically significant.
4. Detailed breakdowns omitted. Available upon request.
# p < .10
** p < .05
*** p < .01

The tendency is also reflected in the majority of second-generation youngsters, but there is a visible trend toward serious labor market engagement among them, especially among boys. For young females, employment is both mostly informal and, overwhelmingly, poorly paid.

## Cross-National Comparisons

It is possible to compare these results with those obtained by CILS in the United States. Family income in late adolescence was derived from the CILS parental survey. The figures, originally given in dollars as of 1996, has been transformed for comparability into euro equivalents for 2010. The results, presented in the first panel of Table 61, indicate a clear bipolar distribution: more immigrant families in the United States in the late 1990s had to live with the equivalent of less than 1,000 euros a month than those in Spain a decade later. Indeed, almost half did. On the opposite side, the proportion of U.S. immigrant families with incomes equivalent to 2,000 euros a month or more doubled that in Spain. The much greater bifurcation of the American immigrant population between high and low human-capital individuals and families and their commensurate incomes is well reflected in these results.

By late adolescence, the majority of immigrant families in the CILS sample already owned their homes. As shown in the bottom panel of Table 61, almost two-thirds did, a figure that falls in-between the immigrant and native samples in Spain (see Table 58). The higher economic resources of high human-capital immigrants in the United States plus greater facilities for home acquisition likely accounts for the observed difference: immigrants in America in the late 1990s doubled the proportion of homeownership of their counterparts in Spain a decade later.

Labor market participation was far more common among second-generation adolescents in the United States than in Spain. As shown in the first panel of Table 62, the American figure tripled the Spanish one (as seen in Table 59), with no significant difference between sexes. Undoubtedly, the greater ability of teenagers to secure jobs in the booming America economy of the late 1990s, as contrasted with the deep Spanish recession of the 2010s, is responsible for much of this difference. In both countries, however, the overwhelming majority of employed respondents did so part-time. As shown in Table 62, 85 percent of American second-generation teenagers worked part-time, a figure that falls right at the midpoint between immigrant and native-parentage youths in Spain (see Table 59). Hence, for the vast majority of

TABLE 61    FAMILY INCOMES AND HOME OWNERSHIP OF SECOND-GENERATION
YOUTHS IN THE UNITED STATES

| | Monthly family income[1] | | | |
|---|---|---|---|---|
| | Less than €1,000 (%) | €1,000–1,499 (%) | €1,500–1,999 (%) | €2,000 or more (%) |
| Girls | 49.65 | 10.89 | 8.30 | 31.16 |
| Boys | 45.63 | 13.28 | 9.53 | 31.55 |
| Total | 47.65 | 12.09 | 8.91 | 31.35 |
| N | 1,096 | 278 | 205 | 721 |
| Chi square = 5.33 (n.s.) | | | | |

| | Home ownership[2] | | |
|---|---|---|---|
| | Owns (%) | Rents (%) | Other (%) |
| Girls | 61.08 | 37.87 | 1.05 |
| Boys | 64.00 | 34.68 | 1.32 |
| Total | 62.49 | 36.33 | 1.15 |
| N | 2,659 | 1,546 | 50 |
| Chi square = 5.10 (n.s.) | | | |

1. Based on CILS parental sample. Dollar figures transformed into 2010 euros.

2. Based on CILS follow-up survey.

children of immigrants in both countries, paid work was basically a supplementary activity while still enrolled in school.

That conclusion is reinforced by the similarity in levels of remuneration for employed youths in both countries. For this comparison, we again transformed CILS dollar figures into 2010 euros. On that basis, over 80 percent of working respondents in the United States earned less than 600 euros a month, and only 4.5 percent in both countries achieved incomes exceeding 1,000 euros. As in Spain, there was a significant difference in income attainment in the United States in favor of males. These common patterns again point to close similarities, in multiple fields, of the adaptation process in both countries.

## ASPIRATIONS AND EXPECTATIONS

Occupational aspirations were measured in the 2012 follow-up survey by an open-ended question asking respondents what job they would like to have by the time they reached 35 years of age. Occupational

TABLE 62  LABOR MARKET PARTICIPATION AND INCOMES OF SECOND-
GENERATION YOUTHS IN THE UNITED STATES

| | Labor Market Participation | | |
| --- | --- | --- | --- |
| | *Working* (%) | *Part-time*[1] (%) | *Full-time*[1] (%) |
| Girls | 37.62 | 87.62 | 12.38 |
| Boys | 37.05 | 82.92 | 17.08 |
| Total | 37.35 | 85.37 | 14.63 |
| $N$[2] | 1,593 | 1,360 | 233 |
| Chi square = 2.23 (n.s.) | | Chi square = 7.04** Cramer's V = .066 | |

| | Monthly earnings[3] | | |
| --- | --- | --- | --- |
| | *Less than €600* (%) | *€600–1,000* (%) | *More than €1,000* (%) |
| Girls | 87.31 | 9.52 | 3.17 |
| Boys | 77.68 | 16.12 | 6.20 |
| Total | 82.69 | 12.68 | 4.62 |
| $N$ | 1,252 | 192 | 70 |
| Chi square = 24.68*** | | Cramer's V = .130 | |

SOURCE: Based on CILS follow-up sample.
1. Among working respondents.
2. Working sample only.
3. Among those working. Dollar figures transformed into 2010 euros.
** p < .01
*** p < .001

expectations were measured by the immediate next question, asking respondents whether they believed they would really achieve this goal. Results are presented in Table 63. Open-ended occupational aspirations were transformed into occupational prestige scales by re-coding them into the PRESCA-2 scale of occupational status, described in previous chapters. The range of the scale is 65–235. As seen in the table, the average aspired score is in the middle of the PRESCA range, corresponding to technical and lower professional occupations. Again, girls have an advantage, exhibiting significantly higher aspirations. There are no major differences by school type or city of residence.

Over 70 percent of children of immigrants in late adolescence believe that they will fulfill their occupational aspirations, there being no significant differences by gender, school type, or city of residence. Hence, we are left with the clear impression of relatively moderate but subjectively reachable goals by the large majority. This orientation does not differ markedly from that of Spanish-parentage youths: as seen in the bottom panel of Table 63, their aspirations are roughly in the same range. Native-parentage girls display the highest occupational goals, but not by a significant margin. Beliefs in the possibility of achieving these goals are about the same, once again confirming the conclusion that children of immigrants and children of natives in Spain belong to the same cultural universe.

Another item in the follow-up survey approached the question of occupational aspirations in a different manner by listing a series of occupations and asking respondents which one came closest to the type of job they would like to have by average age 45. There were some minor differences in the pattern of responses by city of residence and school type, but they pale by comparison with the observed gender gap. Table 64 presents these results. A look at the bottom of the table shows that these differences yield the highest chi square value produced by the analysis so far and the highest coefficient of strength of association, a remarkable .43.

These large differences are due to the marked disparity in occupational choices. Girls are five times more likely to choose nursing as their desired career; boys are ten times more likely to want to become information technicians. At the higher professional levels, three times more females than males aspire to become physicians, lawyers, or professors, whereas males endorse engineering as their vocational choice by a margin of four-to-one. The gendered character of occupations in the Spanish labor market is clearly reflected in these differences. Girls' aspirations are not necessarily inferior to those of boys, they are just different.

This last conclusion is reinforced by the pattern of responses among native-parentage respondents, presented on the right side of Table 64. Once again, it closely corresponds to that observed among second-generation youths: nursing and the trio of medicine/law/academics are, by far, the most common choices among Spanish-parentage girls, whereas boys lean heavily toward engineering and information technology. Gendered differences are less apparent in the lower category of vendors and office clerks and in the higher one of business executives.

It is finally possible to observe the evolution of occupational aspirations over time. Here we encounter contradictory results. Table 65 shows that the proportion aspiring to a professional or executive occupation increased visibly for both sexes between 2008 and 2012. However, the mean and median prestige scores between both years declined

TABLE 63   OCCUPATIONAL ASPIRATIONS AND EXPECTATIONS IN SPAIN, 2012

| | Occupational aspirations | | Occupational expectations | |
| --- | --- | --- | --- | --- |
| | | | Believes s/he will attain aspirations | |
| | Mean status score[1] | N[2] | (%) | N[2] |
| Second generation[3] | | | | |
| Total | 146.31 | 4,485 | 70.31 | 5,255 |
| Gender: | | | | |
| Girls | 148.49 | 2,304 | 69.90 | 2,641 |
| Boys | 144.00 | 2,181 | 70.76 | 2,603 |
| | t-ratio = 3.54*** | | Chi square = 4.75 (n.s.)[4] | |
| School: | | | | |
| Public | 148.47 | 3,386 | 70.0 | |
| Private | 150.89 | 641 | 73.2 | |
| | t-ratio = 1.32 (n.s.) | | Chi square = 3.07 (n.s.) | |
| City: | | | | |
| Madrid | 145.62 | 2,369 | 70.99 | 2,785 |
| Barcelona | 147.10 | 2,127 | 69.55 | 2,466 |
| | t-ratio = 1.17 (n.s.) | | Chi square = 4.26 (n.s.) | |
| Native parentage | | | | |
| Total | 150.66 | 1,639 | 67.68 | 1,906 |
| Gender: | | | | |
| Girls | 152.08 | 758 | 67.66 | 872 |
| Boys | 149.44 | 881 | 67.70 | 1,034 |
| | t-ratio = 1.28 (n.s.) | | Chi square= 9.06* | |
| School: | | | | |
| Public | 150.59 | 1,513 | 67.56 | 1,763 |
| Private | 150.64 | 130 | 70.07 | 147 |
| | t-ratio = 0.01 (n.s.) | | Chi square = 1.04 (n.s.) | |
| City: | | | | |
| Madrid | 147.02 | 797 | 68.17 | 955 |
| Barcelona | 153.60 | 846 | 67.33 | 955 |
| | t-ratio = 3.40*** | | Chi square = 0.63 (n.s.) | |

1. Scores in the PRESCA Scale of Occupational Status. Range: 65–235.

2. Missing data excluded.

3. Joint second-generation sample.

4. Not statistically significant.

* p < .05

*** p < .001

TABLE 64    DETAILED OCCUPATIONAL ASPIRATIONS BY GENDER IN SPAIN, 2012

| Occupations | Second generation | | | Native parentage | | |
|---|---|---|---|---|---|---|
| | Girls (%) | Boys (%) | Total (%) | Girls (%) | Boys (%) | Total (%) |
| Office clerk/ salesperson | 8.78 | 6.11 | 7.45 | 5.96 | 4.05 | 4.90 |
| Nurse | 10.40 | 2.44 | 6.45 | 8.06 | 1.54 | 4.49 |
| Information technician | 2.14 | 20.43 | 11.22 | 2.45 | 16.51 | 10.15 |
| Business executive | 16.17 | 10.91 | 13.56 | 9.11 | 13.32 | 11.42 |
| Engineer | 4.84 | 16.49 | 10.62 | 3.86 | 18.82 | 12.05 |
| Professor | 10.91 | 5.61 | 8.28 | 23.60 | 9.46 | 15.86 |
| Lawyer | 8.09 | 3.44 | 5.78 | 4.56 | 2.90 | 3.65 |
| Physician | 11.10 | 3.83 | 7.49 | 10.05 | 4.73 | 7.14 |
| Other | 27.57 | 30.74 | 29.15 | 35.35 | 28.65 | 30.34 |
| Total | 100.00 | 100.00 | 100.00 | 100.00 | 100.00 | 100.00 |
| N[1] | 2,622 | 2,584 | 5,206 | 856 | 1,036 | 1,892 |
| | V = .428 | Chi square = 951.82*** | | V = .417 | Chi square = 329.07*** | |

1. Missing data excluded.
*** p < .001

by about ten points. The first set of results is in line with those reported in the prior chapter, indicating a significant rise in educational aspirations and expectations over time. The second suggests that, though professional-executive aspirations became more common, they tended to shift toward more realistic levels. This tendency also corresponds to results in Table 64 indicating that only a minority of respondents of both sexes aspired to a prestigious university-level profession (professor, lawyer, physician, or engineer) by age 45. The general trend, therefore, is toward aspirations requiring a university-level education but not necessarily aimed at the top of the Spanish occupational hierarchy.

## Cross-National Comparisons

It is again possible to compare these results with those obtained by CILS in the United States. The occupational prestige scale employed to measure occupational aspirations and expectations there (the Treiman scale) is not the same as that used in Spain, and there is no ready algorithm to transform one into the other. However, we can compare the proportions aspiring to "high" (professional-executive) occupations, those aiming at

TABLE 65  OCCUPATIONAL ASPIRATIONS OF CHILDREN OF IMMIGRANTS OVER
TIME IN SPAIN, 2012

|  | 2008 | 2012[1] |
|---|---|---|
|  | Percent aspiring to a professional-executive occupation in adulthood | |
| Girls | 46.47 | 51.11 |
| Boys | 33.48 | 40.29 |
| Total | 39.86 | 45.74 |
|  | Mean occupational aspirations prestige score | |
| Girls | 158.63 | 148.49 |
| Boys | 152.16 | 144.00 |
| Total | 155.38 | 146.30 |
|  | Median occupational aspirations score | |
| Girls | 158.49 | 141.25 |
| Boys | 138.03 | 131.83 |
| Total | 152.38 | 138.03 |

1. Follow-up sample only.

specific occupations, and those certain that they will reach these goals—
that is, realistic expectations. Table 66 presents the relevant results.

In both countries, females outweigh males in occupational ambition
by late adolescence, but children of immigrants in America surpass their
counterparts in Spain by about 15 percent among both sexes. Forty-six
percent of respondents aimed at professional-executive occupations in
the Spanish second generation versus 63 percent of those in America.
These differences in ideal goals become even more relevant when they
are tallied with realistic expectations in both samples. Children of immigrants in the United States not only aimed higher but were significantly
more confident that they would get there. Ninety percent were "pretty
much" or "absolutely certain" that they would achieve their aims, a
figure that exceeds the corresponding one in Spain by 20 percent.

Therefore, and as we saw with educational goals, there is a notable
gap in levels of ambition between both countries. Although sizable
numbers of Spanish second-generation youths aim high and more than
two-thirds are confident about achieving their aspirations, these figures
are eclipsed by the extraordinarily high expectations of children of
immigrants in America. Once these major differences are taken into
account, the patterned similarities in the adaptation process observed in

TABLE 66  AVERAGE AND SPECIFIC OCCUPATIONAL ASPIRATIONS AND
EXPECTATIONS OF SECOND-GENERATION YOUTHS IN SPAIN AND THE UNITED
STATES

| | Spain, 2012 | | | United States, 1996 | | |
| --- | --- | --- | --- | --- | --- | --- |
| | *Girls* | *Boys* | *Totals* | *Girls* | *Boys* | *Totals* |
| Aspires to a professional or executive occupation (%) | 51.11 | 40.29 | 45.74 | 64.05 | 60.06 | 62.17 |
| | Chi square = 83.15*** V = .128 | | | Chi square = 6.72** | | V = .041 |
| Specific occupational aspiration (%): | | | | | | |
| Office clerk/sales, | 8.78 | 6.11 | 7.45 | 3.43 | 2.31 | 2.90 |
| Nurse | 10.40 | 2.44 | 6.45 | 17.98 | 6.83 | 12.76 |
| Information tech | 2.14 | 20.43 | 11.22 | 3.10 | 10.72 | 6.67 |
| Business exec | 16.17 | 10.91 | 13.56 | 14.83 | 14.82 | 14.82 |
| Engineer | 4.84 | 16.49 | 10.62 | 2.73 | 22.18 | 11.84 |
| Professor | 10.91 | 5.61 | 8.28 | 15.06 | 6.10 | 10.86 |
| Lawyer | 8.09 | 3.44 | 5.78 | 7.83 | 4.73 | 6.38 |
| Physician | 11.10 | 3.83 | 7.49 | 21.46 | 16.66 | 19.21 |
| Other | 27.57 | 30.74 | 29.15 | 13.58 | 15.65 | 14.56 |
| | Chi square = 951.82*** V = .428 | | | Chi square = 651.70*** V = .400 | | |
| Certain or very certain to attain occupational aspirations (%) | 69.90 | 70.76 | 70.31 | 91.75 | 88.38 | 90.14 |
| | Chi square = 4.15*** | V = .128 | | Chi square = 6.72** | | V = .041 |
| $N^1$ | 2,641 | 2,603 | 5,254 | 2,182 | 2,014 | 4,196 |

SOURCES: ILSEG joint follow-up and replacement samples, 2012; CILS follow-up sample, 1996.

earlier results re-emerge: in both countries, girls display significantly higher aspirations, but realistic expectations are about the same for both sexes. There are no sizable differences in either country in the level of confidence of boys and girls about achieving their occupational dreams. (The gender differences in expectations reach statistical significance in the United States, but this is only due to the large sample size.)

These similarities become more remarkable when we consider specific job plans in both countries. As just seen, children of immigrants and children of natives in Spain were very similar in the differential choice of careers expressed by males and females. Table 66 shows that such similarities also hold across the Atlantic, and to an impressive extent. Many more girls than boys in both countries wished to become nurses, physicians, lawyers, and professors; boys leaned strongly toward information technology and engineering. As in Spain, the coefficient of strength of association between job preferences and gender is very strong. This result points to a common cross-national cultural orientation that virtually "assigns" certain occupations to males and others to females. However, the girls' stronger preference for high-prestige jobs such as "lawyer" or "physician" does not point to any disadvantage relative to males in their occupational goals.

DETERMINANTS

In this section, we examine causal determinants of three key outcomes: labor market entry, initial incomes, and occupational aspirations. The first two center on current realities; the third summarizes future goals. By late adolescence, we can argue, future goals center on occupations that are within reasonable reach, given the educational levels already achieved. For this reason, we decided to examine occupations as the most strategic dimensions of ambition at this time.

*Labor Market Entry*

Following past analyses, we examine each outcome through a series of nested regressions, using robust standard errors and deleting missing data list-wise. National origins are entered first, followed by objective and psychosocial predictors. Labor market participation is measured in two different forms: as a dichotomy, with those currently working coded *1* and others *0*; and as an ordinal variable, with full-time employment coded *2*, part-time work *1*, and not working *0*. The first version of this outcome is modeled with a binary logistic regression routine and the second with ordered multinomial logistic regression. Table 67 presents results of the binary regression in three columns: the first is limited to national origins; the second includes all predictors, objective and psychosocial; and the third presents results of the full multinomial regression with all predictors included.

As in prior analyses, we transformed binary logistic coefficients into average marginal effects for ease of interpretation. A single nationality strongly affects labor market entry and that is the Chinese. Relative to the rest of the sample, Chinese-origin respondents are more than 20

TABLE 67  DETERMINANTS OF LABOR MARKET ENTRY AMONG SECOND-GENERATION YOUTHS IN SPAIN, 2012

| Predictors | I[1] | | II[2] | | III[2] | |
|---|---|---|---|---|---|---|
| | AMEs[3] | z-ratio | AMEs[3] | z-ratio | Coeff.[4] | z-ratio |
| National origins:[5] | | | | | | |
| Argentina | | | | | | |
| Bolivia | | | | | | |
| Bulgaria | | | | | | |
| Chile | | | | | | |
| China | .212 | 2.94** | .202 | 2.74** | 1.396 | 3.44** |
| Colombia | | | | | | |
| Dominican Republic | | | | | | |
| Ecuador | | | | | | |
| Equatorial Guinea | | | | | | |
| Morocco | -.052 | -1.93# | | | | |
| Peru | | | | | | |
| Philippines | | | | | | |
| Romania | | | | | | |
| Venezuela | | | | | | |
| Objective traits: | | | | | | |
| Age | | | .044 | 5.66*** | .405 | 5.75*** |
| Male | | | -.025 | -1.79# | | |
| Spanish-born | | | | | | |
| Length of Spanish residence | | | | | | |
| Year in school | | | | | | |
| Knowledge of Spanish | | | | | | |

(continued)

TABLE 67 (continued)

| Predictors | I[1] | | II[2] | | III[2] | |
|---|---|---|---|---|---|---|
| | AMEs[3] | z-ratio | AMEs[3] | z-ratio | Coeff.[4] | z-ratio |
| Hours of school homework | | | -.017 | -1.73# | | |
| Family socioeconomic status | | | | | | |
| Both parents present | | | -.044 | -2.86** | -.409 | -2.88** |
| Lives in Barcelona | | | | | | |
| Attended public school | | | | | | |
| Psychosocial traits: | | | | | | |
| Occupational expectations | | | | | | |
| Familism | | | | | | |
| Intergenerational relations | | | | | | |
| Perceptions of discrimination | | | | | | |
| Self-esteem | | | -.040 | -2.41* | -.385 | -2.43* |
| Wald chi square | 30.54** | | 131.00*** | | 136.00*** | |
| Pseudo-R[2] | .016 | | .073 | | .064 | |
| N = | 2,327 | | 2,327 | | 2,327 | |

1. Predictors limited to national origins. All predictors measured in first survey (2008).
2. All predictors included.
3. Logistic regressive coefficients transformed into average marginal effects. Only significant effects are presented.
4. Ordered multinomial logistic coefficients. Only significant effects on full-time employment are presented.
5. Limited to nationalities with at least fifty cases in the original sample and twenty-five in the follow-up. Others form the reference category.

# p <.10
* p <.05
** p <.01
*** p <.001

percent more likely to be working. This result corresponds perfectly with the lack of interest in the Spanish educational system shown by many Chinese parents and their alternative goal of business success, an orientation transmitted to their young.

When other predictors enter the equation, they yield three important additional effects. Predictably, older age increases the probability of labor market entry; each additional year does so by about 4 percent. On the contrary, having been raised in a two-parent family reduces early employment. Although family socioeconomic status does not have a significant effect, that of family composition is congruent with the predictions of status attainment and segmented assimilation theories on the protective effects of intact families. Relative to other children, this effect reduces the probability of early labor market entry by about 4 percent. Finally, self-esteem also reduces the likelihood of employment, full- or part-time, by a comparable amount. In agreement with theoretical expectations, children who are able to maintain a better self-image in early adolescence are less prone to abandon their studies in favor of low-paid and mostly informal employment. Keeping immigrant families together and protecting children's self-image thus emerge as the key variables preventing premature labor market entry.

## Income

For youths who are already working, a second important consideration is determinants of income. For this analysis, we coded income into the three categories presented in Table 60 and modeled it with multinomial logistic regression in the nested sequence used previously. Results are presented in Table 68. The first model, limited to national origins, shows that, relative to others, youths of Chilean and Ecuadorean origin receive significantly higher incomes, as do Romanians and the Chinese. On the contrary, those from sub-Saharan Africa (Equatorial Guinea) display a large income disadvantage.

Among other predictors, age and sex are paramount. Reinforcing the findings in Table 60, boys receive significantly higher incomes, as do older respondents. Relative to working youths who attended private schools early in life, those who went to public schools are much less likely to be in the higher-income category. Hence, the few respondents who, by late adolescence, had already found stable and better-paid jobs were significantly more likely to be males educated in private schools. With other predictors controlled, the only notable nationality effect

| Predictors | I[1] Coeff.[4] | z-ratio | II[2] Coeff.[4] | z-ratio | III[3] Coeff.[4] | z-ratio |
|---|---|---|---|---|---|---|
| National origins:[5] | | | | | | |
| Argentina | | | | | | |
| Bolivia | | | | | | |
| Bulgaria | | | | | | |
| Chile | 1.879 | 2.12* | 1.546 | 1.75# | 1.587 | 1.72# |
| China | 1.100 | 1.75# | | | | |
| Colombia | | | | | | |
| Dominican Republic | | | | | | |
| Ecuador | .793 | 1.98* | | | | |
| Equatorial Guinea | −12.678 | −16.24*** | −12.920 | −13.89*** | −14.134 | −14.76*** |
| Morocco | | | | | | |
| Peru | | | | | | |
| Philippines | | | | | | |
| Romania | .994 | 1.88# | 1.080 | 1.96# | 1.072 | 1.87# |
| Venezuela | | | | | | |
| Objective traits: | | | | | | |
| Age | | | .404 | 2.62** | .446 | 2.76** |
| Male | | | .814 | 2.87** | .780 | 2.67** |
| Spanish-born | | | | | | |
| Length of Spanish residence | | | | | | |
| Year in school | | | | | | |
| Knowledge of Spanish | | | | | | |
| Hours of school homework | | | | | | |
| Family socioeconomic status | | | | | | |
| Both parents present | | | | | | |
| Lives in Barcelona | | | | | | |
| Attended public school | | | −.984 | −2.30* | −.964 | −2.27* |
| Psychosocial traits: | | | | | | |
| Occupational expectations | | | | | | |
| Familism | | | | | | |
| Intergenerational relations | | | | | | |
| Perceptions of discrimination | | | | | | |
| Self-esteem | | | | | | |

TABLE 68 *(continued)*

| | | | |
|---|---|---|---|
| Cut 1 | 1.473 | 5.569 | 6.604 |
| Cut 2 | 4.082 | 8.370 | 9.424 |
| Wald chi square = | 352.11*** | 364.42*** | 446.23*** |
| Pseudo-$R^2$ = | .032 | .112 | .117 |
| N = | 307 | 307 | 307 |

1. Predictors limited to national origins. All predictors measured in the first survey (2008).

2. Model includes national origins and objective predictors.

3. Model includes national origins, objective, and psychosocial predictors.

4. Ordered multinomial logistic coefficients. Only significant effects are presented.

5. Limited to nationalities with at least fifty cases in the original sample and twenty-five in the follow-up. Others form the reference category.

# p < .10

* p < .05

** p < .01

*** p < .001

correspond to Guineans, and it is highly negative. The size of this coefficient must be interpreted with caution, given the small number of Guineans in the working respondent sample and, hence, the likelihood that a few cases may account for this effect. Nevertheless, its size and direction are worthy of attention.

## Occupational Ambition

To investigate the determinants and evolution of ambition, we modeled occupational aspirations as a continuous variable in PRESCA-2 prestige scores and also dichotomized into "university professional" versus others. Both models are presented in Tables 69 and 70 in three steps: first, national origins only; second, national origins plus all other predictors, objective and psychosocial, except occupational expectations in early adolescence; and third, including this last variable. The inclusion of early occupational expectations alters the meaning of coefficients from net effects on the dependent variable to effects on change over time. Such effects are clearer in the continuous version of occupational goals since they were measured in the same metric in both 2008 and 2012.[5]

Results of the initial model indicate significant differences among nationalities, although they vary across both measures of ambition. Five nationalities register negative effects in both cases, but they are not the same. Children of Moroccan, Romanian, and Chinese origins show lower ambition in the continuous scale but not in the dichotomous measure; the opposite is the case among Chileans and Filipinos.[6] The two nationalities displaying consistently lower aspirations are

TABLE 69 DETERMINANTS OF OCCUPATIONAL ASPIRATIONS (CONTINUOUS SCALE) IN LATE ADOLESCENCE IN SPAIN, 2012

| Predictors | I[1] | | II[2] | | III[3] | |
|---|---|---|---|---|---|---|
| | Coeff.[4] | t-ratio | Coeff.[4] | t-ratio | Coeff.[4] | t-ratio |
| National origins:[5] | | | | | | |
| Argentina | | | | | | |
| Bolivia | | | | | | |
| Bulgaria | | | | | | |
| Chile | | | | | | |
| China | −20.437 | −2.84** | −17.266 | −2.34* | −15.264 | −1.98* |
| Colombia | | | | | | |
| Dominican Republic | −20.606 | −4.68*** | −17.486 | −3.98*** | −16.421 | −3.75*** |
| Ecuador | −8.978 | −3.21** | −6.920 | −2.27* | −7.132 | −2.37* |
| Equatorial Guinea | | | | | | |
| Morocco | −9.035 | −2.16* | −7.254 | −1.72# | −7.066 | −1.71# |
| Peru | | | | | | |
| Philippines | | | | | | |
| Romania | −10.156 | −2.22* | −9.397 | −2.00* | −9.104 | −1.98* |
| Venezuela | | | | | | |
| Objective traits: | | | | | | |
| Age | | | −6.766 | −5.88*** | −5.704 | −5.02*** |
| Male | | | | | | |
| Spanish-born | | | | | | |
| Length of Spanish residence | | | | | | |
| Year in school | | | 4.165 | 2.29* | 3.139 | 1.75# |
| Knowledge of Spanish | | | | | | |
| Hours of school homework | | | 3.545 | 2.92** | 3.241 | 2.69** |
| Family socioeconomic status | | | | | | |
| Both parents present | | | | | | |
| Lives in Barcelona | | | | | | |
| Attended public school | | | | | | |
| Psychosocial traits: | | | | | | |
| Occupational expectations | | | | | .151 | 6.87*** |
| Familism | | | | | | |
| Intergenerational relations | | | | | | |
| Perceptions of discrimination | | | | | | |
| Self-esteem | | | 7.551 | 3.27** | 6.950 | 3.04** |

TABLE 69 *(continued)*

| | | | |
|---|---|---|---|
| Constant | 152.94 | 205.95 | 173.29 |
| F-test[2] | 3.35*** | 4.90*** | 6.85*** |
| $R^2 =$ | .021 | .063 | .087 |
| $N =$ | 2,042 | 2,042 | 2,042 |

1. Predictors limited to national origins. All predictors measured in the first survey (2008).

2. All predictors included, except occupational expectations at Time 1.

3. All predictors, including occupational expectations at Time 1.

4. Ordinary least squares regression coefficients. Only significant effects are presented.

5. Limited to nationalities with at least fifty cases in the original sample and twenty-five in the follow-up. Others form the reference category.

# p < .10

* p < .05

** p < .01

*** p < .001

Ecuadoreans and Dominicans. The Dominican negative effect is quite strong under both model specifications: relative to the rest of the sample, Dominican youths experienced a 21-point net deficit in occupational scores and were 17 percent less likely to aim at a professional-level occupation.

This effect is reduced but remains significant when other predictors enter the model. Other nationality effects are also resilient to the inclusion of objective and psychosocial predictions when aspiration is measured as a continuous variable but not as a dichotomy. Only the negative Dominican effect remains in the latter case. Looking at the second model in both tables, we find that older respondents relative to their school peers have significantly lower aspirations—a net deficit of almost 7 points in the continuous prestige scale. This result corresponds to those for educational attainment, as reported in Chapter 7, and also supports theoretical expectations, as discussed in Chapter 2. In agreement with these expectations, hours of schoolwork in early adolescence and early self-esteem significantly heighten ambition four years later under both specifications.

The dichotomous measure of ambition is also positively affected by family socioeconomic status and better knowledge of Spanish, and it is affected negatively by gender (male). In agreement with results for educational aspirations, boys display lower levels of ambition than girls, controlling for other variables. Early school year also increases occupational aspirations under both models, but this effect, like those of the same variable on educational attainment (see Chapter 7) are attributable to the greater advancement of those interviewed originally in the later years of secondary school.

| Predictors | I[1] | | II[2] | | III[3] | |
|---|---|---|---|---|---|---|
| | AMEs[4] | z-ratio | AMEs[4] | z-ratio | AMEs[4] | z-ratio |
| National origins:[5] | | | | | | |
| Argentina | | | | | | |
| Bolivia | | | | | | |
| Bulgaria | | | | | | |
| Chile | −.141 | −1.65# | | | | |
| China | | | | | | |
| Colombia | | | | | | |
| Dominican Republic | −.168 | −3.18** | −.153 | −2.90** | −.150 | −2.84** |
| Ecuador | −.056 | −1.83# | | | | |
| Equatorial Guinea | | | | | | |
| Morocco | | | | | | |
| Peru | | | | | | |
| Philippines | −.143 | −2.05* | | | | |
| Romania | | | | | | |
| Venezuela | .178 | 1.90# | | | | |
| Objective traits: | | | | | | |
| Age | | | −.032 | −2.46* | −.025 | −1.93# |
| Male | | | −.089 | −4.28*** | −.081 | −4.00*** |
| Spanish-born | | | | | | |
| Length of Spanish residence | | | −.006 | −1.69# | | |
| Year in school | | | .040 | 1.99* | .033 | 1.66# |
| Knowledge of Spanish | | | .060 | 2.42* | .052 | 2.13* |
| Hours of school homework | | | .034 | 2.53* | .032 | 2.40* |
| Family socioeconomic status | | | .031 | 2.06* | .027 | 1.83# |
| Both parents present | | | | | | |
| Lives in Barcelona | | | | | | |
| Attended public school | | | | | | |
| Psychosocial traits: | | | | | | |
| Occupational expectations | | | | | .001 | 4.20*** |
| Familism | | | | | | |
| Intergenerational relations | | | | | | |
| Perceptions of discrimination | | | | | | |
| Self-esteem | | | .048 | 1.87# | .044 | 1.72# |

TABLE 70  *(continued)*

| | | | |
|---|---|---|---|
| Wald chi square = | 24.24* | 97.15*** | 116.43*** |
| Pseudo-R² | .008 | .033 | .038 |
| N = | 2,314 | 2,314 | 2,314 |

1. Predictors limited to national origins. All predictors measured in first survey (2008).

2. All predictors included, except occupational expectations at Time 1.

3. All predictors, including occupational expectations at Time 1.

4. Average marginal affects. Only significant effects are presented.

5. Limited to nationalities with at least fifty cases in the original sample and twenty-five in the follow-up. Others form the reference category.

# p < .10

* p < .05

** p < .01

*** p < .001

When early occupational expectations enter the equation, it becomes the strongest predictor, significantly increasing the $R^2$ coefficient in the continuous measure of the dependent variable. Each point in early occupational expectations increases subsequent aspirations by a net .15 in the PRESCA scale. As noted previously, other effects now become interpretable as affecting change in occupational goals. The pattern of coefficients in these final models are, however, similar to those already observed. The negative Dominican effect remains resilient under all model specifications. In contrast, the Chinese coefficient, which is negative on the continuous version of aspirations, disappears when it is dichotomized into professional-level ambitions versus others. This partially reflects the bifurcation of the Chinese second generation in terms of educational achievement and early labor market entry, as discussed previously.

In the final models, occupational expectations, school homework, and self-esteem emerge as the most powerful predictors of ambition in late adolescence. Since all predictors were measured in the original survey, the order of causality is unambiguous, pointing to the importance of these factors in sustaining high ambition levels. The process is clearly path dependent, with early advantages cumulating over time to produce a final positive outcome.

## Cross-National Comparisons

Parallel results from the CILS data indicate that in the United States, as in Spain, age is the strongest determinant of labor market entry. Vietnamese and other Southeast Asian youths were significantly less likely to be employed and Cuban children more likely, reflecting their access to the Cuban enclave economy of Miami.[7] Age and sex (male) were, as in Spain, the sole major predictors of earnings among working respondents in late adolescence; no other personal factor and no specific nationality affected significantly this outcome.

Cross-national similarities become even more impressive when we examine determinants of occupational aspirations. We coded relevant responses in the CILS follow-up sample in the continuous Treiman occupational prestige scale and dichotomized them, as done previously, into professional-level occupations versus others. Table 71 presents results of the final regressions on both versions of the dependent variable. A comparison between these results and those in the preceding tables shows that the causal process leading to adolescent ambition in both countries is, by and large, the same.

In both countries, professional-level expectations were lower among youths older than their respective class cohorts and were significantly increased by family socioeconomic status and occupational expectations in early adolescence. The positive role of early self-esteem was replaced in the United States by that of good intergenerational relations. Occupational ambition, measured in prestige scores, was again negatively affected by older age and gender (male). In the United States, as in Spain, hours of school homework contributed to higher subsequent expectations. In both countries, only a few national origins retained significant effects once objective and psychosocial characteristics were taken into account.

## DOWNWARD ASSIMILATION

"I had a legal tutor, you know. They wanted to take legal authority away from my mother and put me in a reformatory. Those were difficult years. . . . I got a boyfriend and all I wanted was to be with him; I left school; I slept every day at a friend's house so as not to have to go home and confront my parents."[8] This is Kelly, a 20-year-old Ecuadorean girl brought to Madrid at age 5. Her father was a policeman back home but became a gardener in Spain; her mother works as a store clerk. Her parents have not done poorly economically, but they have lost social status, and they started to lose Kelly when she was 14: "When I was attending the Miguel Delibes (a secondary school in Madrid), I had many problems, you know. I felt that my parents and I were growing apart; I decided to quit . . . studying was not for me." Influenced by her boyfriend, she joined a neighborhood gang. It was composed of Ecuadorean and other Latino kids as well as some Spaniards. She ran afoul of the police and was detained several times. The

TABLE 71  DETERMINANTS OF OCCUPATIONAL EXPECTATIONS AMONG SECOND-GENERATION YOUTHS IN THE UNITED STATES

| Predictors[1] | Professional/executive vs. others[2] | Continuous occupational prestige scale[3] |
|---|---|---|
| Age | –.033** | –1.257*** |
| Male | | –1.566*** |
| U.S.-born | | –1.237* |
| Year in school | | |
| Hours of school homework | | .412** |
| Family socioeconomic status | .029* | .785* |
| Both parents present | | .969* |
| Occupational expectations[4] | .007*** | .272*** |
| Intergenerational relations | .008* | |
| Perceptions of discrimination | | |
| Self-esteem | | |
| National origins:[5] | | |
|   Philippines | .199*** | |
|   Jamaica | .153* | 3.344* |
|   Laos | | –4.114* |
| Constant | | 57.530 |
| Likelihood ratio chi square = 289.98*** | | F = 16.82*** |
| Pseudo-$R^2$ = .061 | | $R^2$ = .120 |
| N = 3,592 | | N = 3,496 |

SOURCE: CILS survey, 1992–93 and 1996.

1. All predictors measured in the CILS first survey, 1992–93.

2. Occupational expectations measured in the CILS second survey, 1996. Figures are binomial logistic regression coefficients transformed into average marginal effects (AMEs). Only significant effects are presented.

3. Occupational expectations measured in CILS second survey and transformed into Treiman prestige scores. Figures are unstandardized ordinary least squares coefficients. Only significant effects presented.

4. Measured in 1992–93 and coded into Treiman scores.

5. Only nationalities having a significant net effect on the dependent variable are presented.

\* $p < .05$

\*\* $p < .01$

\*\*\* $p < .001$

low point came when she was going to be sent to the reformatory: "It was not because I was discriminated against. I have never been discriminated (against) in my life. It was all my own fault—the company I kept." Many of her friends at the time ended up in jail or were deported. Even today, her neighborhood is riddled with gangs, she says.

But, by age 18, Kelly rallied: "I had lost two years of my life; I told myself that I had to quit this or would go down with the others. I did not want to end up like them." Much of the change was due to her parents. From distant and reproachful figures, they became much closer to her. "Things are all right now. My mother is everything to me; more than a mother, she's a close friend. And my father is just that—my father."

She returned to school, graduated from basic secondary, and then enrolled in middle technical school pursuing a degree in business administration. She has already completed her courses and is "in practices" in a private firm. She has earned a scholarship to pursue her career because of good grades at the mid-technical school. "At age 18, life changed for me; I had to start studying; otherwise, it would be all over for me."

Two years later, Kelly felt fairly proud of herself and confident in her future. What seems to have turned her around was the changed attitude of her parents, their strong support, and the terrible fate of other gang members that she witnessed directly. Kelly's story serves well as an introduction to the last subject of this chapter—the incidence and determinants of downward assimilation.

The final step in this analysis consists of construction of a Downward Assimilation Index (DAI), composed of the sum of six indicators of problematic adaptation in late adolescence. Paralleling the analysis in CILS, DAI components are:

1. School abandonment

2. Enrollment in a remedial program (PCPI)

3. Being unemployed

4. Cohabitating or living alone[9]

5. Having had at least one child during adolescence

6. Having been arrested or incarcerated during the preceding three years

As noted previously, there are relatively few signs of problematic adaptation or downward mobility in our Spanish second-generation sample. Nevertheless, it is important to establish the extent to which such trends exist as well as to compare them with those among native-parentage youths. As Kelly's story shows, dangers and pitfalls are present in the lives of many immigrant youths, with serious consequences for those unable to overcome them. The question is how many succumb to these threats. The DAI is a count variable, and, as such, its components are not necessarily correlated. Table 72 presents inter-correlations among the six components, as well as the frequency distribution for the total

TABLE 72  ITEM-INTERCORRELATIONS AND FREQUENCY DISTRIBUTIONS
OF THE DOWNWARD ASSIMILATION INDEX (DAI) IN THE SPANISH SECOND
GENERATION, 2012[1]

|  | I | II | III | IV | V | VI |
|---|---|---|---|---|---|---|
|  | Enrolled in PCPI | Cohabiting or living alone | Unemployed | Has had children | Arrested or incarcerated | Abandoned school |
| I | —— |  |  |  |  |  |
| II | .066 | —— |  |  |  |  |
| III | .053 | .062 | —— |  |  |  |
| IV | .023 | .111 | .016 | —— |  |  |
| V | .062 | .065 | .038 | −.009 | —— |  |
| VI | .065 | .045 | .106 | .142 | .096 | —— |

|  | DAI frequencies | |
|---|---|---|
| Number of incidents | % | Cumulative |
| 0 | 78.42 | 78.42 |
| 1 | 17.25 | 95.68 |
| 2 | 3.34 | 99.02 |
| 3 | 0.79 | 99.81 |
| 4 | 0.16 | 99.98 |
| 5 | 0.02 | 100.00 |

$N = 5,311$

1. Follow-up and replacement samples combined.

Index. As shown, almost 80 percent of the sample has been able to avoid any incident pointing to problematic adaptation, but 20 percent have not, and 5 percent exhibited two or more of such symptoms.

Table 73 presents parallel evidence drawn from our native-parentage sample. There is a remarkable similarity in observed trends, both in inter-correlations among DAI components and in the proportion of incidents indicating downward assimilation. In both samples, a minority has confronted serious difficulties in their teenage years, but four-fifths have managed to avoid them. This result provides final evidence of the convergence between children of natives and children of immigrants in Spain; both appear subject to the same threats and demands.

Despite this general conclusion and being in agreement with the logic of prior analyses, we wish to investigate what factors lead to a greater probability of being in the minority at risk of downward assimilation. For this purpose, we modeled the DAI on the same set of predictors used previously. As a count variable, DAI is not amenable to modeling

TABLE 73 ITEM-INTERCORRELATIONS AND FREQUENCY DISTRIBUTIONS
OF THE DOWNWARD ASSIMILATION INDEX (DAI) AMONG SPANISH NATIVE-
PARENTAGE YOUTHS, 2012

| | I | II | III | IV | V | VI |
|---|---|---|---|---|---|---|
| | Enrolled in PCPI | Cohabiting or living alone | Unemployed | Has had children | Arrested or incarcerated | Abandoned school |
| I | ——— | | | | | |
| II | −.015 | ——— | | | | |
| III | −.054 | .072 | ——— | | | |
| IV | −.011 | −.003 | .020 | ——— | | |
| V | .040 | .085 | .071 | −.125 | ——— | |
| VI | .023 | .103 | .139 | .073 | .234 | ——— |

| | DAI frequencies | |
|---|---|---|
| Number of incidents | % | Cumulative |
| 0 | 76.5 | 76.5 |
| 1 | 19.7 | 96.2 |
| 2 | 3.1 | 99.3 |
| 3 | 0.6 | 99.9 |
| 4 | 0.1 | 100.00 |

$N$ = 1,698

with ordinary least squares or logistic regression. This type of variable approximates a Poisson distribution and is properly analyzed with Poisson regression, provided that it is equidispersed (the variance equals the mean). This is a demanding requirement that is not met by most count variables, including the DAI.

Fortunately, there exists an alternative methodology that avoids this stringent requirement: negative binomial regression (NBR). Table 74 presents results of regressing the DAI on the same set of predictors employed previously using this method. As before, robust standard errors are employed to adjust for the school-clustered nature of the sample. Positive coefficients indicate a *greater* probability of downward assimilation. NBR coefficients can also be transformed into percentages indicating the net increase/decrease in the count of events included in the dependent variable. The table includes this transformation for all significant effects.

A look at the first column of the table, limited to national origins, shows two noteworthy effects: the Chinese are significantly less likely than other nationalities to undergo any incident indicative of downward assimilation, whereas Dominicans are more prone to do so. Being

| Predictors[1] | I[2] Coeff.[5] | % change | II[3] Coeff.[5] | % change | III[4] Coeff.[5] | % change |
|---|---|---|---|---|---|---|
| National origins:[6] | | | | | | |
| Argentina | | | | | | |
| Bolivia | | | | | | |
| Bulgaria | | | | | | |
| Chile | | | | | | |
| China | −1.682# | −81.4 | −1.807# | −83.6 | −1.855# | −84.4 |
| Colombia | | | | | | |
| Dominican Republic | .665** | 94.5 | | | | |
| Ecuador | | | | | | |
| Equatorial Guinea | | | | | | |
| Morocco | | | | | | |
| Peru | | | | | | |
| Philippines | | | | | | |
| Romania | | | | | | |
| Venezuela | | | | | | |
| Objective traits: | | | | | | |
| Age | | | .250*** | 28.4 | .228*** | 25.6 |
| Male | | | | | | |
| Spanish-born | | | | | | |
| Length of Spanish residence | | | | | | |
| Year in school | | | | | | |
| Knowledge of Spanish | | | | | | |
| Hours of school homework | | | −.162* | −15.0 | −.146# | −13.6 |
| Family socioeconomic status | | | −.154# | −14.2 | −.135# | −12.6 |
| Both parents present | | | | | | |
| Lives in Barcelona | | | −.474** | −37.7 | −.501** | −39.4 |
| Attended public school | | | −.261# | −22.9 | −.265# | −23.3 |
| Psychosocial traits: | | | | | | |
| Occupational expectations | | | | | −.003* | −0.3 |
| Familism | | | | | .145# | 15.6 |

*(continued)*

TABLE 74 *(continued)*

| Predictors[1] | I[2] | | II[3] | | III[4] | |
|---|---|---|---|---|---|---|
| | Coeff.[5] | % change | Coeff.[5] | % change | Coeff.[5] | % change |
| Intergenerational relations | | | | | | |
| Perceptions of discrimination | | | | | | |
| Self-esteem | | | | | | |
| Constant | −1.650 | | −3.912 | | −3.055 | |
| Wald chi square = | 19.40 (n.s.) | | 102.72*** | | 121.93*** | |
| Pseudo–R[2] = | .010 | | .044 | | .051 | |
| Alpha[7] = | .903*** | | .571*** | | .520** | |
| N = 1,802 | | | | | | |

1. All predictors measured in the original 2008 survey. Only significant coefficients are presented.

2. Model limited to national origins predictors.

3. Model adds objective predictors.

4. Model adds psychosocial predictors.

5. Negative binomial regression coefficients. Positive coefficients indicate greater downward assimilation; negative coefficients indicate lesser.

6. Limited to nationalities with at least fifty cases in the original sample and twenty-five in the follow-up. Others form the reference category.

7. Alpha indicator of equidispersion. In all models, it is highly significant, indicating high levels of overdispersion (variance > mean).

# p < .10

*p < .05

** p < .01

*** p < .001

Chinese reduces the probability of such incidents by 81 percent relative to the rest of the sample; being Dominican increases it by 94 percent. These effects are consistent with prior findings, but the chi square statistic does not reach statistical significance, indicating that these national origins effects are, by themselves, poor predictors of the dependent variable. The situation changes when objective predictors enter the equation. Among them, the most important are age, family socioeconomic status, and hours of school homework.

Each standard deviation unit in the family socioeconomic status index reduces the probability of downward assimilation by 14 percent, but older youths (relative to their class cohort) are more prone to experience such events. Spending more time on schoolwork in early adolescence also turns out to have a significant inhibiting effect on downward assimilation. With these and other predictors controlled, the Dominican effect disappears, indicating that it is mainly due to low family status and other handicaps affecting that nationality. However, the Chinese effect persists. This indicates that, whether they choose an entrepreneurial or an academic path, Chinese youths in Spain are well poised toward upward mobility as they resolutely avoid any incident that can derail them from their life aspirations.

The introduction of psychosocial predictors leads to additional significant findings. Higher occupational expectations have a beneficial effect, with each additional point in the continuous PRESCA scale reducing the probability of negative events by 0.3 percent. This result adds to those of family socioeconomic status and school homework in pointing to the cumulative character of an upward adaptation path. Three additional effects emerge in this final model. First, familism—indicating tighter intra-family relations—increases incidents of downward assimilation. As shown in prior results, a narrow focus and dependence on the immediate family is *not* conducive to positive adaptation outcomes in Spain. Second, Madrid residents have a higher probability of experiencing negative incidents than those living in Barcelona. And, third, respondents who attended public schools do so at a significantly lower rate. These results were not anticipated.[10] In contrast, the effects of age in increasing the probability of downward assimilation and of family status, school homework, and early occupational ambition in lowering it support prior theoretical predictions and point, once again, to the path-dependent character of the adaptation process.

In agreement with neo-assimilationist predictions, downward assimilation is an exceptional outcome, but those more prone to do so are children who arrived in the country at an older age and, predictably, those raised in poorer environments. Despite the significant intergenerational tensions highlighted in Chapter 6, Chinese youths continue to display positive characteristics, adding to their high educational attainment (see Chapter 7) a strong tendency to avoid events compromising future success. At the other end, Dominican youths are more inclined toward downward mobility, a result directly attributable to a handicapped upbringing in this immigrant community.

## Cross-National Comparisons

It is more difficult to compare these results with those obtained by CILS in the United States because, though the metric of DAI is the same, the index was computed not during late adolescence but only in early adulthood (the final CILS survey).[11] Hence, to differences in national contexts and the time gap between both studies, one must now add a significant distance in average age and maturation at the time when measures of downward assimilation were taken. With this caveat in mind, it is still worth noting that events indicative of downward assimilation in the United States *doubled* those observed in Spain. The first panel of Table 75 presents these results. In particular, respondents experiencing two or more negative events were almost three times more common in the American sample in the early 2000s than in Spain a decade later.

The age gap at the time these measures were taken certainly accounts for at least part of the observed differences, so that by the time the ILSEG sample reaches age 24 (the average age in CILS's final survey), the figures should converge. Nonetheless, the overall advantage of the Spanish second generation is noteworthy. The contrast does not extend, however, to predictors of downward assimilation, since the pattern of similar causal processes noted for previous outcomes holds here as well: negative binomial regressions of DAI in the CILS sample also identifies age as a factor leading to negative life events, and family status and early ambition as factors reducing them.

Each additional year of age increased the count of DAI incidents in the United States by 9 percent; each standard deviation unit in the family socioeconomic status index and higher occupational aspirations in early adolescence reduced them by about 22 percent. Gender (male) significantly increased downward assimilation in the United States, whereas growing up in two-parent families lowered it, reinforcing the effect of family status. In Spain, the direction of gender and family composition effects is the same, but they do not reach statistical significance.

In both countries, significant effects associated with specific nationalities persisted, corresponding to their known modes of incorporation. The Dominican effect in Spain leading to increases in negative events finds its counterpart in comparable influences of Mexican, Haitian, and West Indian origins in the American data. In both countries, immigrant groups characterized by low average human capital and a problematic mode of incorporation tend to be associated with higher incidence of downward assimilation. As also seen in table 75, the resilient Chinese influence inhibiting such outcomes in Spain finds its counterpart in a similar earlier effect among children of early Cubans exiles in the United States.[12]

| | Events Indicative of Downward Assimilation | | | | |
|---|---|---|---|---|---|
| | *None* (%) | *One* (%) | *Two or three* (%) | *Four or more* (%) | N |
| National Origins:[1] | | | | | |
| Chinese/Korean | 67.3 | 16.4 | 16.4 | 0 | 62 |
| Colombian | 63.4 | 27.5 | 9.1 | 0 | 151 |
| Cuban | 65.2 | 25.4 | 8.6 | .8 | 811 |
| Filipino | 61.2 | 29.0 | 9.0 | .7 | 593 |
| Haitian | 47.1 | 31.0 | 19.5 | 2.3 | 97 |
| Mexican | 37.0 | 39.0 | 21.5 | 2.5 | 424 |
| Vietnamese | 56.6 | 29.1 | 13.0 | 2.1 | 200 |
| West Indian | 50.3 | 33.3 | 13.6 | 2.7 | 159 |
| Totals | 58.2 | 28.5 | 12.0 | 1.3 | 3,249 |

| | Principal Determinants of Downward Assimilation[2] | |
|---|---|---|
| | *Coefficient* | *% change*[4] |
| Predictors:[3] | | |
| Age | .086** | 9.0 |
| Male | .179*** | 19.6 |
| Two-parent family | −.342*** | −29.0 |
| Family socio-economic status | −.243*** | −21.6 |
| Early expectations[6] | −.251*** | −22.2 |
| National origin: | | |
| Cuban | −.160# | −14.8 |
| Haitian | .282# | 32.6 |
| West Indian | .381** | 46.4 |
| Mexican | .175* | 19.1 |
| N = 3,148 | Pseudo-$R^2$ = .075 | |

SOURCE: Haller, Portes, and Lynch, "Dreams Fulfilled, Dreams Shattered," tables 2 and 4.

1. Selected nationalities only.

2. Negative binomial regression coefficients.

3. Selected predictors only. All were mearsured in the original CILS survey.

4. Percentage change in the count of events indicative of downward assimilation associated with a unit change in significant predictors by average age 24.

5. Expectations to achieve a professional-executive degree coded 1; else 0. Variable measured in the first CILS survey.

CONCLUSION

This analysis of labor market participation, occupational aspirations, and life course events again yields a positive prognosis for the integration of children of immigrants in Spain. We observe no evidence of mass departures from the educational system and note that, with the exception of some nationalities, early entry into the labor market is exceptional. Occupational aspirations among second-generation youths are no different from their native-parentage peers, and there is, in both cases, a healthy confidence in their future fulfillment. Differences by gender in occupational plans for the future are similar to those observed in other countries.

Though high in absolute numbers, occupational expectations of second-generation youths in Spain fall behind those registered among their peers in the United States. However, the process molding ambition in late adolescence is largely the same in both countries, attesting to the cross-national validity of causal effects. Conversely, incidents indicative of downward assimilation in Spain are about half those observed in the United States. The comparison is at best tentative because of the different life stages of the two samples, but it is still suggestive of a less tense and less problematic adaptation process in Spain—aspirations may not be as high, but school attrition, encounters with the police, and premature childbearing appear less frequent.

Exceptions to this assessment are found among older youths whose profile, in terms of both ambition and achievement, show consistent handicaps, and exceptions are also found among certain nationalities, of which Dominicans are noteworthy, for their low educational attainment, low occupational ambition, and higher likelihood of downward assimilation events. By contrast, Chinese-origin youths are in a class by themselves, marked by their apparent pessimism toward the future and a critical stance toward the Spanish educational system, along with superior educational achievements and a notable avoidance of negative life incidents. This and other unexpected findings, such as the significant differences between Madrid and Barcelona and between public and private schools in several outcomes are worth attention and stand in need of additional inquiry.

For the moment, it suffices to note that the generally positive adaptation results registered by the ILSEG sample over time support the predictions of neo-assimilationism, whereas the consistent differences in such outcomes among children of different nationalities and family backgrounds are in line with expectations from segmented assimilation theory. Results provide no support for the "second-generation advantage" thesis, but neither do they point to a consistent pattern of exclusion and racialization. Instead, children of immigrants in Spain appear to join the universe of young people in that country in a relatively smooth manner—both groups partake, in similar ways, of the opportunities and also of the challenges posed by the country where they have grown up.

# NINE

# Conclusion

*Integration Policies and Their Results*

How do the findings presented in the prior chapters and summarized in their respective conclusions bear on alternative predictions about the Spanish "model" of integration? As seen in Chapter 3, this was not a model at all but rather a patch of pragmatic policies adopted to cope with events as they unfolded. This is why Cebolla Boado and González Ferrer refer to the Spanish immigration experience as "immigration without a blueprint," and it is why Zapata- Barrero refers to the "practical" Spanish approach to the challenges and demands posed by a surging migrant population.[1]

In principle, one could expect that such an unplanned approach to immigrant integration would have negative, if not catastrophic, consequences. From the heights of governments and the academic world, it is almost always deemed necessary to have a "strategy" to deal with new situations and problems because, without pre-planned objectives and means to attain them, it seems impossible to reach satisfactory ends. This is conventional wisdom. However, a long sociological tradition has noted the frequently unexpected and commonly unwanted consequences of the best-designed policies.[2] The rational means-ends paradigm that underlies most policy-making and that is so dear to social scientists of the rationalist tradition often falls prey to unforeseen events as well as unanticipated reactions by the groups affected. By the same token, pragmatic adjustments to present events and improvised solutions may yield, in the end, desirable outcomes.[3]

Based on the results from ILSEG, it appears that the Spanish experience offers a classic illustration of this paradox, especially when compared with the integration experiences of its European neighbors. Indeed, in other countries, such as France, explicit policies have been implemented from the heights of a centralized administration with the explicit purpose of accelerating the integration of immigrant groups and preventing the rise and consolidation of ethnic minorities. Backed by the considerable resources of the French state, the goal was to establish a clear divide between "immigrant" and "French," with little in-between, while facilitating the passage from one to the other as promptly possible. The patent failure of these policies—reflected in the consolidation of ethnic groups, sometimes of a militant reactive character—has been well documented in the empirical literature.[4] Apparently, such rational means-ends policies were implemented in a top-down fashion without consideration of the wishes and needs of the foreign groups targeted by them nor, for that matter, of the attitudes and behaviors of the French native population.[5]

The absence of a pre-existing model of integration in Spain and of governmental policies to implement it appears to have had three important consequences. First, the creation of a social space allowing different immigrant groups to adjust to Spanish society in their own ways and at their own pace without strong external pressures. Second, the absence of governmental incentives for the Spanish population to get involved in the integrative project, thus allowing it to adjust to the presence of foreign minorities in its own ways and at its own pace. Third, tacit acknowledgment and respect for the right-to-exist of foreign cultures created by the absence of direct pressure on their bearers to abandon them in favor of those of the host society.[6]

Such a *laissez-faire* stance was accompanied, as seen in Chapter 3, by a proactive set of policies and programs by regional and local governments as well as school authorities. Nowhere do we find official attempts to bar migrants or marginalize them from public services. School authorities generally took a clear stance to counteract Spanish parents' fears and the decision of some to pull their children from public schools.[7] These efforts were commendable and significant, but the key factor leading to low experiences of discrimination and a rapid integration into the Spanish youth mainstream is that immigrant children were *not* compelled to assimilate, either by the government or by the public at large. Instead, they were allowed to accommodate to their surroundings according to their own ways and to interact with native youths at school and in the streets without major status distinctions.

Hence, here is a case where the absence of a well-designed, rational, long-term integration policy produced results arguably superior to its presence. The lack of an overarching blueprint and the pragmatic approach by Spanish authorities to day-to-day contingencies removed the weight of a top-down integration model that immigrants and their offspring have found so oppressive in other countries. As we illustrated elsewhere, rational means-end policies conceived from the heights of political or economic power and applied without full knowledge and consultation with those affected have a way of exploding in the face of their proponents.[8] For policy interventions toward complex social problems to succeed, they must proceed in short steps, always with an ear to the ground and always with close attention to the reactions and attitudes of the target population. Such an approach has the potential of persuading the population to take a hand in the implementation of desirable goals, rather than actively resist externally designed policies.

## IMMIGRANT ORGANIZATIONS AND THE FUTURE OF THE SECOND GENERATION

Fieldwork for ILSEG was completed in the fall of 2012, about the same time that the economic crisis in the country was deepening. It would have been impossible, for reasons of time and resources, to return to the field in order to investigate how our respondents and their families were coping with this dramatic situation, unexpected only a few years earlier. We knew that, until early 2011, few had returned to their home countries, as noted in Chapter 3. However, the follow-up questionnaire did not incorporate detailed items about the economic crisis and its consequences. To place in context results presented in the preceding chapters, we decided to undertake a series of interviews with representative leaders of immigrant organizations in Madrid and Barcelona in the first half of 2013.

As we have just seen, the balance of ILSEG results yields a consistently positive outlook on second-generation adaptation without evidence of mass downward mobility or reactive ethnicities. In the context of economic crisis subsequently faced by the country, it is worth emphasizing that *something had been done well* with respect to the children of immigrants. However, the implications of this conclusion are not the same if Spanish-bound immigration continues or ceases. In the first case, these results could provide guidance for the design of future policies aimed at immigrants and their offspring. In the second, they would be mostly of historical interest: the integration of the second generation had proceeded along normal and generally positive channels, but now there are no more children to integrate.

The balance of the twenty-five interviews completed with immigrant leaders produced three consistent findings. First, immigrant communities have declined numerically because many migrants have left the country and very few new ones are arriving. Second, despite this, communities still endure and their organizations struggle to survive while everyone awaits the end of the crisis and the return to normalcy. And, third, immigrant leaders support an integration process that combines preservation of the cultures of origin with the adoption of a Spanish identity; almost unanimously they do not see such goals as contradictory.

## Consequences of the Crisis

The accounts given by immigrant leaders came close to what we already knew or could expect: a very rapid rise of unemployment, a drop of salaries, the impossibility of continuing to support families in the countries of origin. All of this has led many migrants to return home or re-migrate to Northern Europe or North America.

To this somber scenario must be added the drastic reduction or disappearance of stable subsidies to immigrant organizations and projects. In the words of a Romanian community leader: "Spain is doing away with its Third Sector." Many organizations have had to abandon their previous offices and move to more modest quarters, and some of the oldest and most respected have disappeared. In this context, immigrant organizations increasingly depend on the contributions of their members, but these have also declined due to general impoverishment. Hence, immigrant organizations' efforts to implement assistance programs to their own communities are jeopardized at precisely the moment when such aid is most needed.

## To Resist and to Endure

Despite all these difficulties, immigrant communities have not disappeared. It is worth noting that, at average age 18, children's integration into Spanish society is a *fait accompli,* especially for those born in Spain or brought at an early age to the country. It is quite difficult for immigrant families with children raised and educated in Spain to uproot them in order to return to their home countries. Of course, there is significant migration of second-generation youths to other European countries or North America, but that tendency does not appear to be any greater among them than among children of natives, a number of whom have also emigrated.[9]

Leaders of immigrant organizations are of the same opinion: 94 percent expected their organizations to survive the economic crisis, and almost 50 percent affirmed that they would be strengthened by it. In the words of a Moroccan leader: "The crisis has made us more solidary." Her own organization has continued to be active and actually expanded its programs. For a Romanian leader: "Life in Spain is better; some Romanians have left, but they will in time return."

In all interviews, immigrant leaders emphasized the sustained assistance that their organizations had received in the past from the Spanish government at all levels—from the central administration to the autonomous communities of Barcelona and Madrid, to municipalities such as Majadahonda, Fuenlabrada, Alcorcon, and others. Although this assistance greatly diminished during the crisis, it constituted additional evidence of why the process of adaptation of immigrants and their young to Spain has followed a positive course. More than 80 percent of immigrant organizations surveyed continue to maintain contact with government agencies, all of them trusting that the present situation would be just a "bump" and that things would return to normal soon. According to an Ecuadorean leader: "Our relations with the community of Madrid have not changed. While financial support has declined, we continue to be in contact, as always. Later on, the situation will improve."

## Selective Acculturation

The great majority of these organizations attempt to keep alive the bonds of its members with their countries of origin. Contrary to the views advanced by Huntington and his European counterparts, immigrant leaders believe that there is no contradiction between maintaining such home country ties and achieving successful integration to Spanish society. This position was shared by Colombian, Dominican, Ecuadorean, Moroccan, Romanian, and even Chinese leaders interviewed in 2013.

This position is in agreement with segmented assimilation in terms of its prediction about the positive effects of selective acculturation. The approach also accords with the generally good intergenerational relations between immigrant parents and children, found in the course of our study, and this depended precisely on a harmonious integration between the present and the past. It is quite possible that the resolute opposition of immigrant organizations and their leaders to the "conflict of civilizations" thesis has something to do with the relatively low perception of discrimination among immigrant parents and their children, as reported in Chapters 5 and 6.

## IMPLICATIONS FOR THEORY

Although we have sought to clarify in each of the preceding chapters the bearing of results from the study on the various theoretical perspectives on immigrant adaptation, it is worthwhile to revisit these implications in summary form. Consistently, our findings provide no empirical support for three of the theses discussed in Chapter 2: resistance to acculturation, second-generation "advantage," and generations of exclusion. Lack of support for Huntington's resistance thesis is not surprising since it is based mostly on ideology rather than on serious empirical research. The other two perspectives were inspired by major field studies, but they suffered from limitations restricting the generalizability of their findings.

The "advantage" argument, advanced by Kasinitz and his colleagues, is grounded on comparisons between immigrant nationalities and domestic minorities generally situated at the bottom of the American socioeconomic hierarchies, such as native blacks and Puerto Ricans.[10] With the bar set so low, it is unsurprising that children of immigrants performed better over a series of outcomes, thus leading to over-optimistic conclusions. The relevant point of reference should have been not disadvantaged and discriminated minorities but native middle-class whites who are conventionally associated with the American mainstream.[11]

The "exclusion" hypothesis, by contrast, is based on a study of a single group—Mexican-Americans—that is also on par, on a number of socioeconomic indicators, with other downtrodden domestic minorities. Though compelling, the "racialization" thesis advanced by Telles and Ortiz does not necessarily apply to all children of immigrants and may easily exaggerate the barriers and failures of other second-generation groups. In their defense, these authors never attempted to generalize their findings beyond Mexican-Americans, and the inclusion of their argument in the family of adaptation theories, reviewed in Chapter 2, is justified mainly by its cogency and by providing a counterpoint to the optimistic "advantage" and assimilationist views.

In contrast, the empirical findings consistently support the age-at-migration hypothesis advanced by Rumbaut, Myers, and others.[12] This support comes in the form of negative age effects on a range of educational and occupational outcomes after controlling for year in school and length of Spanish residence. Children brought at a late age to the country and placed, for that reason, in classrooms with younger peers tend to adjust their aspirations downward and to perform worse academically. Although other factors may be present in these results, they are unlikely to fully explain the negative effects of age-at-migration.

This hypothesis is limited, however, to a single predictor, not contemplating the role of many others, such as gender, family socioeconomic status and composition, place of birth, and ambition in early adolescence. This leaves in play only two general perspectives: neo-assimilationism and segmented assimilation. Through successive chapters, we have seen consistent evidence of a paced process of integration, starting with parents' general desire for their children to stay in Spain and their favorable opinion of the education that the children have received in school, and continuing with low perceptions of discrimination among children and the rapid rise of Spanish self-identities among them. The assimilationist perspective is also buttressed by the lack of systematic differences among nationalities in different measures of ambition and achievement and by the near absence of indicators of downward assimilation in the entire sample. In a sense, the benign prognosis for the future of the Spanish second generation, discussed previously, also counts as general support for this theory.

Yet this is only half of the story. In Chapter 5, we saw that significant differences by national origin persisted among immigrant parents in occupational status and income even after controlling for education, gender, years of Spanish residence, and other individual-level variables. Moreover, these gaps overlap with known differences in the context of reception accorded to different immigrant groups in Spain because of phenotypical traits and linguistic or religious backgrounds.[13]

Such net effects of modes of incorporation among first-generation immigrants are then transmitted to the children via differences in family socioeconomic status, family composition, and related variables. Unlike the case of second-generation youths in the United States, few or no systematic differences in outcome variables remain after controlling for such family and personal characteristics. Certain nationalities, such as Bolivians, Dominicans, Equatorial Guineans, and Moroccans, display patterns of disadvantage, but most of these nationality effects disappear after controlling for socioeconomic status, family composition, age, and gender. Hence, in the case of Spain, effects of modes of incorporation are quite apparent among first-generation parents, but they do not extend to the second generation, except in rare cases.

A second set of results congruent with segmented assimilation are the significant effects of selective acculturation, as indexed by intergenerational relations, on several important outcomes. Good rapport between parents and children in early adolescence, indicative of the presence of a shared culture and language, reduces experiences of discrimination later in life and plays a significant role in educational and occupational attainment. Additional analyses of ILSEG data, not reported in this volume, support this conclusion by showing that fluent bilingual respondents tend to perform educationally ahead of their peers, even after controlling for other predictors. Fluent bilingualism has been employed in past research as a direct indicator of selective acculturation in the second generation.[14]

Hence, though the steady adaptation process portrayed in our results provides evidence supportive of neo-assimilationism, other findings are closely aligned with predictions from segmented assimilation theory, in particular the key role of parental modes of incorporation and selective acculturation. Jointly, the two theories provide an adequate framework for understanding and for synthesizing results of the previous analysis of parents' and children's adaptation processes in Spain.

## CROSS-NATIONAL COMPARISONS

Throughout the preceding chapters, we have sought to compare systematically results of the study conducted in Spain with parallel ones from the project completed in the United States a decade earlier and that served as the original blueprint for ILSEG. By taking advantage of similar research designs and parallel questionnaires, it became possible to address issues concerning similarities and differences in the process of adaptation and the cross-national applicability of concepts and hypotheses developed on the basis of past American research. Specific results of these comparisons have been discussed and summarized in the preceding chapters and need not be repeated here. Instead, we make use of these results for a final reflection on the issues just mentioned. This reflection may be divided into three specific trends.

First, we note the remarkable similarity across countries and over time in a number of outcomes and determinants of immigrant adaptation.

These include the high ambition of immigrant parents; determinants of their occupational achievement and income; the consistent effects of age and gender on measures of second-generation ambition and attainment; the effects of family socioeconomic status and family composition on both psychosocial and objective second-generation outcomes; and the influence of modes of incorporation, as reflected on patterned differences among immigrant parents. These similarities extend to determinants of downward assimilation among children and make it possible to conclude that the second-generation process of adaptation is largely the same in both countries. Hence, selected concepts and hypotheses developed in the American context would apply in Spain as well.

Second, despite these similarities, there are sizable differences in levels of ambition. Whether one considers aspirations or expectations, children of immigrants in America appear to be significantly more oriented toward success. This is not to say that educational and occupational ambitions in Spain are low; they simply pale by comparison with those detected by CILS in the United States. Since early expectations have been shown to be a key predictor of subsequent attainment, it is possible to conclude that, though the status attainment process is essentially the same in both countries, it will yield higher educational and occupational payoffs among children of immigrants in the American context.

Third, there are also divergencies in national self-identities and perceptions of discrimination between the two countries, pointing to a less traumatic and more "even" integration process of second-generation youths in Spain. By average age 18, perceptions of discrimination were far more common among children of immigrants in the CILS survey than among their ILSEG counterparts a decade later. Although the causal process leading to such perceptions is similar in both countries, the resulting absolute levels diverged. Reinforcing these results, national self-identification also differed: four-fifths of Spanish-born second-generation youths identified themselves as Spanish, and, even among the foreign-born, such identities doubled from early to late adolescence. By contrast, identification as unhyphenated Americans actually declined during the same period in the United States, giving way to pan-ethnic labels or even parental nationalities as preferred self-identities. Such differences bring into sharper relief the significance of the ethno-racial hierarchy into which foreign minorities are classified in American society and that impedes their transition to identification with an undifferentiated "mainstream." Spain does not have or has not had time to develop a comparable racial-ethnic framework, thereby allowing youths from the most different foreign origins to join the native majority in a relatively short time.

The value of comparative cross-national research is made evident by these results. They not only allow for tests of validity of concepts and hypotheses developed in one national context into another but also illuminate the very character of such contexts. Studies of immigration and immigrant adaptation conducted exclusively in the United States cannot shed light on key features of the society that foreigners confront with the clarity afforded by a cross-national lens. The competitiveness of American society, the will-to-succeed that it fosters and indeed requires among newcomers, along with the troubled heritage of its racial history are cast into sharp relief by this cross-national comparison.

## LOOKING TOWARD THE FUTURE

As we have seen, for an important group of children of immigrants by average age 18, integration into Spanish society is an accomplished fact. In addition, and based on the words of their leaders, immigrant communities continue resisting the crisis in the expectation of better times ahead. In reality, it is unthinkable that the context of severe economic crisis faced by Spain during the second decade of this century will continue indefinitely. More likely is a gradual recovery, whose signs have become increasingly evident as we pen these lines.

If that is the case, then all the findings from this study will acquire new relevance as a guide to resurgent immigrant flows. Future policies can find inspiration in those that have proven effective so far—combining acculturation to Spanish society with respect and support for the cultures brought from abroad. As repeatedly noted previously, policies of tolerance toward immigrant communities and a proactive orientation toward the goals of their organizations have proven more successful than the enforced assimilationism or even separatist policies implemented elsewhere in Europe.

It is important to emphasize that past policies can be made even more effective by singling out those groups at greater risk of school abandonment and downward assimilation. Youths who arrive in Spain at older ages and are placed in classes with younger peers represent a group at risk. So are children from certain nationalities because of the low human capital and other characteristics of the parental generation. Finally, it would be instructive to pay close attention to the remarkable integration process of the Chinese. It is defined by the premature entrance into the labor market of many—surely to work in their parents' firms or those of other co-ethnics—and significant tensions between generations, together with high levels of academic achievement among those who have remained in school and a notable absence of indicators of downward assimilation. China is today the principal source of out-migration worldwide. Comparing patterns of adaptation of Chinese immigrants and their offspring in different countries of reception will represent a worthwhile endeavor in the future, both for academic and for policy reasons.

# Notes

PREFACE

1. Schneider, "Police Power and Race Riots in Paris"; Entzinger, "Different Systems, Similar Problems."

2. Crul and Vermeulen, "The Second Generation in Europe"; Schneider, "Police Power and Race Riots in Paris"; Cachón, *La España Inmigrante;* Fanning, *Immigration and Social Cohesion in the Republic of Ireland.*

3. Rumbaut, "Turning Points in the Transition to Adulthood"; M. Zhou, "Straddling Different Worlds"; Aparicio, *Hijos de Inmigrantes.*

4. Portes and Rumbaut, *Legacies;* Zhou and Bankston, *Growing up American;* Kasinitz et al., *Inheriting the City.*

5. Portes et al., "Dreaming in Spain."

6. Pajares, "La Inmigración en España"; Cachón, *La España Inmigrante.*

7. See Portes and Rumbaut, *Immigrant America,* 4th ed., and Chapter 3 of this volume.

8. Portes and Rumbaut, *Legacies,* chap. 3.

9. Aparicio and Portes, *Crecer en España.*


CHAPTER ONE: TWELVE LIVES

1. These and the following stories are summaries of selected interviews carried out as part of the qualitative module conducted by the Longitudinal Study of the Second Generation in Spain (ILSEG). All names are fictitious.

CHAPTER TWO: THEORIES OF SECOND-GENERATION
ADAPTATION

1. Office of Immigration Statistics, 2009 *Yearbook of Immigrant Statistics;*
Cachón, *La España Inmigrante.*

2. Portes and Rumbaut, *Legacies;* Aparicio, *Hijos de Inmigrantes.*

3. Rumbaut, "Origins and Destinies."

4. Rumbaut, "Ages, Life Stages, and Generational Cohorts."

5. Portes and Rumbaut, *Immigrant America,* 3rd ed., chap. 2.

6. Ibid.; see also the Preface to this book.

7. Crul and Vermeulen, "The Second Generation in Europe"; Crul, Schneider, and Lelie, *The European Second Generation Compared.*

8. Portes, Fernández-Kelly, and Haller, "No Margin for Error."

9. Alba and Holdaway, *The Children of Immigrants at School.*

10. An exception is the study of the American and British educational systems by Waters and her colleagues that includes a number of ethno-racial groups in both countries. Sources of data employed by these authors are also secondary and mostly cross-sectional, limiting them to speculative conclusions about causes of differences among these ethnic groups. See Waters et al., "Second Generation Attainment and Inequality."

11. Portes and Rivas, "The Adaptation of Migrant Children."

12. Huntington, "The Hispanic Challenge."

13. Ibid.

14. Nijenhuis and Zoomers, "Transnational Activities of Immigrant Organizations in the Netherlands."

15. Cachón, "La España Inmigrante"; Pajares, "La Inmigración en España."

16. Portes and Rivas, "The Adaptation of Migrant Children"; Alba et al., "Only English by the Third Generation?"

17. Aparicio, *Hijos de Inmigrantes;* Portes et al., "Who Are We?"

18. Alba and Nee, *Remaking the American Mainstream;* Portes and Rivas, "The Adaptation of Migrant Children."

19. Hirschman, "America's Melting Pot Reconsidered"; Jacobson, *Whiteness of a Different Color;* Nijenhuis and Zoomers, "Transnational Activities of Immigrant Organizations in the Netherlands."

20. Telles and Ortiz, *Generations of Exclusion.*

21. Ibid.

22. Glazer and Moynihan, *Beyond the Melting Pot;* Glazer, "On Beyond the Melting Pot," 276.

23. Glazer and Moynihan, *Beyond the Melting Pot;* Glazer, "On Beyond the Melting Pot"; Telles and Ortiz, *Generations of Exclusion;* Bonilla and Campos, "A Wealth of Poor"; Bourgois, *In Search of Respect;* Portes and Stepick, *City on the Edge.*

24. Crul and Doomernik, "The Turkish and Moroccan Second Generation in the Netherlands"; Simon, "France and the Unknown Second Generation"; Crul, Schneider, and Lelie, *The European Second Generation Compared.*

25. Alba and Holdaway, *The Children of Immigrants at School.* Interestingly, the lead author advancing this pessimistic view had pioneered, a few years earlier, the much more optimistic approach identified as neo-

assimilationism. See also Waters et al., "Second Generation Attainment and Inequality."

26. Rumbaut, "The Crucible Within."

27. Kasinitz et al., *Inheriting the City.*

28. Kasinitz, Mollenkopf, and Waters, "Becoming American/Becoming New Yorkers."

29. Portes and Zhou, "The New Second Generation."

30. Portes, Fernández-Kelly and Haller, "No Margin for Error"; Portes and Rumbaut, *Legacies,* chap. 3.

31. Rumbaut, "Turning Points in the Transition to Adulthood"; Zhou and Bankston, "Social Capital and the Adaptation of the Second Generation."

32. Portes and Zhou, "The New Second Generation"; Rumbaut, "Turning Points in the Transition to Adulthood"; Zhou and Bankston, "Social Capital and the Adaptation of the Second Generation"; Fernández-Kelly, "The Back Pocket Map."

33. Crul and Doomernik, "The Turkish and Moroccan Second Generation in the Netherlands"; Alba and Holdaway, *The Children of Immigrants at School.*

34. Sewell, Haller, and Portes, "The Educational and Early Occupational Attainment Process."

35. Aldous, "Family, Ethnicity, and Immigrant Youths' Educational Achievements"; Bohon, Johnson, and Gorman, "College Aspirations and Expectations among Latino Adolescents in the United States"; Inoue, *The Educational and Occupational Attainment Process;* Menjivar, "Educational Hopes, Documented Dreams."

36. Kao and Tienda, "Educational Aspirations of Minority Youth"; Portes and Rumbaut, *Legacies,* chaps. 4 and 5.

37. Goyette and Xie, "Educational Expectations of Asian Amercan Youths"; Perreira, Hamis, and Lee, "Making It in America"; Hirshman, "The Educational Enrollment of Immigrant Youth"; Kao and Tienda, "Educational Aspirations of Minority Youth."

38. Glick and White, "Post-Secondary School Participation of Immigrant and Native Youth"; Hao and Bonstead-Bruns, "Parent-Child Differences in Educational Expectations"; Marjoribanks, "Family Background, Individual and Environmental Influences"; Alba and Holdaway, *The Children of Immigrants at School,* chap. 1.

39. Cheng and Starks, "Racial Differences in the Effects of Significant Others on Students' Educational Expectations"; Feliciano and Rumbaut, "Gendered Paths."

40. Perreira, Hamis, and Lee, "Making it in America"; Fernández-Kelly, "The Back Pocket Map."

41. Kao and Tienda, "Educational Aspirations of Minority Youth"; Portes et al., "Dreaming in Spain."

42. Portes and Rumbaut, *Legacies,* chap. 5.

43. The Organization for Economic Cooperation and Development (OECD) has conducted a number of large, statistically representative surveys of secondary students in fifty countries, including all immigrant-receiving nations in Western Europe, North America, and the South Pacific. Results from these

surveys, collectively known as the Program for International Student Assessment (PISA), tend to show higher expectations among children of immigrants than among the native-born of native-parentage. A recent analysis of PISA data for fifteen countries indicates that this advantage is still higher among children who speak a language other than that of the host country at home. Fluency in parental languages facilitates communication across generations and, hence, the transmission of parental ambition to their offspring. See Organization for Economic Cooperation and Development (OECD), "PISA 2006"; Sikora and Saha, "Corrosive Inequality?"

44. Portes and Rumbaut, *Legacies,* chap. 10; Portes, "Tensions That Make a Difference."

45. Hirshman and Falcon, "The Educational Attainment of Religio-Ethnic Groups in the United States"; Telles and Ortiz, *Generations of Exclusion.*

46. Portes, "Tensions That Make a Difference," 573; Rumbaut, "Assimilation and Its Discontents."

47. Portes and Rumbaut, *Legacies,* chaps. 6 and 9; Alba et al., "Only English by the Third Generation?"; Mouw and Xie, "Bilingualism and the Academic Achievement of First- and Second-Generation Asian Americans"; Portes and Hao, "E Pluribus Unum."

48. Rumbaut, "The Crucible Within"; Fernández-Kelly, "The Back Pocket Map."

49. Schneider, "Police Power and Race Riots in Paris"; Entzinger, "Different Systems, Similar Problems."

50. Portes and Rumbaut, *Legacies,* chap. 7; Rumbaut, "The Crucible Within."

51. Altschul, Oyserman, and Bybee, "Racial-Ethnic Self-Schemas and Segmented Assimilation"; Feliciano, "Education and Ethnic Identity Formation among Children of Latin American and Caribbean Immigrants"; Haines, "Ethnicity's Shadows"; Jimenez, "Mexican Immigrant Replenishment"; Aparicio, "La Integración de las Segundas Generaciones en España."

52. Ajrough and Jamal, "Assimilating to a White Identity"; Alba and Islam, "The Case of Disappearing Mexicans"; Dhingra, "Committed to Ethnicity, Committed to America"; Portes et al., "Who Are We?"

53. Bailey, "Language and Negotiation of Ethnic/Racial identity among Dominican Americans"; Feliciano, "Education and Ethnic Identity Formation among Children of Latin American and Caribbean Immigrants"; Morning, "The Racial Self-Identification of South Asians in the United States"; Fernández-Kelly, "The Back Pocket Map."

54. Portes and Rumbaut, *Legacies,* chap. 7; Lopez and Stanton-Salazar, "Mexican Americans"; Schneider, "Police Power and Race Riots in Paris."

55. Ream, *Uprooting Children;* Nesdale and Mak, "Immigrant Acculturation Attitudes and Host Country Identification"; Pahl and Way, "Longitudinal Trajectories of Ethnic Identity among Urban Black and Latino Adolescents."

56. Rosenberg, *Society and the Adolescent Self-Image;* Rosenberg, *Conceiving the Self.*

57. Portes and Rumbaut, *Legacies,* chaps. 7 and 8; Bohon, Johnson, and Gorman, "College Aspirations and Expectations among Latino Adolescents in

the United States"; Kao and Tienda, "Educational Aspirations of Minority Youth"; Hao and Bonstead-Burns, "Parent-Child Differences in Educational Expectations."

58. Edwards and Romero, "Coping with Discrimination among Mexican Descent Adolescents."

59. Portes and Rumbaut, *Legacies*, table 8.6.

60. Yiu, "Calibrated Ambitions"; Portes et al., "Who Are We?"; Flores, "The Increasing Significance of Race in Spain."

## CHAPTER THREE: THE RECENT HISTORY OF SPAIN-BOUND IMMIGRATION

1. According to figures from the Instituto Español de Emigración (IEE), which only include people who emigrated with a work contract, 1,502,028 people left Spain between 1959 and 1973. The majority headed for European destinations (Switzerland, France, and Germany). However, the discrepancy between the official figures and those registered by the respective countries of immigration has led scholars to estimate that the real number of emigrants was 51 percent higher on average. See Garmendia, *La Emigración Española en la Encrucijada*.

2. Aja, Arango, and Alonso, *Inmigración y crisis económica*. Arango and Alonso, "Después del gran boom: La inmigración en la bisagra del cambio," in Aja, Arango, and Alonso, *La inmigración en tiempos de crisis*.

3. Cachón, *La España Inmigrante*; Portes and Rumbaut, *Immigrant America*, 4th ed., chap. 2.

4. Monteserin, Fernández, and Martínez Vega, "Crisis Económica y Nuevo Panorama Migratorio en España."

5. Cebolla Boado and González Ferrer, *Inmigración sin Modelo?*, 47.

6. Ibid.

7. Cachón, *La España Inmigrante*.

8. Ibid.; Alonso, "El Empleo Inmigrante ante la Nueva Fase de Crisis e Integración."

9. Cebolla Boado and Gonzalez Ferrer, *Inmigración sin Modelo?*, 47.

10. Ibid.

11. Instituto Nacional de Estadistica, *National Immigration Survey*.

12. Monteserin, Fernández, and Martínez Veiga, "Crisis Económica y Nuevo Panorama Migratorio en España," 15.

13. Alonso, "El Empleo Inmigrante ante la Nueva Fase de Crisis e Integración," 52.

14. Instituto Nacional de Estadistica, *Padrón Continuo de las Migraciones*.

15. Ioé, "Alumnas y Alumnos de Origen Extranjero"; Defensor del Pueblo, *La Escolarización del Alumnado Inmigrante en España*; Aparicio, "La Integración de las Segundas Generaciones en España."

16. See Aparicio and Tornos, *La Investigación sobre Migraciones en España*; Bardají, *Literatura sobre Inmigrantes en España*.

17. CIDE, *Catorce Años de Investigación sobre las Desigualdades en Educación en España*; CIDE, *Investigaciones sobre educación intercultural realizadas en España entre 1990 y 2002*.

18. Franzé, *Lo que Sabía no Valía;* Juliano Corregido, *Educación Intercultural;* Siguán and Ruiz, *La Escuela y los Inmigrantes.*

19. Franzé, *Lo que Sabía no Valía;* Zapata-Barrero and Burchianti, "Tolerance to Cultural Diversity in Spanish Schools"; Aparicio, "La Integración de las Segundas Generaciones en España"; Rojo, *Asimilar o Integrar?*

20. Etxeberria and Elosegin, "Integración del Alumnado Inmigrante"; Franzé, "Cultura/Culturas en la Escuela."

21. Checa, Checa and Arjona, *La Integración de los Inmigrados;* Cachón, *La España Inmigrante;* Terrén, "Adolescencia, Inmigración e Identidad"; Terrén, "El Sentimiento de Pertenencia Nacional."

22. Carabaña, "El Impacto de la Inmigración en el Sistema Educativo Español"; Garrido Medina and Cebolla Boado, "Rendimiento Educativo y Concentración de Inmigrantes en las Escuelas Españolas."

23. Aja, Arango, and Alonso, *La inmigración en tiempos de crisis;* Cachón, *La España Inmigrante;* Pajares, *La Integración Ciudadana;* Solé and Parella, "The Labour Market and Racial Discrimination in Spain"; Zapata-Barrero, *Diversity Management in Spain.*

24. Cebolla Boado and González Ferrer, *Inmigración sin Modelo?;* Zapata-Barrero, *Diversity Management in Spain,* chaps. 1 and 6.

25. Castles and Davidson, *Citizenship and Migration;* Castles and Miller, *The Age of Migration;* Faist, "Diversity"; Hollifield, "The Emerging Migration State."

26. See Aparicio and Tornos, "Towards an Analysis of Spanish Integration Policy," 231–35.

27. Cebolla Boado and González Ferrer, *Inmigración sin Modelo?,* 47.

28. Zapata-Barrero, *Diversity Management in Spain,* 18.

29. An exception are Arab immigrant communities, which have been closely monitored and subjected to much government interference in the aftermath of the September 11, 2001, events. See Portes and Rumbaut, *Immigrant America,* 4th ed., chap. 9; Lin and Jamal, "Muslim, Arab, and American."

30. See Cachón, *La España Inmigrante;* Cebolla Boado and Lopez-Sala, "Transnational Immigrant Organizations in Spain"; Morales and Ramiro, "Gaining Political Capital Through Social Capital."

31. Zapata-Barrero, *Diversity Management in Spain,* 167.

32. Portes and Rumbaut, *Immigrant America,* 4th ed., chaps. 5 and 10; Alba and Nee, *Remaking the American Mainstream,* chaps. 1–3.

33. Gualda, "Aspiraciónes y Expectativas Educativas y Laborales de Jóvenes Inmigrantes"; Gualda and Jariego Peña, "Adolescentes y Jóvenes Inmigrantes en Huelva y Sevilla (España)."

34. See Firebaugh, *Seven Rules for Social Research;* Guarnizo, Portes, and Haller, "Assimilation and Transnationalism."

35. One such study concludes, for example, that "the banda constitutes a family in the street facing the multiple exclusion processes orchestrated right and left by the (Spanish) state" (Queirolo Palmas, "Bandas Fuera!," 437). This sweeping conclusion is based on seventy-nine interviews with gang members and other relevant actors in the *escena pandillera* (gang scene) in Barcelona and Madrid. No mention is made of the vast majority of second-generation youths who take no part in this scene.

## CHAPTER FOUR: THE LONGITUDINAL STUDY OF THE SECOND GENERATION

1. Rumbaut, "The Crucible Within"; Portes and Rivas, "The Adaptation of Migrant Children."

2. See, for example, the conclusions reached by Kasinitz et al. on the basis of a cross-sectional sample of second generation adults in New York. Kasinitz et al., *Inheriting the City*. For additional comments on this study, see Haller, Portes, and Lynch, "Dreams Fulfilled, Dreams Shattered."

3. Singleton and Straits, *Approaches to Social Research*; Firebaugh, *Seven Rules for Social Research*.

4. Firebaugh, *Seven Rules for Social Research*; Haller, Portes, and Lynch, "Dreams Fulfilled, Dreams Shattered."

5. Firebaugh, *Seven Rules for Social Research*.

6. Singleton and Straits, *Approaches to Social Research*; Portes et al., "Who Are We?"

7. Firebaugh, *Seven Rules for Social Research*. For a discussion of the trade-offs of longitudinal designs in the study of the second generation, see Portes and Rumbaut, *Legacies*, chap. 2.

8. See Portes and Rumbaut, *Legacies*, chap. 2, for a more extensive discussion of the CILS research design.

9. Ibid.; Rumbaut and Portes, *Ethnicities*.

10. Data from CILS are available from the database of the Center for Migration and Development at Princeton University and from the Inter-University Consortium for Political and Social Sciences (ICPSR) at the University of Michigan.

11. See, for example, Crul and Vermeulen, "The Second Generation in Europe"; Crul, Schneider, and Lelie, *The European Second Generation Compared*.

12. For a basic treatise on sampling design, see Kish, *Survey Sampling*. See also Singleton and Straits, *Approaches to Social Research*, chap. 6.

13. Rumbaut, "Ages, Life Stages, and Generational Cohorts"; Portes and Rivas, "The Adaptation of Migrant Children."

14. These are known in Spain as "concerted" schools because they are subsidized by the state and governed by the educational plans and criteria set up by the central government.

15. Aparicio, *Hijos de Inmigrantes*; Gibson and Carrasco, "The Education of Immigrant Youths."

## CHAPTER FIVE: IMMIGRANT PARENTS

1. Instituto Nacional de Estadistica, *National Immigration Survey of Spain*.

2. Portes and Rumbaut, *Legacies*, 73.

3. Ibid., table 2.2.

4. Warner and Srole, *The Social Systems of American Ethnic Groups*.

5. Flores, "The Increasing Significance of Race in Spain"; Portes, Vickstrom, and Aparicio, "Coming of Age in Spain."

6. Flores, "The Increasing Significance of Race in Spain"; Cachón, *La España Inmigrante*.

7. Instituto Nacional de Estadistica, *National Immigration Survey of Spain.*

8. Portes and Rumbaut, *Legacies,* 73; Cachón, *La España Inmigrante;* Aparicio, *Hijos de Inmigrantes.* Latin American and Filipino immigrants are eligible for Spanish nationality after two years of residence because they are citizens of former Spanish colonies.

9. Scores use the PRESCA-2 scale of occupational prestige developed for Spain by sociologists Julio Carabaña and Carmen Gomez-Bueno. The original scale range is 0–270.

10. Carabaña and Gomez-Bueno, *Escalas de Prestigio Ocupacional.*

11. Portes and Rumbaut, *Legacies,* 78–80.

12. Ibid.

13. Borjas, "Economic Theory and International Migration"; Chiswick, "The Effects of Americanization on the Earnings of Foreign-Born Men."

14. Sewell and Hauser, "Causes and Consequences of Higher Education"; Portes and Rumbaut, *Legacies,* chap. 9.

15. Sewell and Hauser, "Causes and Consequences of Higher Education"; Sewell, Haller, and Portes, "The Educational and Early Occupational Attainment Process"; Feliciano and Rumbaut, "Gendered Paths."

16. Portes and Rumbaut, *Legacies,* tables 5.3 and 8.5.

17. This is the common opinion of school principals and other authorities who were queried about this specific finding in the course of fieldwork for ILSEG in 2011.

18. The item components of PSII include the following questions, coded on a four-point scale from "Never" to "Almost Always":

a. Talks to his/her child about what happens in school.

b. Helps his/her child with school homework.

c. Talks to his/her child about what she/he will study in the future.

d. Attends parents' meeting at school.

Responses were added and divided by four, yielding a continuous scale, ranging from 1 (lowest) to 4 (highest).

19. Yiu, "Calibrated Ambitions."

20. Ibid. See also Portes, Vickstrom, and Aparicio, "Coming of Age in Spain."

21. Yiu, "Calibrated Ambitions."

22. Portes and Rumbaut, *Legacies,* table 5.1.

23. Ibid., table 5.4.

24. See the critique by Carina Mood on comparisons of nested bivariate logistic coefficients. Mood, "Logistic Regression."

25. Portes, Parker, and Cobas, "Assimilation or Consciousness"; Rumbaut and Komaie, "Immigration and Adult Transitions."

26. Bohon, Johnson, and Gorman, "College Aspirations and Expectations among Latino Adolescents in the United States"; Rumbaut and Komaie, "Immigration and Adult Transitions."

CHAPTER SIX: THE PSYCHOSOCIAL ADAPTATION OF THE
SECOND GENERATION

1. Schneider, "Police Power and Race Riots in Paris."

2. Rumbaut, "The Crucible Within"; Altschul, Oyserman, and Bybee, "Racial-Ethnic Self-Schemas and Segmented Assimilation"; Portes and Rumbaut, *Legacies*, chap. 8.

3. Portes and Rumbaut, *Legacies*, 155–58.

4. Telles and Ortiz, *Generations of Exclusion*.

5. Ibid.; Portes and Rumbaut, *Immigrant America*, 3rd ed., chap. 5.

6. Portes and Rumbaut, *Legacies*, table 7.6.

7. Portes and Rumbaut, *Legacies*, figs. 6.1 and 6.2.

8. Ibid., table 8.3.

9. Mood, "Logistic Regression"; Heath and Demireva, "Has Multiculturalism Failed in Britain?"

10. Portes and Rumbaut, *Legacies*, table 7.8.

11. Ibid.; see also Edwards and Romero, "Coping with Discrimination among Mexican Descent Adolescents."

12. Zhou et al., "Success Attained, Deterred, and Denied"; Le Espiritu and Wolf, "The Paradox of Assimilation"; Fong-Torres, *The Rice Room*.

13. Portes and Rumbaut, *Legacies*, table 6.5.

14. Ibid.


CHAPTER SEVEN: THE EDUCATIONAL GOALS AND
ACHIEVEMENTS OF THE SECOND GENERATION

1. See the set of theories reviewed in Chapter 2 and summarized in Figure 1.

2. Alba, Sloan, and Sperling, "The Integration Imperative."

3. Portes and Rumbaut, *Legacies*, 252–53.

4. Ibid., table 9.1.

5. Portes and Rumbaut, *Immigrant America*, 4th ed., chap. 4; Zhou, "Growing up American."

6. This is based on special tabulations of CILS-2 data produced for this analysis. Since 2005, all CILS surveys have been in the public domain and are accessible through the websites of the Center for Migration and Development at Princeton University and the Inter-University Consortium for Political and Social Research at the University of Michigan.

7. Field interview conducted as part of ILSEG's qualitative model. The name is fictitious.

8. List-wise deletion is generally considered the most conservative method for handling missing data. Various imputation routines simply inflate the sample size, yielding less rigorous estimates of statistical significance. See Firebaugh, *Seven Rules for Social Research*.

9. When one of the parents was Spanish, the nationality of the foreign-born parent was assigned. In the few cases where parents came from different

countries, the nationality of the father took precedence unless he had left the family.

10. Portes and Rumbaut, *Legacies,* table 9.5.

11. Note that these results come from a multinomial regression model, and, hence, figures in the table are untransformed logistic coefficients.

12. See the discussion of the negative effects of racialization and experiences of discrimination in Chapter 2.

13. Part of this large effect may be due to the relatively small number of Guineans in the follow-up sample. Nevertheless, the size of the effect in comparison with other nationalities requires further attention.

14. Portes and Rumbaut, *Legacies,* table 9.4.

15. Ibid.

16. Kao and Tienda, "Educational Aspirations of Minority Youth"; Feliciano, "Beyond the Family."

17. Buchman and Dalton, "Interpersonal Influences and Educational Aspirations in 12 Countries."

18. Aparicio, *Hijos de Inmigrantes;* Crul and Vermeulen, "The Second Generation in Europe"; Portes et al., "Dreaming in Spain."

19. These results were originally published in Portes et al., "Dreaming in Spain."

20. From ibid. The diagnostics of goodness-of-fit for this model are within an acceptable range.

21. 0 = Basic secondary or mid-level vocational/technical. 1 = Advanced secondary or superior technical. 2 = University degree. 3 = Postgraduate title.

22. 0 = Not enrolled. 1 = Basic secondary or PCPI. 2 = Mid-level vocational/technical. 3 = Advanced secondary or superior technical. 4 = University enrollment and bridge year.

23. The scale ranges from a majority of friends planning to leave school prior to advanced secondary (coded lowest) to a majority planning to attend the university. See Portes et al., "Moving Ahead in Madrid."

24. For a discussion of structural equations models and their indicators of goodness-of-fit, see Maruyama, *Basics of Structural Equation Modeling.*

25. See Kao and Tienda, "Educational Aspirations of Minority Youth"; Portes et al., "Dreaming in Spain"; Haller and Portes, "Status Attainment Processes."

26. Maruyama, *Basics of Structural Equation Modeling.*

27. Field interview conducted in Madrid as part of ILSEG's qualitative module, March 2014. The name is fictitious.

CHAPTER EIGHT: THE ENTRY INTO THE REAL WORLD

1. As noted in prior chapters, statistical significance, as indicated by the chi square statistic, is influenced by sample size. With large samples like the present ones, it is better to rely on Cramer's V coefficient that is indifferent to sample size. In this analysis, we adopt a criterion of .10 as indicative of at least a moderately strong relationship.

2. To avoid clutter, we omit detailed breakdowns of the native-parentage sample by gender, school type, and city of residence, but we indicate when such differences are statistically significant.

3. In Spain, the housing market is dominated by proprietors rather than renters. Contrary to countries of northern Europe, where housing is perceived as a service, the Spanish population, similar in this respect to Americans, perceives home ownership as a prime foundation of economic security and wealth.

4. In-depth interviews with public and private school principals in Madrid and Barcelona, 2008–9.

5. We used expectations rather than aspirations measured in the first ILSEG survey as the more reliable indicator of ambition in early adolescence. The question on ideal aspirations tended to elicit frivolous and non-reliable responses; for this reason, it was substituted by early expectations coded in the PRESCA-2 scale.

6. Occupational aspirations were low for the sizable group of second-generation Chinese who dropped out of school to join the labor market. However, aspirations were quite high for those who remained in school. As seen in Chapter 7, the educational performance of the latter group was above the average for the follow-up sample.

7. See Portes and Stepick, *City on the Edge;* Portes and Shafer, "Revisiting the Enclave Hypothesis."

8. Field interview in Madrid conducted as part of ILSEG's qualitative module, March 2014. Names are fictitious.

9. The overwhelming majority of respondents in the sample live with their parents. In this context, moving out of the parental home to live alone or cohabit is interpretable, at this early age, as a sign of problematic intergenerational relations and dissonant acculturation (see Chapter 2).

10. Children of Asian and European origin were most commonly found in public schools, whereas those of Latin American origin were overrepresented in private (concerted) schools. Such difference may partially account for the observed school effect. We have no ready explanation for the difference between the two cities.

11. For a detailed description of the CILS final survey, see Portes, Fernández-Kelly, and Haller, "No Margin for Error"; Haller, Portes, and Lynch, "Dreams Fulfilled, Dreams Shattered."

12. For analysis of the causes of this relative advantage of the Cuban second generation in the United States, see Portes and Stepick, *City on the Edge;* Haller, Portes, and Lynch, "Dreams Fulfilled, Dreams Shattered."

CHAPTER NINE: CONCLUSION

1. Cebolla Boado and González Ferrer, *Inmigración sin Modelo?;* Zapata-Barrero, *Diversity Management in Spain.*

2. Merton, "The Unanticipated Consequences of Purposive Social Action"; Portes, "The Hidden Abode."

3. Portes, "The Hidden Abode"; Tilly, "Invisible Elbow."

4. Entzinger, "Different Systems: Similar Problems"; Schneider, "Police Power and Race Riots in Paris."

5. Schneider, "Police Power and Race Riots in Paris."

6. Zapata-Barrero, *Diversity Management in Spain;* Aparicio, "La Integración de las Segundas Generaciones en España."

7. Zapata-Barrero, *Diversity Management in Spain.*

8. Portes, *Economic Sociology,* chap. 2; Portes, "The Hidden Abode."

9. Aparicio, "Aproximación a la Situación de los Españoles Emigrados"; González-Ferrer, "La nueva Emigración en Española."

10. Kasinitz et al., *Inheriting the City.*

11. Portes and Rivas, "The Adaptation of Migrant Children."

12. See, for example, Myers, Gao, and Emeka, "The Gradient of Immigrant Age-at-Arrival Effects."

13. Cachón, *La España Inmigrante;* Pajares, "La Inmigración en España."

14. Medvedeva and Portes, *Immigrant Bilingualism in Spain.*

# References

Aja, Eliseo, Joaquín Arango, and Josep Oliver Alonso, eds. *La inmigración en tiempos de crisis*. Anuario de la inmigración en España 2009. Barcelona: Fundación CIDOB, 2010.

————, eds. *Inmigración y crisis económica: Impactos actuales y perspectivas de futuro*. Anuario de la inmigración en España 2010. Barcelona: Fundación CIDOB, 2011.

Ajrough, Kristine J., and Amaney Jamal. "Assimilating to a White Identity: The Case of Arab Americans." *International Migration Review* 41 (2007): 860–79.

Alba, Richard, and Jennifer Holdaway, eds. *The Children of Immigrants at School: A Comparative Look at Integration in the United States and Western Europe*. New York: NYU Press, 2013.

Alba, Richard, and Tariqu Islam. "The Case of Disappearing Mexicans: An Ethnic-Identity Mystery." *Population Research and Policy Review* 28 (2009): 109–21.

Alba, Richard, John Logan, Amy Lutz, and Brian Stults. "Only English by the Third Generation? Loss and Preservation of the Mother Tongue among the Grandchildren of Contemporary Immigrants." *Demography* 39 (2002): 467–84.

Alba, Richard, and Victor Nee. *Remaking the American Mainstream: Assimilation and Contemporary Immigration*. Cambridge, Mass.: Harvard University Press, 2003.

Alba, Richard, Jennifer Sloan, and Jessica Sperling. "The Integration Imperative: The Children of Low-Status Immigrants in the Schools of Wealthy Societies." *Annual Review of Sociology* 37 (2011): 395–416.

Aldous, Joan. "Family, Ethnicity, and Immigrant Youths' Educational Achievements." *Journal of Family Issues* 27 (2006): 1633–67.

Alonso, Josep Oliver. "El Empleo Immigrante ante la Nueva Fase de Crisis e Integración." In *Anuario de la Immigración*, edited by E. Aja, 26–67. Madrid: Bellaterra, 2012.

Altschul, Inna, Daphna Oyserman, and Deborah Bybee. "Racial-Ethnic Self-Schemas and Segmented Assimilation: Identity and the Academic Achievement of Hispanic Youth." *Social Psychology Quarterly* 71 (2008): 302–20.

Aparicio, Rosa. *Aproximación a la Situación de los Españoles Emigrados: Realidad, Proyectos, Dificultades y Retos*. Madrid, OIM España, 2014.

———. *Hijos de Inmigrantes se Hacen Adultos*. Madrid: Observatorio Permanente de la Inmigración, Ministerio de Trabajo e Inmigración, 2006.

———. "La Integración de las Segundas Generaciones en España." In *Juventud e Immigración*, edited by A. Lopez Sala and L. Cachón, 119–36. Tenerife: Gobierno de Canarias, 2007.

Aparicio, Rosa, and Alejandro Portes. *Crecer en España: La Integracion de los Hijos de Immigrates*. Barcelona: La Caixa, 2014.

Aparicio, Rosa, and Andrés Tornos. *La Investigación sobre Migraciones en España*. Madrid: Permanent Observatory of Migration, 2002, http://extranjeros .empleo.gob.es/es/ObservatorioPermanenteInmigracion/Publicaciones /OtrosDocumentos/index.html.

———. "Towards an Analysis of Spanish Integration Policy." In *The Integration of Immigrants in European Societies*, edited by Friedrich Heckmann and Dominique Schnapper, 213–52. Stuttgart: Lucius and Lucius, 2003.

Bailey, Benjamin. "Language and Negotiation of Ethnic/Racial Identity among Dominican Americans." *Language and Society* 29 (2000): 555–82.

Bardají, F. *Literatura sobre Inmigrantes en España*. Madrid: Observatorio Permanente de la Inmigración, 2006.

Bohon, Stephanie A., Monica Kirkpatrick Johnson, and Bridget K. Gorman. "College Aspirations and Expectations among Latino Adolescents in the United States." *Social Problems* 53 (2006): 207–25.

Bonilla, Frank, and Ricardo Campos. "A Wealth of Poor: Puerto Ricans in the New Economic Order." *Daedalus* (1981): 133–76.

Borjas, George J. "Economic Theory and International Migration." *International Migration Review* 23 (1989): 457–85.

Bourgois, Phillippe I. *In Search of Respect: Selling Crack in El Barrio*. Cambridge, Engl.: Cambridge University Press, 1995.

Buchman, Claudia, and Ben Dalton. "Interpersonal Influences and Educational Aspirations in 12 Countries: The Importance of Institutional Context." *Sociology of Education* 75, no. 2 (2002): 99–122.

Cachón, Lorenzo. *La España Inmigrante*. Barcelona: Anthropos Editorial, 2009.

———. "La España Inmigrante: Marco Discriminatorio, Mercado de Trabajo y Políticas de Integración." *Barcelona: Anthropos* (2009): 352.

Carabaña, Julio. "El Impacto de la Inmigración en el Sistena Educativo Español." *Real Instituto El Cano* 63 (2008).

Carabaña, Julio, and Carmen Gomez-Bueno. *Escalas de Prestigio Ocupacional*. Madrid: Centro de Investigaciones Sociologicas, 1996.

Castles, Stephen, and Alastair Davidson, eds. *Citizenship and Migration: Globalization and the Politics of Belonging.* New York: Routledge, 2000.

Castles, Stephen, and Mark J. Miller. *The Age of Migration,* IV Edition. New York: Guilford Press, 2009.

Cebolla Boado, Hector, and Amparo González Ferrer. *Inmigración sin Modelo?* Madrid: Alianza Editorial, 2013.

Cebolla Boado, Hector, and Ana Lopez-Sala. "Transnational Immigrant Organizations in Spain: Their Role in Development and Integration." In *The State and the Grassroots Immigrant Transnational Organizations in Four Continents,* edited by A. Portes and P. Fernández-Kelly, 264–90. New York: Berghahn Books, 2015.

Checa, Francisco, Juan C, Checa, and Angeles Arjona. *La Integración de los Inmigrados: Modelos y Experiencias.* Barcelona: Icaria, 2003.

Cheng, Simon, and Brian Starks. "Racial Differences in the Effects of Significant Others on Students' Educational Expectations." *Sociology of Education* 75 (2002): 306–27.

Chiswick, Barry. "The Effects of Americanization on the Earnings of Foreign-Born Men." *Journal of Political Economy* 86 (Oct. 1978): 897–921.

CIDE. *Catorce Años de Investigación sobre las Desigualdades en Educación en España.* Madrid: Ministerio de Educación y Cultura, 1998.

———. *Investigaciones sobre educación intercultural realizadas en España entre 1990 y 2002.* Madrid: Ministerio de Educación, Cultura y Deporte, 2002.

Crul, Maurice, and Jeroen Doomernik. "The Turkish and Moroccan Second Generation in the Netherlands." *International Migration Review* 37 (2003): 1091–119.

Crul, Maurice, Jens Schneider, and Frans Lelie. *The European Second Generation Compared.* Amsterdam: Amsterdam University Press, 2012.

Crul, Maurice, and Hans Vermeulen. "The Second Generation in Europe." *International Migration Review* 37, no. 3 (2003): 965–86.

Defensor del Pueblo. *La Escolarización del Alumnado Inmigrante en España.* 2 vols. Madrid: Defensor del Pueblo, 2003.

Dhingra, Pawan. "Committed to Ethnicity, Committed to America: How Second-Generation Indian Americans' Ethnic Boundaries Further Their Assimilation." *Journal of Intercultural Studies* 29 (2008): 41–63.

Edwards, Lisa M., and Andrea J. Romero. "Coping with Discrimination among Mexican Descent Adolescents." *Hispanic Journal of Behavioral Sciences* 30, no. 1 (2008): 24–39.

Encuesta Nacional de Inmigrantes 2007 (ENI). http://www.parainmigrantes.info/encuesta- nacional-de-inmigracion-2007/.

Entzinger, Han. "Different Systems, Similar Problems: The French Urban Riots from a Dutch Perspective." *Journal of Ethnic and Migration Studies* 35, no. 5 (2009): 815–34.

Etxeberria, Félix, and Kristina Elosegin. "Integración del Alumnado Inmigrante: Obstáculos y Propuestas." *Revista Española de Educación Comparada* 16 (2010): 235–63.

Faist, Thomas. "Diversity—A New Mode of Incorporation?" *Ethnic and Racial Studies* 32, no. 1 (2009): 171–90.

Fanning, Bryan. *Immigration and Social Cohesion in the Republic of Ireland.* Manchester: Manchester University Press, 2011.

Feliciano, Cynthia. "Beyond the Family: The Influence of Pre-Migration Group Status on the Educational Expectations of Immigrant Children." *Sociology of Education* 79 (2006): 281–303.

———. "Education and Ethnic Identity Formation among Children of Latin American and Caribbean Immigrants." *Sociological Perspectives* 52 (2008): 135–58.

Feliciano, Cynthia, and Rubén G. Rumbaut. "Gendered Paths: Educational and Occupational Expectations and Outcomes among Adult Children of Immigrants." *Ethnic and Racial Studies* 25 (2005): 1087–118.

Fernández-Kelly, Patricia. "The Back Pocket Map: Social Class and Cultural Capital as Transferable Assets in the Advancement of Second Generation Immigrants." *Annals of the American Academy of Political and Social Sciences* 620 (Nov. 2008): 116–37.

Firebaugh, Glenn. *Seven Rules for Social Research.* Princeton, N.J.: Princeton University Press, 2008.

Flores, Rene. "The Increasing Significance of Race in Spain: Discrimination Experiences among Young Immigrants." *Program Report, Center for Migration and Development.* Princeton, N.J.: Princeton University, 2012.

Fong-Torres, Ben. *The Rice Room: Growing Up Chinese-American from Number Two Son to Rock 'n' Roll.* Berkeley: University of California Press, 2011.

Franzé, Adela. "Cultura/Culturas en la Escuela: La Inter-culturalidad en la Práctica." *Suplementos OFRIM* 2 (1998): 43–62.

———. "*Lo Que Sabía no Valía*": Escuela, Diversidad e Inmigración. Madrid: Consejo Económico y Social de Madrid, 2002.

Garmendia, J. A. *La Emigración Española en la Encrucijada: Marco General de la Emigración de Retorno.* Madrid: CIS, 1981.

Garrido Medina, Luis, and Héctor Cebolla Boado. "Rendimiento Educativo y Concentración de Inmigrantes en las Escuelas Españolas." *Presupuesto y Gasto Público* 4, no. 61 (2010): 159–76.

Gibson, Margaret A., and Silvia Carrasco. "The Education of Immigrant Youths: Some Lessons from the U.S. and Spain." *Theory and Practice* 48 (2009): 249–57.

Gibson, Margaret, Silvia Carrasco, Jordi Pámies, Maribel Ponferrada, and Anne Ríos-Pojas. "Different Systems, Similar Results: Youth of Immigrant Origin at School in California and Catalonia." New York: New York University Press, 2013.

Glazer, Nathan. "On Beyond the Melting Pot, 35 Years After." *International Migration Review* 34 (2000): 270–79.

Glazer, Nathan, and Daniel P. Moynihan. *Beyond the Melting Pot: The Negroes, Puerto Ricans, Jews, and Italians of New York City.* Cambridge, Mass.: MIT Press, 1970.

Glick, Jennifer E., and Michael J. White. "Post-Secondary School Participation of Immigrant and Native Youth: The Role of Familial Resources and Educational Expectations." *Social Science Research* 33 (2004): 272–99.

González-Ferrer, Amparo. "La nueva emigración en Española: Lo que sabemos y lo que no." *Fundación Alternativas* 18 (2013).

Goyette, Kimberly, and Yu Xie. "Educational Expectations of Asian American Youths: Determinants and Ethnic Differences." *Sociology of Education* 72 (1999): 22–36.

Gualda, Estrella. "Aspiraciónes y Expectativas Educativas y Laborales de Jóvenes Inmigrantes e Hijos de Inmigrantes Escolarizados." *Trabajo presentado al VI Congreso sobre Migraciones en España*, La Coruña, Galicia, Sept. 2009.

———. "Las Raíces de la Pertenencia y la Identidad en Adolescentes y Jóvenes Inmigrantes en Huelva." In *Integración Social, Escuela y Bilingüismo*, edited by A. Garrido, F. Checa y Olmos, and M. Belmonte García, 223–52. Spain: Icaria, 2011.

Gualda, Estrella, and Maya Jariego Peña. "Adolescentes y Jóvenes Inmigrantes en Huelva y Sevilla (España): Comparativa de los Factores Explicativos de las Aspiraciones y las Expectativas Educativas y Laborales." *VII Congreso Português de Sociologia*, Porto (June 2012).

Guarnizo, Luis E., Alejandro Portes, and William J. Haller. "Assimilation and Transnationalism: Determinants of Transnational Political Action among Contemporary Immigrants." *American Journal of Sociology* 108 (May 2003): 1211–48.

Haines, David. "Ethnicity's Shadows: Race, Religion, and Nationality as Alternative Identities among Recent United States Arrivals." *Identities: Global Studies in Power and Culture* 14 (2007): 285–312.

Haller, Archibald O., and Alejandro Portes. "Status Attainment Processes." *Sociology of Education* 46 (Winter 1973): 51–91.

Haller, William, Alejandro Portes, and Scott Lynch. "Dreams Fulfilled, Dreams Shattered: Determinants of Segmented Assimilation in the Second Generation." *Social Forces* 89 (Mar. 2011): 733–62.

Hao, Lingxin, and Melissa Bonstead-Bruns. "Parent-Child Differences in Educational Expectations and the Academic Achievement of Immigrant and Native Students." *Sociology of Education* 71 (1998): 175–98.

Heath, Anthony, and Neli Demireva. "Has Multiculturalism Failed in Britain?" *Ethnic and Racial Studies* 37 (Jan. 2014): 161–88.

Heckmann, Friedrich, and Dominique Schnapper, eds. *The Integration of Immigrants in European Societies: National Differences and Trends of Convergence*. Vol. 7. Stuttgart: Lucius and Lucius, 2003.

Hirschman, Charles. "America's Melting Pot Reconsidered." *Annual Review of Sociology* 9 (1983): 397–423.

———. "The Educational Enrollment of Immigrant Youth: A Test of the Segmented Assimilation Hypothesis." *Demography* 38 (2001): 317–36.

Hirshman, Charles, and Luis Falcon. "The Educational Attainment of Religio-Ethnic Groups in the United States." *Research in Sociology of Education and Socialization* 5 (1985): 83–120.

Hollifield, James. "The Emerging Migration State." *International Migration Review* 38 (Fall 2004): 885–912.

Huntington, Samuel P. "The Hispanic Challenge." *Foreign Policy* 141 (Mar.–Apr. 2004): 30–45.

Inoue, Yukiko. *The Educational and Occupational Attainment Process: The Role of Adolescent Status Aspirations.* Washington, D.C.: University Press of America, 2006.

Instituto Nacional de Estadistica. *Padrón Continuo de las Migraciones.* Report. Madrid: INE, 2012.

——. *National Immigration Survey of Spain.* Madrid: INE, 2007. Selected tabulations.

Ioé, Colectivo. "Alumnas y Alumnos de Origen Extranjero: Distribución y Trayectorias Escolares Diferenciadas." *Cuadernos de Pedagogía* 326 (2003): 63–68.

Jacobson, Matthew. *Whiteness of a Different Color: European Immigrants and the Alchemy of Race.* Cambridge, Mass.: Harvard University Press, 1999.

Jimenez, Tomas R. "Mexican Immigrant Replenishment and the Continuing Significance of Ethnicity and Race." *American Journal of Sociology* 113 (2008): 1527–67.

Juliano Corregido, María Dolores. *Educación Intercultural: Escuela y Minorías étnicas.* Mexico: EUDEMA Universidad, 1993.

Kao, Grace, and Marta Tienda. "Educational Aspirations of Minority Youth." *American Journal of Education* 106 (1998): 349–84.

Kasinitz, Philip, John H. Mollenkopf, and Mary C. Waters. "Becoming American /Becoming New Yorkers: Immigrant Incorporation in a Majority Minority City." *International Migration Review* 36 (2002): 1020–36.

Kasinitz, Philip, John H. Mollenkopf, Mary C. Waters, and Jennifer Holdaway. *Inheriting the City: The Children of Immigrants Coming of Age.* Cambridge, Mass., and New York: Harvard University Press and Russell Sage Foundation, 2008.

Kish, Leslie. *Survey Sampling.* New York: Wiley, 1967.

Le Espiritu, Yen, and Diane L. Wolf. "The Paradox of Assimilation: Children of Filipino Immigrants in San Diego." In *Ethnicities: Children of Immigrants in America,* edited by R.G. Rumbaut and A. Portes, 157–86. Berkeley and New York: University of California Press and Russell Sage Foundation, 2001.

Lin, Ann Chich, and Amaney Jamal. "Muslim, Arab, and American: The Adaptation of Muslim Arab Immigrant to American Society." In *The Religious Lives of American Immigrants: Past and Present,* edited by R. Alba and A. Raboteau. New York: Russell Sage Foundation, forthcoming.

Lopez, David E., and Ricardo D. Stanton-Salazar. "Mexican Americans: A Second Generation at Risk." In *Ethnicities: Children of Immigrants in America,* edited by R.G. Rumbaut and A. Portes, 57–90. Berkeley: University of California Press, 2001.

Luján, Néster. *Cuento de Cuentos: Origen y Aventura de Ciertas Palabras y Frases Proverbiales.* Vol. 1. Barcelona: Ediciones Folio, 1993.

Majoribanks, Kevin. "Family Background, Individual and Environmental Influences, Aspirations and Young Adults' Educational Attainment: A Follow-up Study." *Educational Studies* 29 (2003): 233.

——. "Learning Environments, Family Contexts, Educational Aspirations and Attainment: A Moderation-Mediation Model Extended." *Learning Environments Research* 6, no. 3 (2003): 247–65.

Maruyama, Geoffrey M. *Basics of Structural Equation Modeling*. Thousand Oaks, Calif.: Sage, 1997.

Medvedeva, Maria, and Alejandro Portes. "Immigrant Bilingualism in Spain: An Asset or a Liability?" *International Migration Review* (forthcoming 2016).

Menjivar, Cecilia. "Educational Hopes, Documented Dreams: Guatemalan and Salvadoran Immigrants' Legality and Educational Prospects." *The Annals of the American Academy of Political and Social Sciences* 620 (2008): 177–93.

Merton, Robert K. "The Unanticipated Consequences of Purposive Social Action." *American Sociological Review* 1, no. 6 (1936): 894–904.

Ministry of Education. *Datos y Cifras del Curso Escolar 2011/2012*. http://www.mecd.gob.es/educacion-mecd/.

Monteserin, Susana Alba, Ana Fernández Asperilla, and Ubaldo Martínez Vega. "Crisis Económica y Nuevo Panorama Migratorio en España." *Estudios. Fundación 1 de Mayo* 65 (2013): 17–18.

Mood, Carina. "Logistic Regression: Why We Cannot Do What We Think We Can Do and What We Can Do About It." *European Sociological Review* 26 (2009): 67–82.

Morales, Laura, and Luis Ramiro. "Gaining Political Capital Through Social Capital: Policy-Making Inclusion and Network Embeddedness of Migrants' Associations in Spain." *Mobilization: An International Journal* 16, no. 2 (2011): 147–64.

Morning, Ann. "The Racial Self-Identification of South Asians in the United States." *Journal of Ethnic and Migration Studies* 27 (2001): 61–79.

Mouw, Ted, and Yu Xie. "Bilingualism and the Academic Achievement of First- and Second-Generation Asian Americans: Accommodation With or Without Assimilation?" *American Sociological Review* 64 (1999): 232–52.

Myers, Dowell, Xin Gao, and Amon Emeka. "The Gradient of Immigrant Age-at-Arrival Effects on Socioeconomic Outcomes in the US 1." *International Migration Review* 43, no. 1 (2009): 205–29.

National Institute of Statistics. Annual Surveys of the Economically Active Population. http://www.ine.es/dyngs/INEbase/en/operacion.htm?c=Estadistica_C&cid=1254736176918&menu=ultiDatos&idp=1254735976595.

———. Continuous Register of Inhabitants (Padrón Continuo), 2012. http://ine.es/inebaseDYN/cp30321/cp_resultados.htm.

Nesdale, Drew, and Anita S. Mak. "Immigrant Acculturation Attitudes and Host Country Identification." *Journal of Community and Applied Social Psychology* 10 (2000): 483–95.

Nijenhuis, Gery, and Annelies Zoomers. "Transnational Activities of Immigrant Organizations in the Netherlands." In *The State and the Grassroots: Immigrant Transnational Organizations in Four Continents*, edited by A. Portes and P. Fernández-Kelly, 236–63. New York: Berghahn Books, 2015.

Office of Immigration Statistics. *2009 Yearbook of Immigration Statistics*. Washington, D.C.: Department of Homeland Security, 2010.

Organization for Economic Cooperation and Development (OECD). "PISA 2006: Science Competencies for Tomorrow's World," 2007. http://www.oecd.org/unitedstates/39722597.pdf.

Pahl, Kerstin, and Niobe Way. "Longitudinal Trajectories of Ethnic Identity among Urban Black and Latino Adolescents." *Child Development* 77 (2006): 1403–15.

Pajares, Miguel. "La Inmigración en España: Sus Causas y las Políticas con los que se Gestiona." In *Las Migraciones en el Mundo,* edited by F. Checa Olmos, C. Checa, and A. Arjona, 175–92. Barcelona: Icaria, 2009.

———. *La Integración Ciudadana: Una Perspectiva para la Inmigración.* Barcelona: Icaria Editorial, 2005.

Perreira, Krista M., Kathleen Hamis, and Dohoon Lee. "Making It in America: High School Completion by Immigrant and Native Youth." *Demography* 43 (2006): 511–36.

Portes, Alejandro. *Economic Sociology: A Systematic Inquiry.* Princeton, N.J.: Princeton University Press, 2010.

———. "The Hidden Abode: Sociology as Analysis of the Unexpected." *American Sociological Review* 65, no. 1 (2000): 1–18.

———. "Tensions That Make a Difference: Institutions, Interests, and the Immigrant Drive." *Sociological Forum* 27 (Sept. 2012): 563–78.

Portes, Alejandro, Rosa Aparicio, William Haller, and Erik Vickstrom. "Moving Ahead in Madrid: Aspirations and Expectations in the Spanish Second Generation." *International Review* 44 (Winter 2010): 767–801.

Portes, Alejandro, Adrienne Celaya, Erik Vickstrom, and Rosa Aparicio. "Who Are We? Parental Influences on Self-Identities and Self-Esteem of Second Generation Youths in Spain." *Revista de Investigaciones Sociologicas* 70 (Jan.–Apr. 2012): 9–37.

Portes, Alejandro, Patricia Fernandéz-Kelly, and William Haller. "No Margin for Error: Educational and Occupational Achievement among Disadvantaged Children of Immigrants." *Annals of the American Academy of Political and Social Sciences* 620 (Nov. 2008): 12–36.

Portes, Alejandro, and Lingxin Hao. "E Pluribus Unum: Bilingualism and Loss of Language in the Second Generation." *Sociology of Education* (1998): 269–94.

———. "The Price of Uniformity: Language, Family and Personality Adjustment in the Immigrant Second Generation." *Ethnic and Racial Studies* 25, no. 6 (2002): 889–912.

Portes, Alejandro, Robert N. Parker, and Jose A. Cobas. "Assimilation or Consciousness: Perceptions of U.S. Society among Recent Latin American Immigrants in the United States." *Social Forces* 59 (Sept. 1980): 200–224.

Portes, Alejandro, and Alejandro Rivas. "The Adaptation of Migrant Children." *The Future of Children* 21 (Spring 2011): 219–46.

Portes, Alejandro, and Rubén G. Rumbaut. *Immigrant America: A Portrait.* 3rd ed. Berkeley: University of California Press, 2006.

———. *Immigrant America: A Portrait.* 4th ed. Berkeley: University of California Press, 2014.

———. *Legacies: The Story of the Immigrant Second Generation.* Berkeley and New York: University of California Press and Russell Sage Foundation, 2001.

Portes, Alejandro, and Steven Shafer. "Revisiting the Enclave Hypothesis: Miami Twenty-five Years Later." *Research in the Sociology of Organizations* 25 (2007): 157–90.

Portes, Alejandro, and Alex Stepick. *City on the Edge: The Transformation of Miami.* Berkeley: University of California Press, 1993.

Portes, Alejandro, Erik Vickstrom, and Rosa Aparicio. "Coming of Age in Spain: Self-Identification, Beliefs, and Self-Esteem in the Second Generation." *British Journal of Sociology* 62 (2011): 387–417.

Portes, Alejandro, Erik Vickstrom, William J. Haller, and Rosa Aparicio. "Dreaming in Spain: Parental Determinants of Immigrant Children's Ambition." *Ethnic and Racial Studies* 36 (Apr. 2013): 557–89.

Portes, Alejandro, and Min Zhou. "The New Second Generation: Segmented Assimilation and Its Variants." *Annals of the American Academy of Political and Social Sciences* 530 (1993): 74–96.

Queirolo Palmas, Luca. "Bandos Fuera! Escuela, Exclusion y Espacio Publico." *Revista Española de Sociologia* 21 (2014): 25–46.

Ream, Robert K. *Uprooting Children: Mobility, Social Capital, and Mexican American Underachievement.* New York: LFB Scholarly Publishing, 2004.

Rojo, Luisa Martín. "¿Asimilar o Integrar? Dilemas ante el Multilingüismo en las Aulas." Madrid: Ministerio de Educación y Cultura, CIDE, 2003.

Rosenberg, Morris. *Conceiving the Self.* New York: Basic Books, 1979.

———. *Society and the Adolescent Self-Image.* Princeton, N.J.: Princeton University Press, 1965.

Rumbaut, Rubén G. "Ages, Life Stages, and Generational Cohorts: Decomposing the Immigrant First and Second Generations in the United States." *International Migration Review* 38 (Fall 2004): 1160–1205.

———. "Assimilation and Its Discontents: Ironies and Paradoxes." In *The Handbook of International Migration: The American Experience,* edited by Charles Hirschman, Philip Kasinitz, and Josh deWind, 172–95. New York: Russell Sage Foundation, 1999.

———. "The Crucible Within: Ethnic Identity, Self-Esteem, and Segmented Assimilation among Children of Immigrants." *International Migration Review* 28 (1994): 748–94.

———. "Origins and Destinies: Immigration to the United States since World War II." *Sociological Forum* 9 (1994): 583–621.

———. "Turning Points in the Transition to Adulthood: Determinants of Educational Attainment, Incarceration, and Early Childbearing among Children of Immigrants." *Ethnic and Racial Studies* 28 (Nov. 2005): 1041–86.

Rumbaut, Rubén G., and Golnaz Komaie. "Immigration and Adult Transitions." *Future of Children* 20 (2010): 39–63.

Rumbaut, Rubén G., and Alejandro Portes, eds. *Ethnicities: Children of Immigrants in America.* Berkeley: University of California Press, 2001.

Schnapper, Dominique. *L'europe Des Immigrés: Essai Sur Les Politiques D'immigration.* Paris: Editions François Bourin, 1992.

Schneider, Cath L. "Police Power and Race Riots in Paris." *Politics and Society* 36, no. 1 (2008): 133–59.

Sewell, William, Archibald O. Haller, and Alejandro Portes. "The Educational and Early Occupational Attainment Process." *American Sociological Review* 34 (1969): 82–92.

Sewell, William, and Robert M. Hauser, "Causes and Consequences of Higher Education: Models of the Status Attainment Process." *American Journal of Agricultural Economics* 54 (Dec. 1972): 851–61.

Siguán, Miquel. "Inmigrantes en la Escuela." *Revista Textos de Didáctica de la Lengua y de la Literatura* 23 (2000): 13–21.

———. *La Escuela y los Inmigrantes.* Buenos Aires: Paldós, 1998.

Sikora, Joanna, and Lawrence J. Saha. "Corrosive Inequality? Structural Determinants of Educational and Occupational Expectations in Comparative Perspective." *International Education Journal* 8 (2007): 57–78.

Simon, Patrick. "France and the Unknown Second Generation: Preliminary Results on Social Mobility." *International Migration Review* 37 (2003): 1091–1119.

Singleton, Royce, and Bruce C. Straits. *Approaches to Social Research.* 4th ed. New York: Oxford University Press, 2005.

Solé, Carlota, and Sonia Parella. "The Labour Market and Racial Discrimination in Spain." *Journal of Ethnic and Migration Studies* 29 (2003): 121–40.

Telles, Edward, and Vilma Ortiz. *Generations of Exclusion: Mexican Americans, Assimilation, and Race.* New York: Russell Sage Foundation, 2008.

Terrén, Eduardo. "Adolescencia, Inmigración e Identidad." *Juventud e Inmigración: Desafíos para la Participación y la Integración* (2007): 86.

———. "El Sentimiento de Pertenencia Nacional entre los Adolescentes de Familias Immigradas." *Papers* (2011): 91–116.

Tilly, Charles. "Invisible Elbow." *Sociological Forum* 11, no. 4 (1996): 589–601.

Warner, Lloyd, and Leo Srole. *The Social Systems of American Ethnic Groups.* New Haven: Yale University Press, 1945.

Waters, Mary C., and Karl Eschbach. "Immigration and Ethnic and Racial Inequality in the United States." *Annual Review of Sociology* (1995): 419–46.

Waters, Mary C., Anthony Heath, Van C. Tran, and Vikki Boliver. "Second-generation Attainment and Inequality: Primary and Secondary Effects on Educational Outcomes in Britain and the U.S." In *The Children of Immigrants at School: A Comparative Look at Integration in the United States and Western Europe,* edited by Richard Alba and Jennifer Holdaway, 120–59. New York: New York University Press, 2013.

Yiu, Jessica. "Calibrated Ambitions: Low Educational Ambition as a Form of Strategic Adaptation among Chinese Youths in Spain." *International Migration Review* 47, no. 3 (2013): 573–611.

Zapata-Barrero, Ricard. *Diversity Management in Spain: New Dimensions, New Challenges.* Manchester, Engl.: Manchester University Press, 2013.

Zapata-Barrero, Ricard, and Flora Burchianti. "Tolerance to Cultural Diversity in Spanish Schools, Discourses and Practices." Report. Barcelona: Pompeu Fabrega University, 2011.

Zhou, Min. "Growing up American: The Challenge Confronting Immigrant Children and Children of Immigrants." *Annual Review of Sociology* 23 (1997): 63–95.

———. "Straddling Different Worlds: The Acculturation of Vietnamese Refugee Children." In *Ethnicities: Children of Immigrants in America,* edited by

R. G. Rumbaut and A. Portes, 187–227. Berkeley and New York: University of California Press and Russell Sage Foundation, 2001.

Zhou, Min, and Carl Bankston. *Growing up American: How Vietnamese Immigrants Adapt to Life in the United States*. New York: Russell Sage Foundation, 1998.

———. "Social Capital and the Adaptation of the Second Generation." In *The New Second Generation*, edited by A. Portes, 197–220. New York: Russell Sage Foundation, 1996.

Zhou, Min, Jennifer Lee, Jody A. Vallejo, Rosaura Tafoga-Estrada, and Yang Soa Xiong. "Success Attained, Deterred, and Denied: Divergent Pathways to Social Mobility in Los Angeles' New Second Generation." *Annals of the American Academy of Political and Social Sciences* 620 (Nov. 2008): 37–61.

# Index

Pages referring to a figure or a table are followed by *f* or *t*, respectively.